MUSIC

iS THE

WEAPON

OF THE

FUTURE

MUSiC iS THE WEAPON OF THE FUTURE

Fifty Years of African Popular Music

by Frank Tenaille

translated by Stephen Toussaint
and Hope Sandrine

photographs by Akwa Betote

Lawrence Hill Books

Library of Congress Cataloging-in-Publication Data
Tenaille, Frank.
  [Swing du caméléon. English]
  Music is the weapon of the future : fifty years of African popular
music / Frank Tenaille.—1st ed. in English.
      p. cm.
  Translation of: Le swing du caméléon.
  Discography: p. 277
  Includes bibliographical references (p. 289) and index.
    ISBN 1-55652-450-1
    1. Popular music—Africa—History and criticism.
  2. Musicians—Africa. I. Title.
    ML3502.9 .T4613 2002
    781.63'0967—dc21   2002001515

*Cet ouvrage, publié dans le cadre d'un programme d'aide à la publication,
bénéficie du soutien du Ministère des Affaires étrangères et du Service
Culturel de l'Ambassade de France aux Etats-Unis.*
This work, published as part of a program of aid for publication,
received support from the French Ministry of Foreign Affairs and the
Cultural Services of the French Embassy in the United States.

All photographs © Akwa Betote

TRANSLATORS: Stephen Toussaint and Hope Sandrine
TRANSLATION COPYEDITOR: Jerome Colburn, Publication Services, Inc.
TRANSLATION PROOFREADER: Sue Feldman

COVER AND INTERIOR DESIGN: Lindgren/Fuller Design

Originally published in 2000 by Actes Sud, France, as *Le Swing du caméléon,
musiques et chansons africaines 1950 - 2000*

To Neige Neyron-Bourret;
to El-Hadj Djeli Sory Kouyate,
the greatest balafonist in Manding country;
to Wendo Kolosoy, Prince of the Rumba.

CONTENTS

WORLD SOUND

LEAVING THE TWENTIETH CENTURY

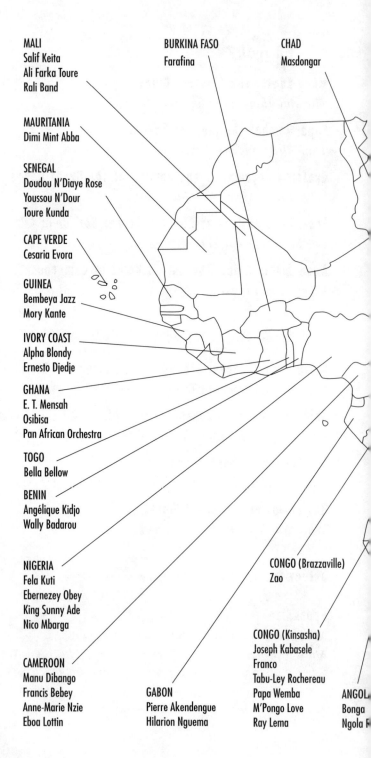

MALI
Salif Keita
Ali Farka Toure
Rali Band

BURKINA FASO
Farafina

CHAD
Masdongar

MAURITANIA
Dimi Mint Abba

SENEGAL
Doudou N'Diaye Rose
Youssou N'Dour
Toure Kunda

CAPE VERDE
Cesaria Evora

GUINEA
Bembeya Jazz
Mory Kante

IVORY COAST
Alpha Blondy
Ernesto Djedje

GHANA
E. T. Mensah
Osibisa
Pan African Orchestra

TOGO
Bella Bellow

BENIN
Angélique Kidjo
Wally Badarou

NIGERIA
Fela Kuti
Ebernezey Obey
King Sunny Ade
Nico Mbarga

CONGO (Brazzaville)
Zao

CONGO (Kinsasha)
Joseph Kabasele
Franco
Tabu-Ley Rochereau
Papa Wemba
M'Pongo Love
Ray Lema

CAMEROON
Manu Dibango
Francis Bebey
Anne-Marie Nzie
Eboa Lottin

GABON
Pierre Akendengue
Hilarion Nguema

ANGOL
Bonga
Ngola F

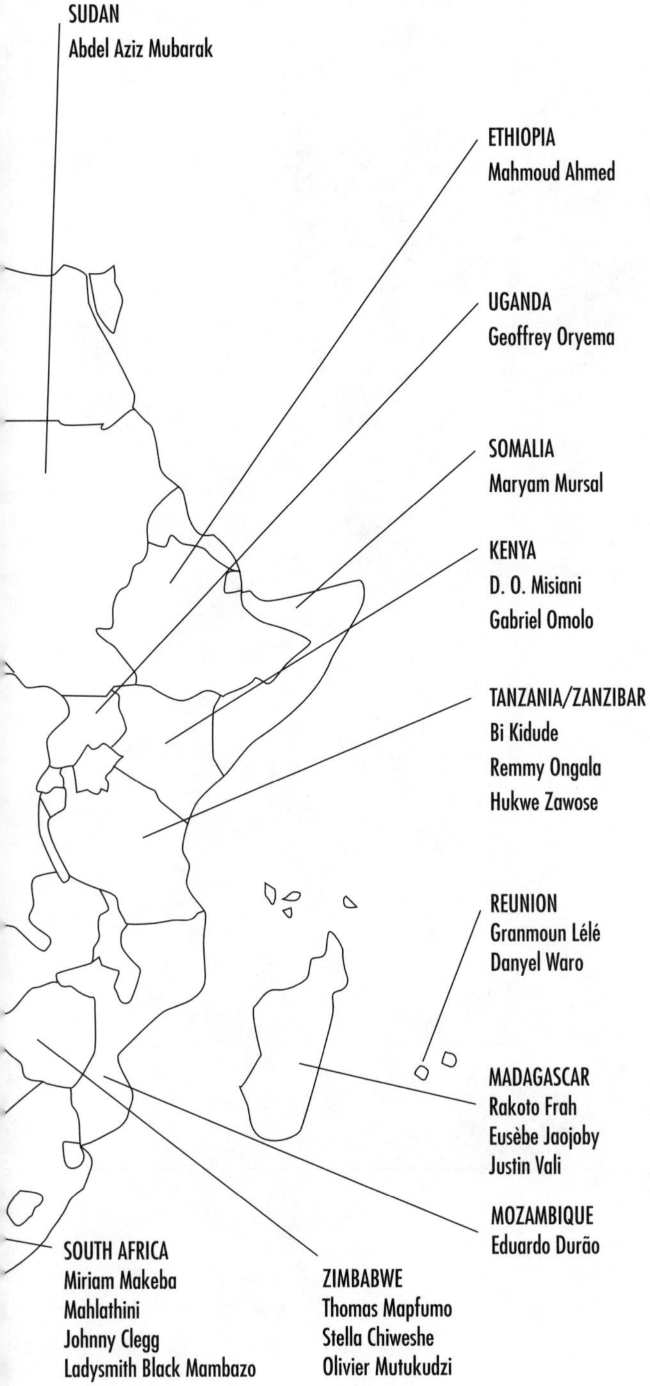

SUDAN
Abdel Aziz Mubarak

ETHIOPIA
Mahmoud Ahmed

UGANDA
Geoffrey Oryema

SOMALIA
Maryam Mursal

KENYA
D. O. Misiani
Gabriel Omolo

TANZANIA/ZANZIBAR
Bi Kidude
Remmy Ongala
Hukwe Zawose

REUNION
Granmoun Lélé
Danyel Waro

MADAGASCAR
Rakoto Frah
Eusèbe Jaojoby
Justin Vali

MOZAMBIQUE
Eduardo Durão

SOUTH AFRICA
Miriam Makeba
Mahlathini
Johnny Clegg
Ladysmith Black Mambazo

ZIMBABWE
Thomas Mapfumo
Stella Chiweshe
Olivier Mutukudzi

introduction

As is well known, Africa always brings something new.

—RABELAIS

In African stories, where the past is retold as if it is the present, there is at times a certain chaos that disturbs Western minds—but we find ourselves right at home.

—AMADOU HAMPATE BA[1]

It don't mean a thing if it ain't got that swing.

—DUKE ELLINGTON

I f we go by the first recordings, "modern" African music has been around for a century.[2] But for a continent where *Homo habilis* hunted antelope and hippopotamus on the soil of present-day Tanzania over 400,000 years ago, a single century is a modest period of time, which explains why the music has not been taken very seriously. Nevertheless, it has proven to be the ideal popular vehicle for the hopes, sorrows, and contradictions of a modern Africa said to have started off on the wrong foot.

---

[1] "Caractéristiques de la mémoire africaine," *Histoire de l'Afrique,* vol. 1 (Jeune Afrique).

[2] The first recordings appeared in Tanganyika (a German territory) in 1902. Western wind instruments, guitars, and banjos arrived on the African coast in the early twentieth century. In the 1920s, the phonograph and 78-rpm record player spread into central Africa. The British firm Gramophone (with the labels Zonophone and HMV) set up shop in South Africa in 1922. Five years later, the East African Broadcasting Service opened in Kenya. Radio stations began operating in West Africa and Madagascar in the 1930s. The first recording studio, Gallotone Records, was formed in South Africa in 1934.

For some years now, the music of Africa has inspired an astonishing craze throughout the world, after having traveled, in two decades, from small dance halls in Bamako, Lagos, and Kinshasa to the biggest stages in the world with Salif Keita, Mory Kante, and Youssou N'Dour as its intermediaries. What happened? What was at stake in this maelstrom of rhythms, languages, instruments, and chants?

These traveling showmen have captured in music the torments, hopes, and disappointments of the century. Their words are as pale as a shroud, as red as spilled blood, as black as the mine, as green as the forest, and, when reflecting happy times, as multicolored as the peoples of Africa themselves. Their notes exhale the sweat of toil, the musk of passion, and the fragrance of festival. Their tempos are as languid as an evening in the village, or as speedy as the late-night "drugstore" where you can drown your fate in drink.

These singers and musicians have thus become invaluable chroniclers. Between the tom-tom and the Internet, these present-day griots have been the witnesses to a convulsive era, the ferry captains of memory, the clown parodists of tradition. This, their saga—of the red dirt lanes and corrugated metal roofs of ghettos, of pandemic wars, of peoples swindled out of grand collective hopes[3]—quietly traces the path of a broad cluster of lives swept along the wind's four courses, a journey set within a labyrinth of savannas and forests, of villages and cities, of languages, aromas, and landscapes, of myths and gods.[4] As John Cage said, "Music is secondarily an affair of music." And, as Zanzibar, prince of the Bikutsi, asserted, "There's nothing better than dying well-groomed."

---

[3] It would be difficult to discuss Africa's music and its collective hopes without evoking the figure of Thomas Sankara, former guitarist for the Missils International Band, who in 1983 became the president of a West African nation rechristened Burkina Faso (meaning "the country of honest men"). Sankara had pushed for the creation of an all-female national orchestra, a stance symbolic of his belief in the emancipation of women.

[4] This passage deliberately paints an image of sub-Saharan Africa. There are cultural artifacts, however, that suggest an historical interdependence between the musical styles of the several regions of Africa. Examples of musical exchange can be easily spotted in the Manding tradition, in Tuareg music, among the Gnawa of Morocco (descendants of black Bambara slaves), or in East Africa via the taarab.

THE
SWEET SMELLS
OF
iNDEPENDENCE

... And Lumumba Was Dancing the Cha-Cha-Cha

Joseph Kabasele and the Rise of the Congolese Crucible

Doctor Nico in 1982, introspective as usual.

Mobutu said: "Does Rochereau realize the magnitude of a song?" Because the newspaper will not be bought by the old lady in the street unless she uses it to wrap her donuts. But a song goes everywhere. The housewife, even while crushing her cassava and making *attiéké* [couscous] out of it, she listens to the song. The street does not have to make any effort to understand its meaning.

—TABU-LEY ROCHEREAU[1]

In February 1960, a sensuous song was heard over the airwaves:

> *Indépendance cha-cha, Tozoui,*
> *O Kimpwanza cha-cha, Tubakidi,*
> *O Table ronde cha-cha, Tua gagné o,*
> *O Dipanda cha-cha, Tozui e e.*
> (Here we are, independent at last!
> Long live Liberty, cha-cha!
> Victory at the political roundtable!
> Long live Independence,
> We have won.)[2]

Its writer and singer was Joseph Kabasele, a songsmith with a tenor voice whose performance tours had helped to make Africa better known to Europe, accompanied by his group, African Jazz. And this man had a

---

[1] Interview with the author in 1993. Tabu-Ley Rochereau, "beautiful voice in B major," born in 1940, has composed more than two thousand titles. He brought to Congolese music a focus on the lead guitar, innovations such as the James Brown–style intro, and several brilliant singers, of whom Mbilia Bel remains the most famous. He is considered father of "boucher" soukous, based on the acceleration of the rhythm of the rumba "à papa" under the influence of the twist and the jerk.

[2] "Indépendance cha-cha," Philips, 1960.

friend Patrice Lumumba, the forty-five-year-old poster child of emerging Congolese nationalism, who baffled the colonial powers.

Africa was in turmoil. Since the Third Interterritorial Congress, held at Bamako in September 1957, which had proclaimed that "independence of the people is an inalienable right," several countries had put that objective on their agenda. Lumumba, leader of the Congolese National Movement, despite all the snares devised by Western forces, was at last able to wrest from the Belgian colonial power an agreement to grant his country its freedom. He won this concession at the Brussels Roundtable Conference—a series of negotiations that took place in January for an independence that would not be declared until June 30.

This context underscores how much, in that six-month interval, this anthem of Kabasele's, recorded on the Philips label, would strike a chord in an Africa tormented by the decolonization process—and the resonance it would have later when Patrice Lumumba, seven months after becoming president, was assassinated; and became forever, along with Amilcar Cabral, Kwame Nkrumah, Mehdi Ben Barka, and a few others, one of the founding fathers of twentieth-century Africa.

It was just a song, but with its refrain it was worth many a speech—so clearly did its simple words crystallize the communal consciousness and the hopes of an entire people.

When he wrote "Indépendance cha-cha," Joseph Kabasele was already a colossal musical figure. Born in Matadi in 1930, he developed his musical skills, as did most artists from the Belgian Congo, in a Catholic church choir (in his case that of the Missionaries of Scheut), after his uncle, Abbot Malula—himself a playwright, author, composer, and future cardinal—recognized the promise in his nephew's voice and encouraged him to develop it. Academic events would further encourage the youth's vocation. Expelled from school during his sophomore year (in 1949) for bad behavior, the teenaged Kabasele joined an a cappella group, the Voice of Concord, and chose the Afro-Cuban sound over religious music, deducing that his future resided in that musical style so rich in potential.

Between 1950 and 1960, the music of the two Congos (Congo-Brazzaville, now the Republic of the Congo, and Congo-Léopoldville, later known as Zaire, and now the Democratic Republic of the Congo) went through a crucial period. In the capitals, situated on either side of the river, and linked by ferry, a music was born that incorporated traditional rural dance and song, the rhythms of West Africa (highlife) and Europe (like the polka), influences from colonial brass bands and songs of the religious choirs. Linked to the *Congo-bars* (taverns), the music flourished, the number of bands grew, and an industry came into being. The electrification of instruments, together with the influence of jazz and Caribbean music, fostered the emergence of central Africa's famous musical crucible, of which the "Congolese Tino Rossi" would be the figurehead.

The rise of African Jazz,[3] in which Kabasele involved his childhood friends, was a foundational moment for the music, symbolic of its metamorphosis from a form used mainly for collective rituals to one that henceforth functioned as entertainment. The importance of this group was due to these facts: it reflected the emerging tastes of an urban public whose manners and customs were breaking away from those of the countryside; it expressed the multiculturalism of the ethnic groups whose paths crossed in the capital; and it accommodated foreign influences, especially those of Cuban music (the rumba, pachanga, and cha-cha-cha), with which Kabasele was smitten.

"Grand Kalle," as Kabasele was known, would direct his band as if on a mission. "I have always seen a responsibility in everything I do. As far as the music is concerned, without tooting my own horn, I believe that I am the mainspring of modern music in my country. In several respects, I have contributed to its promotion. And when they called me '*Grand*' (big) or even '*Vieux*' (old), even though I was barely in my twenties at the time, it wasn't pejorative. The people wanted to make me responsible. As for me, I have always had my own responsibilities, and I have tried to keep pace with the major bands of my country, for they have

---

[3] African Jazz would be a proving ground for numerous talents, including the guitarists Mwamba Dechaud, Tino Barosa, and Nico Kassanda; the Zimbabwean saxophonist Isaac Muskewa; the luminous flautist Edo Clary; and all those who would spend longer or shorter stays in the band, after the manner of Manu Dibango, hired in Brussels, who stayed in Kinshasa for three years beside the master. A Cuban/Congolese synthesis, the music of African Jazz makes reference to the Cuban group La Sonora Matancera, especially in its flute and piano technique. The African Jazz disbanded in 1968, and Kalle passed away in 1982.

had an influence throughout all of Africa, in accordance with this apos-
tolate of mine."[4]

Along with a refined sense of melody, Kabalese had a gift for flushing
out new talent. Throughout his career he continued to assemble an alliance
of an impressive number of musicians,[5] who, through label rivalries[6]
and dancing competitions, would have their own progeny in turn. The
most famous of his spiritual sons were Tabu-Ley Rochereau, who would
create the Africa Fiesta National ensemble, and the guitarist Kassanda
"Doctor" Nico, whom Jimi Hendrix privately called one of his major
inspirations. Kabasele's influence was a musical taproot that would
nourish African creativity up to the present.

A saga's worth of groups, soloists, speakers, and dancers would arise
under the haughty vigilance of President Mobutu Sese Seko, who
remembered that, at the very moment when Kabasele, Lumumba's future
Secretary of State for Information, was writing his hit "Indépendance
cha-cha," he [Mobutu] had been chosen almost by accident to be the secretary who took notes during the independence negotiations with the
Belgians. Having become the henchman of the Western financiers, and
placed in power by a coup, Mobutu always showed a kind of jealousy
toward performers, as if he envied them the popular adulation they had
garnered, which relied only on the ephemeral power of a song.

In any case, Mobutu, via the men of his clan, did not refrain from
pushing performers to write "revolutionary" songs that bragged about
the merits of his presidency—or at least from reminding them of the
civic virtue of self-censorship.

Tabu-Ley Rochereau would test this system of patronage at his own
risk in 1993. This great renewer of Zairean music, a disciple of Kabasele,

---

[4] Interview in 1973 on Tele Zaire with Lukezo Luani for the show *Chronique musicale.*
[5] Among the groups said to play in Kabasele's style (in contrast to the other current
groups represented by Franco, more "roots" in treatment), the most famous were
Vox Africa (backing Bombenga), Africa Fiesta Sukisa (backing Doctor Nico), the
Maquisards (with Sam Mangwana), Empire Bakuba (particularly with Pepe Kalle,
Dilu, and Papy Tex), Zaiko Langa-Langa (with Manuaku, Papa Wemba, and Nyoka
Longo contributing), and Les Bantous de la Capitale (in Brazzaville).
[6] Those labels (Ngoma, Opika, Loningisa, Olympia, Papadimitrou, La Voix de son
maître, Philips, Vita, Epanza-Makita, Esengo) were for the most part owned by Greeks,
who would have a recording monopoly in that region for a number of years.

composed a song called "Le glas a sonné" (The Bell Has Tolled), included on an album destined for international release and produced by Peter Gabriel. In this song Rochereau said that instead of fighting all day long for government positions, "it is time for a truce so that we can worry about hospitals, schools, jobs." Some remarks in the Lingala language referred to the great ancestors (Lumumba among them), whom the author asks, "Why have you turned your back on us?"—before concluding with a prophetic sentence in French: "*Le dernier mot appartient au peuple seul*" (The last word belongs to the people alone).

The government would interpret the song as a veiled threat. It accused Rochereau of "subversion"—and threatened him so menacingly that he was forced to seek political asylum in France. "Sir" Rochereau had already suffered some painful ordeals at the hands of the soldiers of the "Man with the Leopard Skin Hat." In 1991 his wife was killed under very mysterious circumstances. In September 1992, soldiers robbed his house in Kinshasa and raped one of his daughters, only fourteen years of age. And throughout his long career he had been the object of various plots originated by Mobutu's men, designed to compel him to sing the praises of the president. "And then he [Mobutu] would tell his men to ease up and receive me. Congratulations and all that... sometimes, a small envelope.... Me, I only wanted to save my skin. My geopolitical origin did not give me a choice. I come from the region of Mulele, the first to conduct a rebellion against Mobutu after the death of Lumumba. It lasted five years before it was put down. Since then, everyone from that region is on edge, even if they have no political afterthoughts. Nobody from there lives beyond a certain level without the consent of the government. Me, I've always kept some distance between politics and myself. But my fame in Africa has always been considered a threat to the president."[7]

Is it the old antagonism of griot and government with a modern twist? It's easy to come to that conclusion in Zaire, as in all of Africa. Houphouët-Boigny, Sekou Toure, Kenneth David Kaunda, etc.—all would display, each in his own way, a dissuasive seduction vis-à-vis the artists. The singer-songwriter has precarious dealings with the chief, the latter always trying to prove his superiority.

---

[7] Interview with the author in 1993.

In the case of Mobutu, one would think that psychologically he never came to terms with the fact that Lumumba and the author of "Indépendance cha-cha" were friends and linked to the birth of the Congo's modern identity. He sometimes tried blindly to capture some of the aura of the musicians. Symptomatic was his attitude toward the guitarist Doctor Nico, the one Zairean musician (along with Kabasele) who can be said to have never enjoyed favors from the government during his musical career, or to have composed anything for it. In September 1985, Doctor Nico fell into a coma in Kinshasa. Mobutu[8] gave the order to rush Nico to a hospital in Brussels, where the "guitar hero" would ultimately die. Was this a way to maintain ambiguity regarding a supposed relationship between the government and the deceased? Was it an act of magnanimity, or of psychoanalytic transference? Who says that music is innocent.

---

[8] Mobutu died in 1997 after fleeing Kinshasa. A fascinating and shocking documentary by Thierry Michel, *Mobutu, roi du Zaïre* (1999), examines his thirty years of dictatorship.

E. T. Mensah: The King of Highlife

The Influence of Colonization on Music

King Sunny Ade, 1989.

Gentlemen, hold on tight to your wives,
Fathers and mothers, hold on tight to your daughters!
The calypso is damn seductive!
If they leave you,
It won't be Bobby's fault!

—"GENTLEMAN BOBBY,"
A HIT BY BOBBY BENSON

Much of modern African music is indebted to the musical instruments of colonization brought over by sailors, soldiers, and missionaries. The bugle, the flügelhorn, the harmonica, the accordion, the banjo, and the harmonium often preceded the teaching of harmony and religious musical education. It was in the bars that these instruments were diverted from their original purposes and adapted to a new life. The story of Ghanian highlife illustrates this phenomenon. In the 1920s, most forts on the Gold Coast had garrison bands that added some local melodies to their military march repertoires. The popularity of acoustic guitars would further change the scene. These were brought by Kru sailors from Liberia who worked on boats that shuttled between England, the United States, the Caribbean, and African ports. They were adapted to the technique of sanza (thumb piano) or harp players: the strings were plucked rather then strummed. This gave rise to numerous guitar bands[1]—either traveling groups or groups linked to those drinking

---

[1] Kro music developed in Freetown (Sierra Leone) in the 1950s and 1960s. Named after the Krio, or Creole, language (descended from the dialect of freed slaves who returned to Africa from 1807 on), Kro was a brass-band style reminiscent of the New Orleans genre and also a local calypso style, a kind of pre-highlife. Its most famous representative was the Maringar Band, headed by Ebernezar Calender, a coffin maker, who died in 1985. These "guitar bands" wedded the guitar to drums, banjos, triangles, scraped condensed-milk cans, and shekeres (dry gourds covered with a net of shells). It should be noted that at around the same time a similar music was developed on the Kenyan coast with the addition of bottleneck guitar, called "dry music."

spots that, a few seasons earlier, had been the birthplace of the sweet and light palm-wine music.[2]

Afterward came the big urban bands whose repertoire of waltzes, foxtrots, quicksteps, cakewalks, and ragtime made the Western colonialists, the "high-up," and the black elite all dance. The time of highlife had come! Named, it is said, after a local expression—"When I play this music, I feel high, very highlife"—it's a fusion of the jazz idiom and osibi, a percussion-based dance of the Akan, a people whose civilization centered around gold. And it would soon have as its unrivaled "king" Emmanuel Tetty Mensah.

Born in 1919, E. T. Mensah took organ and saxophone classes during his high school years at the establishment of a certain Joe Lampley (a fascinating character who had accumulated enough money to put together a band of about sixty players—on fifes at first, and other wind instruments later). By 1939, Mensah had become a pharmacy technician at the Gold Coast hospital in Accra and started playing in various local groups. A Scottish sergeant known as "Leopard" took note of him and invited him to join Leopard and His Black and White Spots—a mixed group, just as the name suggests.

At the time, World War II was raging. The Allies were massing troops and supplies on the Gold Coast to ensure against future invasions. The group played mostly jazz, swing, and other popular European dances in canteens and European clubs until the end of the war, when the soldiers departed, leaving the black public, who were greater fans of highlife, to become the authorities on it.

By then Mensah had opened his own pharmacy, and he had put together the Tempos Dance Band, another group polished in front of a uniformed public. Now he could finally dedicate himself to his passion. In the 1950s, imported Trinidadian calypso records and Afro-Cuban instruments (maracas, bongos, and congas) modified the dynamics of the local sound. A quiet fusion occurred, merging the African American rhythm and percussion with raw local sounds. Mensah's group pushed

---

[2] Palm-wine music reached an international audience thanks to S. E. Rogie, a Sierra Leonean musician who passed away in 1994. He was the author of such inimitable songs as "My Sweet Elizabeth" and "Dead Men Don't Smoke Marijuana."

this alchemy further than any other bands, and the Ghanian public was spellbound by the new style. It also became popular in Sierra Leone, Guinea-Conakry, Liberia, Nigeria, and even England, growing so renowned that in 1956, Louis Armstrong, while staying in Accra during his African tour, asked to play with Mensah. This was a great tribute to this prolific composer, who also owed his fame to the fact that, since 1958, Ghana had been governed by Kwame Nkrumah, one of the great Pan-African activists and a man who used music as a tool for the affirmation of national culture. Highlife also owed its popularity among the youth to its lyrics, often tied to current events. Whether sung in English, Fante, Twi, Ewe, Efik, or Hausa, its joking themes essentially dealt with day-to-day life and questions about the greater good. Highlife could be particularly biting and caustic in its social commentary.

By the 1960s, highlife, popularized by numerous bands (among the most famous were the Ramblers International and the Professional Uhuru), had generated a rich progeny, both in and outside Ghana. Several offshoots would emerge outside of Africa: the "burgher" highlife of Pat Thomas of Hamburg and the pop highlife of the London group Osibisa.[3] But it was, above all, in immense Nigeria, with a population at that time of eighty million, that the genre would branch out—turning into a national idiom in the hands of people such as Robert "Bobby" Benson and "Cardinal" Jim Rex Lawson.

Even though the Biafran civil war dealt it a severe blow,[4] highlife, like a hydra, continued multiplying, utilizing the limitless possibilities of traditional percussion and modern acoustics. One descendant went on to develop a tremendous momentum: juju music, whose name refers to what

---

[3] As a teenager Teddy Osei obtained a scholarship from Nkrumah, who was impressed by his saxophone playing, to study at the London Royal College of Music; in 1970 he formed Osibisa, which made the British hit parade with its Afro-rock. Their records became well known in the United States, Japan, and Europe.

[4] From 1967 to 1971, the region of Nigeria that was under Ibo control attempted to become independent under the leadership of Colonel Ojukwu, unleashing the Biafran war, which resulted in two million deaths. Although it was represented as a war between the Catholic Ibo and Muslim Nigerians, it was really caused by the despicable negligence of Northern politicians and oil interests. In time, highlife music was largely taken over by Ibo groups from the Lagos region. Leaders of these groups ranged from Chief Stephen Isita Osadebe to the passionate Oriental Brothers.

whites used to call the blacks' "magical" medicine as well as to the "joo-joo-joo" sound of the gbedun drum, which, over several decades, expressed the ascendancy of traditional rhythms. Juju, inaugurated by Baba Tunde King, strengthened its vocabulary with a series of percussion instruments associated with Yoruba initiation rites. In particular, the talking drum—hourglass-shaped, carried under the arm, and beaten with a curved stick to produce a sound that conforms to the tonal characteristics of the Yoruba language—would become one of the rhythmic signatures of this music.

A subtle mix of technology and the sacred, of worldwide influences and timeless rhythms, highlife gradually became more and more sophisticated. Bobby Benson kidnapped jazz and opened new avenues. Tunde Nightingale introduced the ukulele, the banjo, and the small samba drum. I. K. Dairo and his Blue Spots Band innovated with the accordion and experimented with mixing rhythms from different regions. "Chief Commander" Ebenezer Obey innovated with *miliki,* a melodious highlife based on several guitars. "King" Sunny Ade[5] integrated dobro guitar and synthesizer effects, eventually perfecting his "Synchro-System D," which permits each instrument to play its part without overlapping those of the others, the harmony being based on the subtle variations of the arrangements. These two major ambassadors of juju at the international level heralded an even more forceful explosion of regional schools and styles. These variations, made possible by the amplification of guitars, talking drums, congas, shekeres, agidigbos, and other bongos, were demonstrated in turn by "Sir" Shina Adewale and his Super Stars International, "Prince" Adekunle and his Western Brothers, "Doctor" Orlando Owoh and his African Kenneries Beat International, and others.

The latest craze to date is fuji music, derived from the Yoruba Muslim tradition and led by "Chief" Kollington Ayinla and "Chief" Sikuru

---

[5] Born in 1947 of royal Udoh blood, Chief Sunday Adeniyi, alias "King" Sunny Ade, produced hundreds of albums with his impressive group African Beat and organized powerful international tours. A brilliant manager, he directed a myriad of businesses (labels, video, film, night clubs, oil, and so forth). With a silky voice, ingenious guitar playing, and thought-provoking rhythms and harmonics, the "chairman" also owed much of his charisma to his lyrics, through which he conveyed the rich, spiritual Yoruba heritage.

Ayinde Barrister, which incorporates the bata drum dedicated to the god Shango in Yoruba ceremonies. Barrister (who, for a time, had to take refuge abroad in order to avoid being arrested by the military) envisioned a "sound" based on the Muslim Ramadan songs, augmented by apala chorus, sakara music, and percussion—a philosophical fuji, which he preemptively called "fuji garbage," to beat the critics to it. Today, along with reggae, it is the favorite music of young Nigerians.

Miriam Makeba: The "Click-Click Girl"

South African Music Between Silence and Exile

Miriam Makeba, 1993.

Satisfied with the gifts of honey and meat,
   the women clap and keep the beat
Since after the hunt, the hunters will be the
   ones who dance.
They tie the ears of an antelope—
Dry and full of resonant hollows—
Around their ankles
To give rhythm to the dance.

         —"THE HUNTERS' DANCE,"
            BUSHMAN SONG

Zenzile Ka Makeba Ka Gqwashu Ngu Vama Ngxowa Bantana Balomi Xa Ufuna Bafabulisa Uba Then Geha Ibotile Yotywala Sqiba Ukutsha Sithathe Izisha Sizilahle Singalalawu Singam Sqwashu Singama Nenekasi Singama Nagmala Nghiti, known worldwide by the name of Miriam Makeba, has had a strange destiny. In 1932, at the age of eighteen days, she began a six-month stay in prison with her mother, who was accused of manufacturing *umqombothi*—a beer made with malt and corn flour, the sale of which helped support the family. A few years later, her father, a Xhosa, disappeared. Her grandmother brought her up in a small dry mud hut, so Makeba understood common ghetto life, with its joys, violence, and constant humiliation by the white man. Her mother was forced to live far away, because she worked as a domestic servant in Johannesburg.

Makeba's mother played the sanza, the tom-tom, and the harmonica; she sang traditional airs and dance tunes, notably those of the healers, with a clear, strong voice. She was an *isangoma*, a medium who interpreted the *izinthola* (the bone joints), as well as shells, and rocks, and spoke with the *amadlozi* (the spirits). Her animist philosophy would profoundly influence her daughter and determine most of the decisive choices she would make about her life.

In 1948, apartheid[1] was enacted, and from then on black children were forbidden to go to school after the age of sixteen. As a teenager Makeba had to work as a maid. She also participated in a chorus that indiscriminately rehearsed a repertoire of gospel, Xhosa, Sotho, and Zulu songs. For black South Africans, the syncretism of their original cultures with those of the British and Afrikaans was a natural thing. Thanks to her pure voice, which earned her the nickname of "Nightingale," she was recruited in 1952 by the Manhattan Brothers, one of the most popular groups in the country, and went on to form the Skylarks, a quartet of women. This fan of Billie Holiday and Ella Fitzgerald, whom she discovered thanks to their records, made nine dollars each for her own first records, and earned nothing from their sale. In 1959, furthering her reputation, she formed African Jazz and Variety, a group that played mbombela, a mix of jazz and traditional rhythms. While in that group she was discovered by a film producer, who asked her to perform two songs for a documentary. The movie, *Come Back Afrika,* named after the anthem of the African National Congress (ANC), the principal force of black resistance, was an indictment of apartheid and won the Critics' Prize at the Venice Film Festival. To promote the film, Makeba traveled to Italy, then to the United States, where Harry Belafonte took her under his wing and introduced her to the most talented black performers of the time.

When Makeba opened at the Village Vanguard, the famous New York jazz club, before Sidney Poitier, Duke Ellington, Nina Simone, and Miles Davis, her voice was heard. The American media christened her "the Click-Click Girl"[2] and launched her career.

Meanwhile, the situation in South Africa had worsened. On March 21, 1960, the police opened fire on participants in a demonstration against restrictions imposed on the movements of blacks—"the Sharpeville mas-

---

[1] "Apartheid" summarizes the program of the Afrikaner nationalists after they assumed power in 1948: racial segregation, imposed in housing (creating ghettos), school, work, and day-to-day life.

[2] She got this nickname because of a song that used clicks—the implosive consonants belonging to the Khoisan ("Bushman" and "Hottentot"), Xhosa, and Zulu languages.

sacre." When the smoke cleared, eighty-eight victims lay dead or wounded, among them members of the Makeba family.

Following her premonitions, Makeba's mother decided to send Bongi, Miriam's daughter, to the United States with jazz artist Hugh Masekela. Shortly thereafter, Makeba's mother died, and the singer wanted to go home to organize a decent funeral for her. When she went to the South African consulate, however, the bureaucrats there made it clear to her that, though she might be the darling of the American media,[3] to them she was just a "Kaffir." a disdainful employee stamped her passport "invalid." This clash made her an exile—the first in a long list including Dollar Brand (the future Abdullah Ibrahim), Hugh Masekela, Chris McGregor, Dudu Pukwana, Letta Mbullu, Jonas Gwangwa, Louis Moholo, and Julien Bahula.

The 1960s marked the beginning of the end of the black South African urban music that had flourished for a time in neglected cracks of apartheid's racial walls. The most obvious sign was the fate reserved for Sophiatown, a multiracial neighborhood in Johannesburg. Despite difficulties, over a period of twenty years an incredible bouquet of musical styles and theatrical performances had developed there, influenced by music newly arrived from America and Europe as well as that brought by the migrants working in the factories and mines. This milieu was an unauthorized melting pot that gave rise to hybrid musical styles such as majuba jazz—a combination of marabi, kwela, and American jazz that would be the ancestor of the mbaqanga popularized in the 1980s by Mahlathini and Johnny Clegg, among others. This blossoming urban culture—an embodiment of the new black identity, as magazines such as *Drum, Bambu World, Zonk,* and *Golden City* would rightly observe—apartheid erased with bulldozers, condemning the musicians to silence, exile, or the uncertainty of the *shebeens,* the local ghetto bars.

---

[3] Her appearance in the New York clubs would open doors. *Newsweek* wrote: "She sings with the smoky tones and delicate phrasing of Ella Fitzgerald, and when the occasion demands she summons up the brassy showmanship of Ethel Merman and the intimate warmth of Frank Sinatra." *Time* magazine added: "She is probably too shy to realize it, but her return to Africa would leave a noticeable gap in the U.S. entertainment world, which she entered a mere six weeks ago."

Meanwhile, on the other side of the Atlantic Ocean, Miriam Makeba would experience again the brutal reality that had thrust her into the long tunnel of exile, as *realpolitik* trampled on the great humanist sentiments that had accompanied her arrival in the United States. East–West relations being what they were, the racists of South Africa had free rein. As proof, while she was performing a concert at Carnegie Hall, ANC leader Nelson Mandela was arrested, later to be condemned to life in prison. Makeba, despite being seen singing at President Kennedy's birthday with Marilyn Monroe, or denouncing the crimes of apartheid in front of the General Assembly of the United Nations, would find herself in the FBI's sights. Her crime? She had allied herself with the Black Power movement, which had become radicalized after Martin Luther King's assassination. To make matters worse, she was in love with one of the leaders of the Black Panthers, Stokely Carmichael. That fact would eventually cause her to lose her recording contracts; she would also be shunned by artists who earlier had delighted in her company. Constant police surveillance forced her and Carmichael, now her husband, to take refuge in Guinea-Conakry at the invitation of President Sekou Toure. Her ongoing saga would be punctuated by several marriages, a plane crash, car accidents, a battle with cancer, a coup d'état, and the death of Bongi... events that would sometimes be revealed in the intonation and modesty of her singing.

The violence Makeba endured contrasts with her timid character. Trying to explain the secret of her resiliency and calm strength, she wrote: "In the West the past is like a dead animal. It is a carcass picked at by the flies that call themselves historians and biographers. But in my culture the past lives. My people feel this way in part because death does not separate us from our ancestors. The spirits of our ancestors are ever-present. We make sacrifices to them and ask for their advice and guidance."[4] It's no surprise then that, whatever the ups and downs of international show business [which swindled her more than most], the African continent has always seen itself in the woman it affectionately calls "Mama Africa." Here is proof that modern African music, passing

---

[4] In Miriam Makeba and James Hall, *Makeba: My Story* (New York: New American Library, 1987), p. 2.

through the sieve of time, has maintained its memory and its pride. This permanence enabled the singer of "Pata-Pata"[5] to return in the 1980s to her original plan, beginning with her participation in the *Graceland* tour organized by Paul Simon, and climaxing with her homecoming, after thirty-one years of exile, to a liberated South Africa.

---

[5] Written in 1956, the song "Pata-Pata" ("Touch-Touch" in the Zulu/Xhosa language) was inspired by a traditional dance, accompanied by whistles, that is sexually suggestive because each dancer touches the other all over the body following the rhythm of the music. In 1967, Makeba recorded the song with an arrangement that blended mbombela (South African jazz) and kwela (a cocktail of traditional urban rhythms) with soul music. It became the first international African hit.

Bembeya Jazz and the Syliphone Elephant

The Era of National Pride in Guinea

*Still playing, a guitarist from Bembeya Jazz is
borne aloft in triumph by the audience, 1989.*

To save his head, Diakouma improvises the words and the melodious sound that accompanies them. The King tells him: "Bala fasseke" (I authorize you to play the balafon). Since then, Diakouma is called "Bala Fasseke" (Player of the Balafon). Meanwhile, Soundjata's army is getting stronger: he successfully obtains the secret of invincibility from the king of Sosso, who could be killed only with the spur of a white rooster.

— YOUSSOUF TATA CISSE AND WA KHAMISSOKO[1]

In Niagassola, in the northeast of Guinea, the Kouyate family preserves in a mud case the Sosso-bala, an eight-hundred-year-old balafon (xylophone with gourd resonators). This instrument, along with a leather bonnet and a pair of wrist jingles, once belonged to Soumaworo Kante, last ruler of the Sosso kingdom and ancestor of the hunter-smiths. Legend has it that Soumaworo Kante gained his power through the magic of this balafon, played by his slave, Diakouma Doua, who, before being captured, had been the griot of the king's nemesis, Soundjata Keita. Soundjata defeated Soumaworo for good in 1235, at Kirina on the left bank of the Niger, and went on to found the Mali Empire. The famous balafon he gave to Diakouma, the "Bala Fasseke."

The instrument's creation was inspired by the spirits, and it remains in working condition (only two bars and one calabash have been replaced). But the Sosso-bala is played only at night, and is under the constant watch of a guard—the *beletigui*. It is considered the ancestor of all the balafons on the continent of Africa.

This moment in history, known throughout West Africa, expresses well the inextricable, fantastic, and extraordinarily precise character of the Manding oral tradition, whose eldest daughter, genealogy, nourishes

---

[1] *La Grande Geste du Mali,* by Youssouf Tata Cisse and Wa Khamissoko (Karthala-Arsan, 1988).

a large part of its heroic epic. And one of the chosen lands of that epic is Guinea-Conakry.

The 1960s were the tumultuous years of independence. French Guinea had been at the forefront of Pan-Africanism, voting "No" to the referendum on the French Commonwealth proposed by General De Gaulle in 1958. The ex-colonial power retaliated by trying to strangle its economy. In that context, for Guinean president Sekou Toure, music became the vehicle for asserting national identity. The Art Direction project created an artistic group in each of the country's 2,422 administrative units, 236 counties, and 34 states. In 1959, at the request of the president, Keita Fodeba[2] created *Les Ballets Africains,* whose aims included defending "a Pan-African vision that privileges encounters and multiethnicity." This view would spread through other countries of Africa[3] and turn artistic codes, genres, and catalogs upside down, fostering a new generation of artists. On the musical front, the strategy of multiethnicity would generate altogether unprecedented working arrangements that motivated figures such as Kante Facelli, who later died in a plane crash, but not before ensuring that Guinean musicians had a leg up on their neighbors for a long time.

In each city, bands would spring up and challenge each other in high-powered competitions. The top eight groups among them were "nationalized" and gained financial support from the state. The Horoya Band, Keletigui and His Tambourinis, Balla and His Baladins, the Super Boiro Band, Djoliba National, Camayennc Sofa, and the instrumental and choral ensemble *Voix de la Revolution* (Voice of the Revolution)

---

[2] An ardent nationalist since 1947, Keita Fodeba created the Fodeba-Fancelli-Mouangué. The ensemble was later renamed the African Ballet, then the National Ballet of the Republic of Guinea. In 1957, he became interior minister, before falling victim to Sekou Toure's paranoia about a "plot." He was put in prison in 1969, where he died.

[3] In September 1960, Mali became independent. On the airwaves, the voice of the blind griot Bazoumana Cissoko urged the exiles to return to the country, where Modibo Keita had taken power. The former schoolteacher knew the importance of art as a teaching tool. Guided by Guinea's example, he also pushed for creation of more musical groups. Some brilliant bands would result, among them the Regional Orchestra of Mopti, the Negro Band of Gao, the Super "Biton" of Segou, and the National Instrumental Ensemble.

were the most dynamic and renowned in Guinea—and West Africa. The most revolutionary band was the Amazons of Guinea (still active today), which originated in the women's police brigade. After starting with drums, mandolins, violins, and cellos, they adopted electric guitars, a jazz organ, a drum set, and horns.

Thus, hundreds of musicians practiced every day, played profusely, and saw their work marketed by the state firm Silly Phone (later Syliphone), with its elephant symbol (elephant is *silly* in Manding), mascot of the president's former party. This label would market modern Manding music over the whole continent.

The main figure in this revival was Ibrahima Kouyate Sory Kandia, child of Fouta-Djalon, whose sublime mezzo-soprano voice, together with his compositions, represented the high point of the renewal of the Manding heroic epic. He was supported in his work by outstanding musicians such as the dazzling kora player Diabate Sidikiba and El-Hadj Djeli Sory Kouyate, the greatest balafonist the Mande have ever known.[4]

Bembeya Jazz was born a thousand kilometers from Conakry, in the small town of Beyla. In 1961 the band formed as nothing more than a group of talented youngsters whom the governor, Emile Kwande, pushed to organize. The group took its name from the local river, the Bomboya, which runs between Diakolidougou and Beyla, and in the Guerze language means "twines in the water."

From the beginning, Bembeya Jazz aimed to create modern music based on traditional melodies. Thus, for example, they decided to replace the bolon—a type of kora with three strings, in the griot style of the lords—with a string bass with a similar sound, ultimately to be replaced

---

[4] "Traveling Ambassador of African Music" and "The Bard of Medieval Africa," according to the Guinean newspapers. When Kouyate Sory Kandia died at the age of forty-four from a heart attack on Christmas 1977, all of Africa mourned his death as if they had lost a family member. Kandia had been heard throughout the world, especially in New York. Related to Kouyate Kandia and a kindred spirit on stage, El-Hadj Djeli Sory Kouyate is a direct descendant of Bala Fasseke Kouyate, the famous griot counselor of Soundjata Keita, King of the Manding. As such he received his first balafon at the age of twelve as the scepter of his lineage. At eighty-two years old, he is still active.

by an electric bass. In 1966 the group relocated to the capital, Conakry, and became "nationalized." By now a glowing swing machine, its members were chosen as ambassadors of the young republic during important meetings of what was then called the Third World. The meetings of the Tri-Continents in Cuba (1965), the Pan-African Festival in Algiers (1969), and FESTAC (the Festival for Black Arts and Culture) in Lagos (1977), provided an opportunity for all that brass to shine.

This innovative big band took the rich Manding tradition to new heights, but did so didactically. It attracted its first notice through compositions recounting the story of Samory Toure who, from 1888 to 1898, led the resistance against the colonial troops of Borgnis-Desbordes, Boylebe, Gallieni, and others—before being captured and exiled to the Gabonese island of N'Jole, where he died on June 2, 1900. The music formed a type of opera, based on eyewitness accounts and songs collected from the oldest griots.

Bembeya also hosted many excellent musicians and singers—as adversity would demonstrate. In 1973, on the road to Dakar, Bembeya lost Aboubacar Demba Camara, called "The Dragon," in a car accident. An idol even in a country where the collective was exalted in the name of ideology, this great singer—proclaimed No. 1 on the continent by the BBC—was the darling of all West Africa. As proof of his popularity, a hundred thousand people, all dressed in white, accompanied his remains to the cemetery of Camayenne while the Camp Boiro military band led the procession playing "Boloba," the Manding anthem of valiant warriors. Simultaneously, funeral processions were organized in Zaire, Senegal, Upper Volta, Mali, and Liberia. The losses of the melodious accompanist Mamady Camara, called "Old," and the bassist Mory Kouyate II, were among the band's somber twists of fate. But Bembeya continued a transformative course as an informal conservatory. Ashkeen Kaba, founding member and trumpeter, constantly hired new musicians, and the singing of the leader Salikou Laba was reinforced in 1978 by the new voices of Youssef Bah, Sekouba Diabate, and Sayon Diabate. The group's dancers also doubled as backup singers.

Rooted in a rich and fertile musical tradition, Bembeya Jazz has, through the years, managed to update its style without leaving its spiritual roots. For a while, it was hunting for a "mestizo" style influenced by

Franco, Fela Kuti, Manu Dibango, and others—not to mention Cuban music, which inspired so much imitation in Africa. But in the 1980s it started reworking its sound in the direction of folkloric roots.

Although its discography displays great activity, Bembeya Jazz, like many of its brethren in Africa, suffered from a cultural environment governed more by "*le système D*"[5] than by professional rationality, and its state support was withdrawn in 1984. Despite all the obstacles, it has sung in all languages of the country with themes ranging from the social (one of its hits, "Whiskey-Soda," talks about the bad effects of alcohol) to the political (another hit, "O.U.A.," castigates apartheid), passing along epic tales or evoking more picaresque realities. On top of all this it succeeded in founding a modern classical orchestral school. At a time when world music is rediscovering the merits of great musical patrimonies, these are no small accomplishments.

---

[5] *Translator's note:* The phrase "*le système D*" is not readily translatable into English, and expresses a uniquely French attitude. An example of French ingenuity, cunning, and resiliency, it is the act of finding a way around any obstacle, finding a loophole in any rule, turning a situation to one's own advantage. People who do this well are not considered dishonest, but rather extremely clever.

Francis Bebey, Pierre Akendengue: The Metropolitans

The Children of Négritude

Francis Bebey, his eyes closed, and his guitar, 1984.

This power often takes the name of universality. Assimilation, as a political tool, is a product of the cultural vocation of the Latin peoples. They readily admit that all men are alike and are created equal—so long as they assimilate into the colonial mass, melt into *their* history and submit to *their* values and to *their* cultural authorities—and, of course, they have to renounce all that is not from the Latin genius, and particularly their own cultural and spiritual values.

—ALIOUNE DIOP[1]

While modern African music was conceiving new sounds in Kinshasa and Brazzaville, in Paris, in the tumultuous May of 1968, Francis Bebey was distinguishing himself as a middle-aged musician at the American Center for Students and Artists at 261 Boulevard Raspail.[2] It was a place where, for a five-franc cover, the young French folk crowd met at hootenannies engineered by Lionel Rocheman. Singing in Douala, French, and English, the Cameroonian Bebey offered them a musical array inspired by Bantu songs and Pygmy polyphonies. He played assiko (a Cameroonian version of highlife) influenced by the jazz he heard as a young man studying in New York, where he had composed his first piece, "Lake Michigan in the Summer." He came to Paris in 1956 and became a reporter for the SORFOM (*Société de radiodiffusion de la France d'outre-mer,* the Overseas French Radio Broadcasting Society, ancestor of RFI, Radio-France International), then joined UNESCO to develop its musical department.

---

[1] *Présence Africaine,* November 1947.
[2] The Center, which had weekly concerts from 1965 to 1977, and whose director was also a percussionist, was also one of the places where modern African dance won its first devotees, through pioneer teachers such as Ahmed Tidjani Cisse, Buem, and Lucky Zebila.

The son of a Baptist pastor who played harmonium and accordion, and raised on Bach and Handel, Bebey ended up an educator. Through his many activities as a composer and writer, he became a proselytizer of traditional African music, largely unknown in France. He once said, "I wanted, at all costs, blacks to become conscious of their music and non-Africans to become aware of our existence. If you do not know this African music, you may never understand the black man, because his life, his philosophy, his past, present, and future are incorporated in what he expresses musically, whether it is music for listening or for dancing."

Indeed, Bebey used the sounds of all the instruments of central Africa—mouth bow, sanza, flute, and harp. He took inspiration from African myths and imagination to compose his songs. He opened new avenues, such as the humorous song, which provided him with several hits, including "La Condition Masculine," "Agatha," "Divorce Pygmée," and "Le Troisième Bureau." In 1972, Philips offered him a recording contract for the album *Idiba*, in which he included arrangements by his childhood friend, Manu Dibango. Upon its release, he dedicated the first vinyl copy to Leopold Sedar Senghor, president of Senegal. The gesture was not in vain. Senghor was one of the principal figures of the *négritude* (blackness) movement, which, both before and after World War II, was dedicated to literary, artistic, and political plans to promote "the common values of black civilization."

This movement had several magazines to trumpet its cause, including the stellar *Présence africaine*, created in 1947. Around its founder, Alioune Diop, it gathered the brightest of the engagé intelligentsia, both white (Jean-Paul Sartre, André Gide, Albert Camus, Michel Leiris, Theodore Monod, Emmanuel Mounier, Paul Rivet) and black (Aimé Césaire, Birago Diop, Jacques Rabemannajara, Richard Wright, René Depestre, Mongo Beti, and others).

For Francis Bebey, the movement was more than a vocation. It was his way of enlisting in the continuation of that earlier struggle, for the farther African music got from its soil, the more it had to prove its relevancy and contemporaneity. At the time, it was still largely confined to being picked apart by ethnomusicologists or caricatured by the cinema. Although the Western imagination was beginning to revise its representations of black, Arab, and Indo-Chinese natives in proportion to the assertiveness of their claims to self-determination, the exchange between North and South was still unequal.[3]

Pierre-Claver Zeng Akendengue of Gabon, who arrived in France in 1964 to finish his studies, similarly struggled for recognition. In his case, his passion for music was born at Bessieux College,[4] a religious institution at Libreville whose program included sight singing, Gregorian chant, and the guitar—an instrument to which he would adapt the technique of the seven-stringed ngombi harp and which he would use in his first compositions. His songs chronicled the social life of the capital, Libreville, and of Port-Gentil, situated at the mouth of the Ogooué River, which carries cargoes of precious woods, notably *okoume*. Eager for musical connections, Akendengue became a member of the *Petit Conservatoire de la Chanson*,[5] hosted on television by the singer Mireille. This small,

---

[3] One can follow these changes of perception through Art Nouveau, certain composers (Debussy, Poulenc, and Milhaud), surrealism, the birth of ethnology, a literature influenced by pan-Africanism. World War I and its Senegalese machine gunners, jazz, the black and Caribbean bands on the banks of the Seine or at the Joliette in Marseilles, and finally the defeat of Nazism all contributed to the rise of doubts about Eurocentrist thinking. The independent countries of the 1960s, which exported their cultures in the name of their new nationalities, would shuffle the cards even further. In the 1970s, the connection between music and international politics became closer. A counterculture symbolized by the big pop festivals chose its heroes from Kingston (Bob Marley and the reggae movement), the United States (Black Power), India, and Tangiers. The principal figures of this dissident culture and their followers would have a hand in the black music wave at the beginning of the 1980s, when the French heritage, interpreted in Lingala, Bambara, or in Boby Lapointe's wordplay, played itself out. The airplane and the immigrant home created new musical alchemies among the transplants from Africa and the Caribbean. A variety of musicians, studios, stages (the Traditional Art Festival of Rennes, the Spring Festival of Bourges, the Mongrel Musics of Angoulême, the White Nights for Black Music in Marseilles, the Theater of the City of Paris), labels, media (from *Actuel* to *Libération*) have made France a revolving door for the musical genres of the world (cf. *Les Musiques du monde en question,* Babel–Maison des cultures du monde, 1999).

[4] The influence of religious institutions on African music is considerable. Three main artists of modern Gabonese music, it turns out, studied at Bessieux: Hilarion N'Guema (founder of Afro Success), Damas-Ozimo (founder of the Sphinx Orchestra), and Pierre Akendengue.

[5] This experiment would be re-created at Libreville by Akendengue when he hosted his *Carrefour des arts* (Crossroads of the Arts) from 1988 to 1992. Housed in the Saint-Exupéry French Cultural Center, it launched many local careers.

effervescent woman, seduced by the young man's songs, would play a decisive role in his career by urging him to sing in his native language, Myene. That encouragement reinforced his hitherto-fragile commitment to a modern African music that draws directly on its heritage, as his first 45-rpm record would show. This famous piece, "Le Chant du coupeur d'okoume" (Song of the Okoume Woodcutter), had the air of a poetic manifesto.

Like Francis Bebey, Pierre Akendengue would have to go to an "alternative" setting to find ears willing to listen to his cause—specifically those of Pierre Barouh, who, thoroughly alienated from the music available at the time, had just founded the Saravah label with the motto, "Some years you just don't feel like doing anything." A group of daring liberals became active with him, among them Jacques Higelin, Brigitte Fontaine, David McNeil, and Jean-Roger Caussimon. In the bosom of this family, in the studio of the Rue des Abbesses in Paris, Akendengue produced the albums *Nandipo* (1974), *Afrika Obota* (1976), *Eseringila* (1978), *Owende* (1979), before switching to a major label (CBS), and then creating his own label, symbolically called Ntche (The Country), in Gabon.

Francis Bebey and Pierre Akendengue were undeniably at the forefront in African music's quest for recognition. The two composers spent a lot of energy seeking acknowledgment from the North, whose cultural norms they had inherited. Along with others of the same generation, they lived through a period of contradictory dynamics: a Europe walled up in its privileges, and an Africa that, through its new generations, was becoming aware that it could only rely upon its own strengths. As an example of this gap, in the 1980s, Francis Bebey represented Africa at the *Haut Conseil de la Francophonie* (High Council of the French-Speaking World) created by François Mitterrand. This was an appropriate turn of events for a writer-musician who had never seen any contradiction between the delicacies of French and the defense of Africa's national languages and dialects, essential tools of any cultural affirmation.

At the same time, globalization was pushing aside the myth of French superiority, a fact expressed by the new generations in Dakar and Abidjan, who had their eyes riveted on New York, Tokyo, or Sydney. That uneasiness was voiced by Bebey's Gabonese counterpart in the album

Maladalité. "This title is because Africa is in the condition of a bedridden patient [*malade alité*] in need of assistance. To cure an illness it has to be diagnosed. It is up to us Africans to snap out of it, jumpstart it. The main project, at home, is the cultural one. Africa has suffered from an eclipse of identity. We have been reduced to a savage, folkloric part of the scenery, to which you have to add the economic and military system that has governed us. This has debased the image of Africa. There are great spiritual forces in Africa. There is the animist Africa and the profoundly religious Africa. I believe that it is up to us to capture this spirituality and, in the process of give and take, offer it to others."[6]

For all that, the pleas of these luminaries of modern African music—for a multiethnic look at the continent and, above all, for a fruitful dialogue between tradition and modernity—remain strong. Thus, with Francis Bebey, if his voices, sanzas, and flutes are once again blazing paths through the savannas, and if his compositions are fragrant with the night-time stillness of the village while his words capture its myths, he nonetheless never tires of pointing out that the griots were the first to weave the "web" (i.e. the Internet). He establishes a correlation between the most intimate African imagination and the present (see the album *Dibiye,* 1998): the Pygmy pulse suggestive of the trip-hoppers, the incantatory chant echoing the hypnotic sound of dance music, and the reminiscence of a sublime *"Stabat Mater Dolorosa"* evoking some familiar spirits of the brush.

For his part, Akendengue, in collaboration with Hugues de Courson, formerly of the famous folk group Malicorne, released *Lambarena,*[7] one of the most original world music albums of the decade. It is a kind of oratorio in homage to Albert Schweitzer—theologian, winner of the 1952 Nobel Peace Prize, founder of the hospital at Lambaréné in Gabon, doctor, Bach expert—who at times left to play concerts in Europe, the proceeds from which financed his insolvent hospital. But Albert Schweitzer displayed no interest in African traditional music, and when he practiced

---

[6] From an interview with J. Thiefaine, *Paroles et musique,* January 1996.
[7] The premiere included 150 musicians and singers. It took six months to prepare and three months in the studio with a budget of 1.5 million francs, donated by an arts foundation.

his organ, he took the unusual step of closing all the windows—an odd-ity that prompted Akendengue to ask: "If he had opened the window to listen to the vibrant indigenous music, what shock would that have caused? What mélange could have resulted?" These questions led Courson and him to imagine an animist saga that merges the songs and rhythms of the Gabonese forest with the architecture of Bach, the unrivaled rhyth-mist—a footnote to history, which never settles its scores.

Rakoto Frah: The Wizard Merlin of the Sodina

The Malagasy Musical Entity

Rakoto Frah, 1996, with a bouquet of flowers offered for his birthday.

Nothing is better than family.
He who owns a bull has meat;
He who owns a rice paddy has mud;
He who has fat in reserve can have light at night;
But he who has a family has everything.

— MALAGASY SONG

I n the shantytown neighborhood of Anitihazo-Isotry in Antananarivo lives Philibert Rabezaoza Rakoto, better known as Rakoto Frah. This small man, with missing teeth and a straw hat glued to his head, represents Malagasy music. Born sometime between 1920 and 1923, he followed in the footsteps of a father who was a singer at the royal court of the Merina dynasty, which had unified Madagascar and whose palace rises above the capital. Introduced early to the sodina flute, he started getting invitations at a very young age to play at the countless gatherings that gave rhythm to Malagasy daily life, from block parties to circumcisions.

Today there is a special place reserved for him during the ceremonies of the return of the dead (*famadihana*), one of the most spectacular national rituals dedicated to the spirits. For the Malagasy, the living and the dead coexist in a visible and invisible world. The invisible realm is populated by the ancestors, who are endowed with magical powers and are custodians of the practices, customs, and *fady* (taboos)—in short, they are the keepers of social harmony.

To become an ancestor, it is not enough just to have died. First, the skeleton has to be cleansed of all impure flesh. Decomposition takes place in a temporary sepulcher under the watchful eye of a guardian. Then, when the *ombiasy* (sorcerer/healer) orders it, the bones are very carefully cleaned, wrapped in a silk shroud (*lambamena*), and interred in a permanent tomb. Even then, every five years the dead are exhumed in order for them to meet with the sun, the source of life. The rituals can last from two days up to a week, with guests numbering in the hundreds, and often include offerings, sacrifices of zebus, and libations, all testifying that death is also a renewal.

These burial feasts turn into a pretext for a good deal of music and song.[1] During the long days of joyful remembrance, the musicians have to prove their talent and imagination. In the region of Antandroy (known as "the country where the water hides"), groups with three or four voices sing in epic fashion *bekos*—songs that retrace the life story of the deceased. Rakoto Frah's improvisational talent, his ability to adapt to each family's tradition, and his mastery of the flute made him one of the most sought-after musicians for these ceremonies.

But he was also one of the first to travel abroad to help export Malagasy music. Leaving behind his work as a baker and blacksmith, he went to perform with the National Orchestra in sub-Saharan Africa, North Africa, Australia, India, the Soviet Union, and Europe. Then, after a conspicuous absence during the dictatorial "socialist" regime of Didier Ratsiraka, he reappeared on the international scene in the 1980s. Always even-tempered, he was a little surprised to find himself resurrected as a father figure for a new generation, who banded together to pay for his dental work. As a rugby fan, he leads his flute-and-percussion band in the stadium during the national team's games. He is the Malagasy culture's tie between modernity and tradition. That tradition includes one of the world's richest musical legacies, in which a number of world music producers have developed an interest in the past few years—surprised, in this age of mingling styles, that Madagascar has been living this way for eons.

---

[1] The cost of these ceremonies, as well as the bill for the tombs—impressive esplanades fenced by tall walls with zebu horns and *aloalos* (carved totems that recount the life of the deceased) rising above them—can be shocking. But for the Malagasy people, since "life is transitory and death is eternal," it is justified. Ancestors are regularly consulted and honored, and they can be capricious if not totally unpredictable. It is advisable to soothe them with offerings of rice, honey, rum, zebus, and music. The possession rituals depend on healers, who are consulted once the therapeutic recipes of Western and traditional medicine have failed. They usually diagnose the existence of evil spirits, which must be banished. In all exorcisms, the voices are backed by instruments—drums, bamboo rattles, marovany, mandolins, and accordions—that "lift" the evil spirit (the *bilo*).

In fact, as far as music is concerned, Madagascar long ago set itself apart from the rest of the African continent. The oldest island in the world displays some amazing singularities: the highest concentration of indigenous plants, fascinating lemurs (primeval primates who live in trees), and a wide range of topography and climates. In the musical realm, it also displays a fascinating uniqueness. Its eighteen different ethnic groups each have their own diverse instrument-building traditions, collective practices, playing techniques, and song styles—yet they all have a common flavor.

The smooth richness of Malagasy, the island's Malayo-Polynesian language, provides the link. Madagascar's uniqueness is due to its late settlement (though still before the Christian era) and its layers of migrant cultures. These include Indonesians who arrived from across the sea before the ages of Indonesian Hinduism and Islam (presumably via the outrigger canoe so characteristic of the coasts); African Bantu; Islamic Swahilis; Yemeni traders; Portuguese, English, and French pirates; and so on. A melting pot of musical instruments, the island's artful sounds rendered Kurt Sachs, one of the pioneers of ethnomusicology, speechless in 1938. He wrote, "You see, side by side, the Stone Age rattle, the Arabian hurdy-gurdy, the 18th-century European viol, and the modern accordion."[2]

Modern groups have put this incredible diversity to good use. They use a bit of polyphony here, some vakisova (street choirs with a very social repertoire) there. Elsewhere, the seventeenth-century European violin, which became the lokanga bazaha (the "foreign" lokanga), is at the heart of the *mpilalaos:* "classical" orchestras without which no festival worthy of the name could take place. Jean Emilien is fond of the kabossy (a lute with three to six strings), whose trapezoid shape recalls the mandolin. Sylvestre Randafison and Justin Vali have brought international renown to the valiha (a zither on a bamboo tube that sounds somewhat like a harpsichord), as Bekamby did with the marovany, another

---

[2] The songs of Madagascar traveled for the first time to the modern West at the World Exposition of 1900, an occasion for France to appreciate the importance of her colonial empire. It was there that Maurice Ravel found the inspiration for his *Chansons Madécasses.* For its part, Pathé-Marconi has recorded there since 1935, inaugurating a long line of local producers.

type of zither on a wooden trunk. Rossy was inspired by the street theater (*hiragasy*) and by the royal brass sections. The ecologist D'Gary adapted marovany music for the guitar. Regis Gizavo adapted the gorodo, a Hohner-type button accordion (Malagasy musicians like to file the blades to make it adapt to the vocal scale, calling it a "castrated accordion"). Eusèbe Jao-joby internationalized the salegy, a 6/8 rhythm reminiscent of the rattle of possessed women and the clapping of hands at funerals. Vaovy, the group led by Jean-Gabin Fanovona, reintroduced the neotraditional island sound of the Antandroy, "the thornbush people." The Salala trio reen-acts the jousts of Antandroy herdsmen. Erick Manana and Sola Razafindrakoto fascinate with their picking technique...

With his striking array of flutes, protected by plastic duct pipes, Rakoto Frah in concert is accompanied by various musicians of all regions, and is thus a little all-over-the-place. Is it any wonder that he was chosen to play for General De Gaulle during his visit to the colony? And that, for forty years, his likeness has adorned those 1,000-*ariatry* bills that he so rarely has in his own possession? Nevertheless, this musician—who, according to Ornette Coleman, has one of the most seductive phrasings of anyone in the world—doesn't care for such fame.

> *On earth, where we are only passing through,*
> *Everything has its time,*
> *A time to cry,*
> *And then a time to laugh,*
> *A time to stay,*
> *And the time to leave.*[3]

For him, the spirit world is always the most important one. Thus, between concerts, he dedicates himself to transmitting his knowledge of the traditional arts to the new generation, so they, too, can proudly travel the planet, honoring through their transit these famous ancestors with fatally musical ears.

---

[3] From "Any Indray Andro," translated by Michele Razafitrimo-Randrianivosoa, from an album by Feo-Gasy (a group consisting of Rakoto Frah and five singer-musicians) called *Tsofy Rano* (Les Nuits atypiques/Mélodie).

THE SALT

OF THE

EARTH

Thomas Mapfumo and the Ancestors' Mbira
in Zimbabwe

National Liberation Music in Southern Africa

Thomas Mapfumo, 1986.

Oh! grandmothers! Oh! mothers! Oh! boys!
There is a snake in the forest!
Mothers, grab a hoe!
Grandmothers, grab a hoe!
Boys, grab an axe!

—CHIMURENGA SONG

n April 1980, Zimbabwe declared independence. To celebrate the
event, Thomas Mapfumo and his group, the Blacks Unlimited, were
joined by no less than Bob Marley and the Wailers in front of a sell-
out crowd at Rufaro Stadium in Salisbury (to be renamed Harare)—a
concert marking the turn of history's page after a seven-year struggle for
national liberation.

The presence of the "pope" of reggae was not a mere coincidence. A
few months before, Marley had made his first trip to Ethiopia and, at a
retreat in a Jamaican Rasta community there, composed the song "Zimbabwe," explicitly about the liberation struggle. And it was this song that
a hundred thousand people were now singing in unison during the
encore at Rufaro Stadium.

As for Thomas Mapfumo, he embodied the seven years of struggle in
what was up until then called Rhodesia. The fight was led by two organizations, the ZANU (Zimbabwe African National Union) of Robert Mugabe
and the ZAPU (Zimbabwe African People's Union) of Joshua Nkomo,
against a white colonial power that, allied with South Africa, had free rein
over the mines (copper, gold, chrome, tungsten, coal, and so forth), the
tobacco and cotton fields, and the livestock of the land. The harsh struggle, in a country of seven million people, claimed thirty thousand dead,
fifteen thousand maimed, two hundred and fifty thousand exiled, and
one million people displaced.

To face a superbly equipped white army, the black militants practiced
all the guerrilla tactics known throughout the world, but above all they

used the weapon of consciousness raising, relying on the spiritual resources of the Shona and Ndebele, the two majority ethnic groups. From this philosophy, Thomas Mapfumo ("Spear" in Shona) and his guitarist Jonas Sithole would crystallize a music that was destined to become the anthem of the emancipation movement in the shantytowns of Salisbury and Bulawayo as well as in the countryside. The music would be widely disseminated by Radio Mozambique, Radio Zambia, Radio Cairo, Radio Moscow, and underground recordings.

Born in 1945, Thomas Mapfumo knew what he was talking about. He grew up in the middle of the Tribal Trust Lands, rundown reservations abandoned by the white colonists. He followed his parents into the township ghettos of the capital; and it was there, while listening to broadcasts of the soul music and rock 'n' roll that was inspiring youths at the other end of the world, that he sensed the power of music.

The mbira would be his alchemical tool. In use since the Monomotapa dynasty of the sixteenth century, this lamellaphone usually has twenty-two strips of metal, mounted on a wooden resonator and played with the thumbs. In the Shona culture, this sanza, when played in groups of several instruments along with a calabash rattle (the hosho), had a special purpose: it was the instrument-medium that permitted contact with the spirits during possession dances. The missionaries had no doubt about it: they called its crystalline themes "the music of Satan." Transposing the cyclic sounds of this instrument, Mapfumo devised a new style incorporating repeated guitar and bass riffs and triplets played with the hosho on a cymbal, the whole accompanied by a vigorous bass drum. Chimurenga music was born. Through it Mapfumo would channel the frustrations and humiliations of his people.

Although banned by Ian Smith's racist regime, the songs were broadcast secretly. Thanks to them, many youths joined the resistance. They also earned their composer several months of imprisonment—although the authorities were unable to charge him with a tangible crime, since the words of the Chimurenga songs were cloaked in the parables and metaphors so treasured by the national languages of Zimbabwe.

After independence, the hypnotic beat born of the mbira would be the signature sound of Zimbabwean pop. Stella Rambisai Chiweshe (the first woman who used the mbira, formerly reserved for men, onstage),

Oliver Mutukudzi, Bhundu Boys, Devera Ngwena, the Four Brothers, Comrade Chinx, and Chiwoniso were the music's major figures.

Zimbabwe was not the only country where music was used to fight against the cultural alienation born of colonial oppression. A similar process unfolded in the Portuguese colonies prior to the 1974, toppling of the heirs of the Salazar regime, especially in Angola, the richest province of that empire. As in Rhodesia, the first expressions of the rebellion were coupled with the first indigenous modern music. The layout of the capital, Luanda, vigorously embraced the social divisions of the colonial system: whites lived in the center, whereas workers and domestics lived in the unpaved quarters: the *musseque* ("built on sand" in Kimbundu). Between the two zones were areas reserved for the "assimilated": state workers, employees, traders, and artists, often of mixed origin. Traditional music had been tolerated in the 1930s and 1940s—particularly during Carnival—but when a popular liberation movement emerged in the 1950s, centered on the MPLA (*Movimento Popular da Libertação de Angola*), native culture was outlawed. At the same time, in the *turmas* (youth groups that got together to sing and dance), an Angolan national identity was taking shape—an *Angolanidade* that advertised itself as interethnic and interracial, like the contemporary *négritude* movement, whether in America, in the Caribbean, or in Africa.

Inspired by tradition, groups sought to renew it: Duo Ouro Negro, Escola de Samba de José Oliveira Fontes Pereira, Kimbandas do Ritmo, Eliaas Dia Kimuezu, and especially Ngola Ritmos, a school founded in 1947 and named after Ngola Kiluanje, ruler of the kingdom of Ndongo, who had led a rebellion against Portuguese colonization in the sixteenth century. Alumni of the school would almost all become nationalist militants. Under the tutelage of Liceu Vieira Dias, the Ngola Ritmos brought Mbundu music "up to date." Liceu found inspiration for his *lamentos* in the chants of Besangana women and funeral lamentations. He adapted regional dances, most notably the semba, a derivative of the Kazukuta rhythm, and also the basis of the famous Brazilian samba, thanks to the slave trade.[1] His guitar harmonizations tamed the circular rhythms of

---

[1] The triangular trade (between Africa, Europe, and the Americas) linked to the transport of slaves fostered an extraordinarily rich diaspora of the imagination. On

the marimba (the xylophone dear to the Mbundu) and the sanza kissanje. The solo guitar in counterpoint to the voice, which enhanced the rhythm guitar; the use of the dikanza (a scraped-stick instrument somewhat like the Brazilian reco-reco) to keep a counter-rhythm; the drums; and the dialogue between lead vocal and chorus—all these particulars made up the much-copied style of Ngola Ritmos. Yet they had only a decade to enjoy this creativity. In 1959, Liceu Vieira Dias and Amadeu Amorim were sent to the concentration camp of Tarrafal, at the end of one of the Cape Verde Islands, from which they would not return until ten years later. José Maria, in turn, was arrested in 1961 and forced into the army.

It was with the armed actions of the MPLA that the music began to play a pivotal role in mobilization[2] and in the rehabilitation of the stifled memory of identity. The colonial powers tried to limit its impact, going so far as to ban Carnival,[3] but the economic vigor of the colony thwarted the government's intentions, because the trade in coffee, cotton, and beer since the mid-1960s funded a rising number of radios,

---

the musical front, the blues of the slaves would inspire the majority of popular styles in the United States. And one need only open one's ears in the West Indies, in Latin America (specifically in Peru, Ecuador, Venezuela, Colombia, and on the banks of the Rio de la Plata), as well as in the Indian Ocean, to find identical effects. The unique vodun culture rooted in Benin, Togo, and Nigeria (called the Shango cult in Trinidad, Santería in Cuba, Vodun in Haiti, Obeah in Jamaica, and Bayou in New Orleans) includes close to one hundred million people. These diaspora cultures gave rise to modern musical styles that, from the Cuban rumba to the Haitian kompas, are coming back in turn to the dance floors of Africa.

[2] All the leaders of nationalist movements of the Portuguese colonies, Agostinho Neto (Angola), Samora Machel (Mozambique), and particularly Amilcar Cabral (Guinea-Bissau and Cape Verde), himself an honorable morna musician, expressed throughout their writings a special interest in the role of culture in an occupied country. In Cape Verde, it was through the combination of literature and music that the national identity was affirmed. Beginning in 1935, the first theories appeared in poem collections and in magazines like *Claridade,* which questioned assimilation or imposed values. The great popular poets such as Eugene Tavares (1867–1930) took up the baton and became lyricists for the mornas and the coladeiras, giving these popular musical forms a legitimacy that was never again denied.

[3] Carnival was forbidden from 1961 to 1968, and numerous artists were exiled. After independence, Carnival was permanently set on the March 27, in remembrance of the victory of the MPLA (and Cuban forces) over South African troops.

record shops, nightclubs, and commercial transactions with Portugal. This contradiction allowed for the expression of a certain African aesthetic in Luanda.

Thus, a new generation of artists, tuned in to the frequencies of the world, emerged in Angola and in exile. Some had close ties to the key figures in the renewal of Portuguese popular music, including José Afonso (who lived in Angola and Mozambique), composer of "Grândola Vila Morena," the anthem that signaled the beginning of the "Carnation Revolution" in Lisbon in April 1974, which ended thirty-two years of Salazarism.[4]

Barcelo de Carvalho, today known as Bonga, was one of this generation. "With my group, Kissueia, we sang about the reality of Angola under colonial rule, the poverty, the shantytowns, the lack of milk for the kids, the whole filthy aspect of real life. We asked the question why a country so rich in gold, diamonds, and coffee could be in such a catastrophic situation." But his involvement in the struggle put his life in danger. In 1966, he had to leave Luanda for Lisbon, where he felt better protected after becoming the national champion in the 400-meter dash. Still, because of his connection to the nationalist movement, he remained a target of the PIDE, the state political police, and finally had to leave for The Netherlands. There, finding many exiled musicians, including some Cape Verdeans, he cut some of the most significant albums of modern Angolan music.

---

[4] In addition to the Portuguese influence, the African musicians had also been inspired by artists of the Brazilian *tropicália* movement (Gilberto Gil, Chico Buarque, Caetano Veloso, Maria Bethânia, Milton Nascimento, etc.), who had also experienced the harshness of dictatorship and become interested in their African roots. Gil participated in the FESPAC (Pan-African Cultural and Film Festival) in Lagos in 1977, and later in "voodoo" musical sessions.

Franco: "You Go in OK, You Come out KO"

The Second Wave of the Congolese Sound

Franco with his guitar, 1983.

Night-Kinshasa is a woman in labor, pushing every night, scream after scream, in a bath of sweat and blood. Night-Kin is also an erect phallus, always erect, sign that the city is awake. This city rises because it knows how to take hold of its hunger with both arms and drape it in velvet, laughter, and mockery.

—VINCENT LOMBUNE KALMASE[1]

1978. After the open-air market of Kasavubu, Matonge is the pulsing heart of Kinshasa, a city of four million inhabitants from four hundred different ethnic groups. The city is the capital of a country that is four times the size of France, and has been ruled since 1965 by the dictator Mobutu Sese Seko Kuku Ngbendu Waza Banga. In keeping with the proverb "a fish rots from the head," Kien-Kiese (translated: Kin Joy) is nothing but one vast grabfest ruled by the famous, apocryphal "Article 15" of the constitution—"*Démerde-toi!*" (Do what you have to do.) In this enormous social pressure cooker governed by "*le système D*" and closely guarded by the lone political party's Revolutionary Agitation Groups, Matonge is a safety valve for letting off steam, a free zone for irony, so as not to go crazy. It is in this maze of cement buildings and concession huts that modern Zairean (previously "Congolese" and, after Mobutu's death in 1997, once again Congolese) music has always been created. In this court of miracles one can, for what little cash one has, find live crocodiles and smoked monkeys, car parts, medicine, *kadhafis* (gasoline in liter bottles),[2] foreign currency, illegal drugs, and most of all, beer, girls,

---

[1] From the novel *Errances ou le quêteur de rebuscences* (1988), excerpted in *Revue noire*, no. 21 (June 1996).

[2] The African metropolises are rich in slang and vernacular expressions, in the local languages as well as in their adopted Western counterparts. Examples of Kinshasa French expressions are *un tetanos* (tetanus): a rusted-out taxi; *un tais-toi* (be quiet): hush money; *prendre le train de 11 heures* ("take the 11 o'clock train"): to run away; *avoir le soleil* (to have sunshine): to have hemorrhoids; *un deserteur* (deserter): a husband

and music. Enlisting the big names in song for the price of a quart and an ad, bars like the Primus, the Skol, the Castel, and so on, carry on their turf wars. Wearing the *"abas-cost"* (*à bas le costume* [down with the suit] because of Mobutu's decree that the *boubou,* or tunic, should be worn as part of his cultural authenticity policy), men come to pick up *mingandos* (rural women who have come to sell their charms) or to meet their "second offices" (mistresses). The music pours loudly from the *ngandas* (clubs) and from the speakers in front of music stores that sell bootleg tapes. Night after night, these clubs become factories churning out new titles that enlarge the reputation of the musicians.

Modern popular music is always born from a combination of dubious regulations, social rule breaking, artificial paradises, tribal loyalties, and a collective need to flout inevitable fate a little. In this light, Matonge, a jumbled warehouse of rhythms, is another one of those places around the planet where history has transformed "crap" into musical gold—like New Orleans during Reconstruction, Athens after the tragedy of the Turkish expulsion of 1922, Buenos Aires full of immigrants, and the dancehall Paris of La Bastoche.

In this Dadaist world, violent and hearty, streetwise and generous, just to survive the blows and counterblows of the "struggle for life" is a proud achievement. And François Luambo Makiadi, a.k.a. L'Okanga La Ndju Pene Luambo Makiadi, and better known as Franco, has become one of the legends of this place. After starting in the 1950s in the footsteps of the Zairean guitarist Tino Barosa, wizard of the patengue style, a cross between the pachanga (post-cha-cha-cha) and the merengue (Dominican salsa), Franco set his stamp on the rumba odemba, a fast rumba enriched by folk elements and spiked with a guitar technique that consisted in embellishing with two notes around a theme introduced by the kalimba, a local sanza.

For his journey through the storms, Franco used a high-powered engine: OK Jazz (Orchestre Kinois de Jazz),[3] a group with which this son

---

who has left his home; *voir mystique* (see mystical): blurry vision; *un long crayon* (long pencil): an intellectual; *le retour* (the return): coins; *coop* (for cooperation): corruption or negotiations; *tailler le caillou* (sharpen the stone): to work things out.

[3] OK Jazz was born in 1956. It was named after Oscar Kashama, owner of the OK dancing bar. It became a musical entity in 1962 at the insistence of Luamba François and Longomba Lukuli, alias "Vicky" Longomba, who had had valuable experience at

of the Lower Congo would imaginatively combine native rhythms and Cuban influences, all based on the rhythmic flow of popular language, giving birth over several decades to hits such as "Mario,"[4] "Marie-Catherine," "Bana Motoba," "Ngala ya petit bolingo," "Attention Na SIDA," and about a hundred albums.

In 1965, after a political-financial debacle knocked the young OK Jazz to the mat, Franco saved the instruments from the creditors' talons and reformed the group under the name TPOK Jazz (*Tout-Puissant* [Almighty] OK Jazz), a way of declaring his unbridled ambition. This rebirth signaled the beginning of a fiery competition with other groups, particularly the Africa Fiesta National led by the innovative Tabu-Ley Rochereau, who would establish himself as stylistic heir to the great Kabasele. And what a battle! Each band had its fans, who had at their fingertips its repertoire, its genealogy, its drama, and its breakups and relationships, just as if it were a soccer team. And, of course, the stylistic challenges and farcical feuds[5] were driven by songs and answer songs that were subject to the exegesis of all Kinshasa.

But of all the signs of musical allegiance, the dances were the most decisive. Each band tried to impose its own, which had to resist whatever fashions swept by, or else demonstrate its ability to reinvent itself. The media[6] kept a close watch on the dance wars and commented on them endlessly. Dances with scrumptious names arose, the most memorable

---

Decca, the most dominant label in Africa. It would take several pages to name all of those who worked with Franco and ultimately founded their own bands.

[4] In "Mario," a woman complains of her boyfriend's ingratitude after she has given him everything: "Because of the beauty products, my skin has become smooth. / Tomorrow, when I get cancer, / when I fade, you will leave me. / Mario, I have had enough. / Mario's parents think he takes care of me, / while it is I who dresses, feeds, and puts him up. / Leave my house, Mario! / Why is there this ransom for love?" (Franco, "Mario," African Sound Music, 1987.)

[5] A competitor once called Franco a "fake millionaire," to which he answered in a sung address: "You were a public rotten corpse / that stunk all day long. / I brought you out of your putridity. / Today I, Franco, become your enemy!" (Franco, "Chicotte," Epanza Makita, 1968.)

[6] In a uniquely Congolese custom, the press has always devoted major stories to music. In 1978, it published a census: there were 1,200 bands in Zaire, one for every 20,000 inhabitants! Another distinctive aspect of the local scene was the existence of local recording studios, record presses, and musical producers.

being the apollo (from the TPOK Jazz), the boucher (Africa Fiesta National), the cavacha and the choquez retardé (slow grind) (Zaiko Langa-Langa), the griffe-coucou (cuckoo's claw) (Viva la Musica), the makassi calculé (Empire Bakuba), the mobylette (Africa Fiesta Sukisa), and the crapeau-crapeau (Stukas). Most of these dances were comical or sexually suggestive in their choreography.

It was from his headquarters, his club Le 1, 2, 3, in a building he had had constructed on Khetule Avenue, that Franco directed the TPOK Jazz project. On the first floor were the offices of *Yé*, a weekly magazine dedicated to music; on the second, a restaurant and bar; on the third, the offices of "Uncle Yorgho"—Franco himself. This was where he looked after his several businesses and where he housed UMUZA (*Union des Musiciens Zaïrois*), of which he was the president. It was the nerve center for perpetual machinations in and around the Zairean musical world. It was from here that Franco also ruled his band with an iron hand, recruiting and firing talented musicians, adapting to the hazards of international showbiz, and organizing tours to Europe and the United States.

As far as anyone can tell, Franco owed his professional longevity to his talent as a social commentator and satirist. Songs like "Makambo Mazali Bourreau," "Lettre au DG" (Letter to the Director), "Très Impoli" (Very Impolite), and "Très Faché" (Very Angry) were sharp little musical morality plays that Franco's public ate up. Though well aware he was no paragon of virtue himself, Franco decried moral decay and perversion, admonished loose women, and reprimanded the young "strays" besotted with the West. All the same, he never let the appearance of virtue get in the way of the cunning he needed to get by in Mobutu's Zaire, especially since, as a member of the ruling party, he occasionally found himself fencing with the "leopard" power, and sometimes losing. In 1978, Mobutu made him appreciate just how small a prison cell could be.

Franco lost his father at the age of ten and had to quit school early to help his mother sell donuts at the market of Ngiri Ngiri. During this time he lived in the street, and earned him the right to sing rawly about the harshness of a society drained by the cupidity of the powerful, economic crises, and the ever-present *baksheesh* (*madesu ya bana*, a society whose values have been corrupted). His lyrics, with their rude verbiage, and his music, with its hypnotic, aggravating rhythms, elucidate a Congolese urban world in total upheaval, and a social free-for-all marked by the urgency of hunger and want. Still, he always used the derision so peculiar to *Kin la Frondeuse* (Kinshasa the Mudslinger) to soften tragedy. For example, he once, as if attempting to musically exorcise AIDS[7] (*SIDA* in French), called it "*Syndrome Imaginaire pour Décourager les Amoureux*" (an imaginary syndrome to discourage the amorous)—all while many of the singers and musicians of the prolific Kinshasa musical milieu were succumbing to the disease.

---

[7] Franco died on October 12, 1989, in Brussels. He was buried a few days later at the Gombe cemetery in Kinshasa, accompanied by a million mourners. No one mentioned the famous "imaginary syndrome to discourage the amorous." Even so, AIDS has been the subject of many songs in an Africa, whose leaders long refused to acknowledge the seriousness of the epidemic in their own countries. For example Remmy Ongala, a Tanzanian star, promoted the practice of using condoms in "Mambo kwa soksi" (Things in Socks), a song that was banned from the radio until it became popular with teenagers.

Fela Kuti: "The Man Who Carried Death in His Pouch"

The Quest for the Nigerian Afrobeat

Fela Kuti (in front of a banner reading "Blackism a Force of the Mind").

There is only one civilization and one culture that we can transmit to others: ours.... Our task, if we believe in our civilization and in ourselves, is to boldly lead the African people on the same path that we are following, and, in doing this, we are sure that we will fulfill our duty toward them.

—GOVERNOR OF UGANDA, 1938[1]

Winter 1983. The slogans "Blackism: Force of the Mind" and "Pan Africanism Will Save the World," in bright letters and signed MOP (Movement of the People) span the stage. Is it a political meeting? You might think so. But the instruments on the stage, and the glistening colors of the ten thousand people assembled in a lighthearted atmosphere under a huge tent set up in a field not far from the Balard station of the Paris Métro, indicate another type of event: a performance by the band Egypt 80, led by the "Black President," also known as Fela Anikulapo Kuti, "the man who carries death in his pouch," the star of Afrobeat music—a combination of highlife, hard bop, and African free jazz. Catlike, nervous, an instigator, agitator, and redeemer—for twenty years he has disrupted, intrigued, charmed, and provoked controversy.

The impressionistic lyricism of his music cannot be separated from his political views, as the Western entertainment industry would like to do. In Africa, many advised him to cool down his militant talk. "Brother, you're not being reasonable," they said. All doors would be open to him, they said, if he'd just get with the program. But though he paid dearly for his refusal to give in, Fela never dropped his guard, and now he has become the mouthpiece for the resentments of the biggest and most important African nation (with more than one hundred million people) and the bard of a Pan-Africanism that evokes memories of Kwame Nkrumah and Sekou Toure in the 1960s.

---

[1] From the inaugural speech of Makerere University, May 21, 1938.

It is because of all this that a Fela concert—encompassing at once a "happening," a jazz session, a soul-funk show reminiscent of James Brown's, and Yoruba ritual incantations—is worth the trip. On the Balard stage, five saxophones, three percussionists, a drummer, and four singers are cooking up a throbbing, enchanting pulse. A canvas of basses woven with percussion threads and brass riffs serves as backdrop to the lead saxophone, the chorus, and the psalmlike chant that make Fela's long pieces so unique. With jabbing words and acid themes, his songs (such as "International Thief Thief") explicitly denounce neocolonialism and the control of the African economy by multinational corporations, especially in Nigeria.

> *Na true I want talk again o*
> *If I dey lie o*
> *Make land punish me o*
> *Make Ifa dey punish me o*
> *Make Osiris punish me o*
> *Make Edumare punish me o*
> *All African Gods o well well*
> *Long time ago*
> *Long long time ago*
> *African man we no dey carry shit*
> *We dey shit inside big big hole*
> *For Yoruba-land na "Shalanga"*
> *For Igbo-land na "Onunu-insi"*
> *For Hausa-land na "Salga"*
> *For Ashanti-land na "Tiafi"*
> *For Gaa-land na "Yarni"*
> *[…]*
> *I read about one of them inside book*
> *Them call him name na I.T.T.*
> *Them go dey cause confusion*
> *   (Chorus:) Confusion*
> *Cause inflation*
> *   (Chorus:) Inflation*
> *Cause corruption*

> *(Chorus:) Corruption*
> *Confusion, Inflation, Corruption*
> *Them get one style wey them use*
> *Them go pick one African man*
> *A man with low mentality*
> *Them give am million naira bread*
> *To come and find position here*
> *[...]*
> *Like Obasanjo and Abiola*
> *(Chorus:) International Thief Thief*
> *I.T.T.*
> *International rogue*
> *We go fight them well now*
> *We don tire to carry anymore of them shit*[2]

Other songs follow: "Authority Stealing" and "Upside Down," which criticize the current African dictators; "Unknown Soldier," a song that calls for the unity of a much-divided continent. Fela knows what he is talking about. Dozens of times he has been dragged in front of the courts, and he has lived his life at the crossroads of the social, political, and historical contradictions of his country. His hopes, failures, and triumphs are ambiguous, just like those of a continent confused by foreign "independences." When he was seven, a *babaláwo*, a practitioner of the Ifa oracle, warned his mother: "The child will be stubborn, impetuous, unbridled.... His path will be strewn with pitfalls...turbulence and violence.... His wives will be numerous.... He will live in poverty alongside beggars and thieves. His friends will be fugitives...and he will be branded an 'outlaw.' For he will flout laws, go counter to the taboos of men and the god of the *oyinbo*." He concluded, "And he will perish by their hand."[3] More or less, Fela's life would verify the prophecy.

---

[2] Fela, "ITT (International Thief Thief)," a twenty-four-minute song originally recorded in 1980 (EMI Music Editions); later included in the album *Original Sufferhead/ITT* (Barclay-Universal). Ifa: Yoruba god of divination. Edumare: Yoruba supreme god. Obasanjo and Abiola were both Nigerian heads of state.
[3] Carlos Moore, *Fela, Fela: This Bitch of a Life* (London: Allison & Busby, 1982).

In a country such as Nigeria, whose economic center, Lagos, is an ungovernable human maelstrom, Fela's strength is fed by the past. Born, like his relative, the Nobel Prize–winning writer Wole Soyinka, in Abeokuta, a county seat in the state of Ogun, a region rich with oil, Fela had deep, ancestral ties to Yoruba culture. A people with a rhythmic language, passionate temperament, sophisticated spiritual beliefs, and complex political and social institutions, the Yorubas, according to historian Cheikh Anta Diop, emigrated in antiquity from the Nile to southeastern Nigeria. There they founded a powerful state of more than thirty million people before separatism and fratricidal wars divided it and the slave trade struck it a fatal blow. Christianity and Islam, in their turn, also put their stamp on Yorubaland.

Fela, in his quest for personal and collective identity, had always made a big deal of this history. His father, the Reverend Ransome-Kuti, Anglican pastor, principal of a grammar school, first president of the Nigerian educators' union, had passed it on to him. In case his son couldn't follow in his own footsteps, he also passed on to him his taste for the piano—a family passion started by Fela's paternal grandfather, who had been a pioneer of the Yoruba Christian Church and a composer who, in the 1930s, recorded close to twenty-five 78-rpm records of Africanized religious music. His mother also had an enterprising spirit, having founded at the start of the 1940s the Nigerian Women's Union, which mobilized against "politicos," won the battle for women's right to vote, and developed friendly ties with Mao Tse-tung and Kwame Nkrumah, president of neighboring Ghana and leader of the Pan-African movement.

But before finding his own voice, Fela traveled, studied, listened, and garnered points of view from England, Ghana, and the United States. In the States he learned of the Black Power movement, which made him aware of his "Blackism" and pushed him to define his Africanist convictions in his music.[4]

Back in a country festering with corruption and torn apart by the terrible Biafra War, Fela put his ideas into practice with his group Africa

---

[4] A meeting with Sandra Taylors, a member of the Black Panthers; books by black authors (notably Malcolm X); and a range of influences including Miles Davis, Martin Luther King Jr., The Last Poets, and Nina Simone—all helped determine Fela's path.

70, whose first hit, the aptly named "Jeun Ko'Ku" (variously translated as "Eat and Die" and "Chop and Quench"), revealed his intentions. Then, in 1974, the saga of the "Republic of Kalakuta" began. This cooperative community in the neighborhood of Ikedja, one of the poorest in Lagos, consisted of Fela's house, his brother's "clinic," and an empty lot next door. The name was the same as that of a cell in which the musician had been incarcerated for "corruption of minors and possession of cannabis."[5] A self-governing land, the "republic" became the target of a succession of military groups in power who were enriching themselves from the nation's oil exports. Because the recording industry had found the task too embarrassing, Fela decided to produce his own albums, at the rate of eight per year, with each album-pamphlet irritating the authorities, who kept trying to tame him and temper his passion. The peak of uniformed vindictiveness came in February 1977, when an army of a hundred soldiers invaded Fela's "republic." Everything was destroyed by fire. Fela and his friends were beaten. Many of his wives were raped. His mother was thrown from the second floor.[6] And when the singer brought a lawsuit, an investigating commission determined that the incident was the work of "unknown soldiers." Fela answered with his album *Kalakuta Show*, whose cover art depicts the tragic event.

Fela's troubles with the authorities didn't end there. He continued to have constant run-ins with both formal and informal powers (for example, the Lagos gangs, with whom he no longer sympathized), even though one might think that his international notoriety might have protected him a little. Finally, in 1984, his running battle with the government again came to a head. As he was leaving for a tour in the United States, he was arrested under a trumped-up charge and then condemned to five years in prison. This time, though, his international renown at last brought him some

---

[5] Several of Fela's singers and dancers had run away from home to join Africa 70, thus giving rise to these accusations. On Fela's return from exile in Ghana on February 20, 1978, he decided to marry the twenty-seven women of his group to avoid allegations of pimping.

[6] His mother, seventy-eight years old, died from her wounds a year later. Fela had a replica of her coffin, carried by his wives, placed at the entrance of the government palace. A few weeks before the sack of Kalakuta, Fela had upset the authorities who organized FESTAC (Festival for Black Arts and Culture) by staging a "sit-out" at Kalakuta that had attracted the majority of the press and foreign artists.

measure of protection. A European coalition was mobilized. In France, artists organized under the code name "Operation Jericho" and gave a series of concerts in Europe; the newspaper *Paroles et musique* gathered signatures from hundreds of artists and published them during the Spring Festival of Bourges. This European lobbying on Fela's behalf helped win his eventual release from jail, after he had served only twenty months of his term.

A few months after his release, a new album surfaced: *Teacher Don't Teach Me Nonsense.* In the song "Look and Laugh," Fela proposed to set the record straight:

> *Since long time I never write new tune,*
> *Long time I never sing new song.*
> *Many of you go dey wonder why*
> *Your man never sing new song.*

His explanation followed, targeting the corrupt Nigerian governments that succeeded each other, the foreign governments that had a stranglehold on the country's economy, and the reality that never changes. He concluded:

> *Which-e kind wayo* [deceit] *be that?...*
> *When them come, burn burn my house*
> *All my property burn-u, burn-u dem-o*
> *Beat-e beat-e me, kill my mama...*
> *Look at our television and listen to our radio in Nigeria*
> *When dem do dem nonsense finish, newspaper self go join*
> *My own be say, too many overseas things and our own too small*
> *When dem go do our small sef, dem go be ye-ye things* [when they
>   cover local things a little, they cover inconsequential topics]
> *No plans, no set, no ideas inside dem, dem go dey copy overseas dey go*
> *Government this, government that, in their ties, lace and dungarees*[7]

---

[7] *Translator's note:* Fela is evoking the endless news coverage of government maneuvering, and depicting the Westernized and elite African dressing styles the politicians are always seen wearing.

Ah! Looku, looku, looku [look], *lafu, lafu, lafu* [laugh]
   [repeats]
Se, I no know what dem do inside television,
Police uniform come important pass [becomes more important
   than] *the food-u for this country,*
Go to court and the big-big [fancy] *English, and still, dem do dem*
   nonsense [corruption],
1809 [law] *book dem go bring to judge case of 1980*
Government people still dey enjoy with police supporting
Nigeria still dey where he dey [stuck in the same place], *problems*
   still plenty more.
Looku, looku, looku, lafu, lafu, lafu.[8]

Afterwards, between international tours, prolific recordings, and concerts in his Lagos club, The Shrine, Fela developed more fully the possibilities of his Afrobeat, keeping equal distances between the tradition of highlife and technological advances in sound and fusion, until his death on August 2, 1997, at the age of fifty-nine. His funeral sparked antigovernment protests defying the military regime.

Two years later, some of Fela's most important songs were finally released in France[9] as originally recorded. From a distance, one can appreciate in these songs the power of his African saga, brimming with chiaroscuri, ghosts, and modern myths: a musical work-in-progress that could have been the soundtrack of a novel by Amos Tutuola,[10] another native of Abeokuta, in whose works monsters have names like "smelling-ghost," "spirit of prey," "flash-eyed mother," and "long white creatures." His novels throb with ridiculous words stirred by Ubuesque situations. Fela's

---

[8] "Look and Laugh," a seventeen-minute song, from *Teacher Don't Teach No Nonsense* (Mercury, 1987). *Translator's Note:* Many thanks to Michael Veal for providing the transcription.

[9] His collected work was reissued in 1999 by Barclay under the guidance of Francis Kerketian. Fela's afrobeat legacy has had few claimants except for his son Femi and his former drummer Tony Allen.

[10] Amos Tutuola, author of *The Palm-Wine Drinkard* (1952), was, along with Wolé Soyinka (1986 Nobel Prize–winner for literature after being jailed and exiled), Chinua Achebe, and Ken Saro-Wiwa (hanged by the military), a prominent figure of Nigerian literature.

work sounds like a strange oratorio in which the topic is the black man's—
or simply man's?—reappropriation of his own destiny. This goal explains
why music and its magnetic power is a spiritual vehicle particularly suited
for the reality of a disconcerted Africa, and seen therefore as a useful
tool by Fela Kuti: "Music is the weapon of the future / music is the weapon
of the progressives / music is the weapon of the givers of life."

Mahlathini, "King of the Groaners," and Johnny Clegg, "The White Zulu"

The Soweto Stewpot on the Hot Coals of Apartheid

Mahlathini and the Mahotella Queens, 1998.

For centuries we have been artificially separated from the rest of Africa. We are discovering its culture. We are becoming Africans.

—BARBARA MASEKELA,[1] SOUTH AFRICAN
AMBASSADOR TO FRANCE, 1995

1964. Robben Island is a fortress in the icy waters off the Cape, a prison where the clank of pickaxes, the rattle of chains, and the barking of dogs are part of the daily routine of men condemned by apartheid to decades of imprisonment. Blacks, Indians, and "coloreds" are called kaffirs, coolies, and hotnots here. Brutalities and tortures, blows from cudgels and rubber hoses, are common. Above are airplanes and countless seagulls; below are dolphins. It is in this Kafkaesque universe ruled by racist Afrikaner minutia that Nelson Mandela, leader of the African National Congress (ANC), the principal force of underground opposition, has been imprisoned.[2]

Meanwhile, Simon Nkabinde, a child of the province of Natal who has grown up in the township of Alexandra (the urban residential zone reserved for Blacks), is noticed by Rupert Bopape, from the black label Gallo,[3] one of the key men in the local music industry. Renamed

---

[1] Speech given in May 1995, at a meeting of one hundred South African artists at La Villette in Paris.

[2] Sentenced to life in prison, Mandela was transferred in 1982 to the Polls Moor Prison near Cape Town, and freed in February 1990. Apartheid was abolished on June 30, 1991. Countless African songs took Mandela and apartheid as themes (one-third of all the songs sent to the RFI [Radio France International] *Découvertes* competition, for example). The biggest hits included "L'Esclave" (The Slave) by Papa Wemba, "Sisi Mandela" by Tabu-Ley Rochereau, "Soweto" by Sam Mangwana, "Apartheid" by Zao, "Zimo" by Sam Fan Thomas, "Nelson Mandela" by Koko Ateba, "Espoir à Soweto" (Hope in Soweto) by Akendengue, "Apartheid" by Xalam, "Soweto" by Super Diamono, "Apartheid Is Nazism" by Alpha Blondy, "Nelson Mandela" by Youssou N'Dour, and "La honte de l'humanité" (The Shame of Humanity) by Kante Man Fila.

[3] Eric Gallo's South African label has been recording "tribal" music since the 1930s and is still the biggest record company on the continent.

Mahlathini (meaning "bush on his head"), this street singer is associated with three young women: Hilda Tlubatla, Mildred Mangxola, and Nobesuthu Shawe, who will ultimately come to be known as the Mahotella Queens. Around this time, a new musical genre is emerging. Mbaqanga— named after a meatless stew that contains pumpkin, cabbage, and yeast— will become the soundtrack of a black population enduring the injustices of an ever-worsening apartheid. This mbaqanga combines everything that urban African music has been over the last several decades: marabi from the 1920s, kwela from the 1940s, sax-jive or majuba from the 1950s, and imitations of highlife, American pop, and rhythm and blues.[4] On this ground Mahlathini, whose impressive, rugged bass voice groans and roars, and the Queens, singers and dancers with an insatiable energy, will prove themselves remarkable entertainers. Their colorful, generous, and eccentric performance style is right on target, taking its inspiration from the world of migrant labor. Workers in the mines have long been entertaining themselves during breaks by having dance contests and vocal or instrumental duels. The choreography of these competitions is often inspired, although not infrequently with an ironic distance, by Zulu, Xhosa, Sotho, or Swazi traditions. John Bengu, called Phuzhushukela (Sugarwood) first put this style on stage in 1950; Mahlathini and his associates exploit it under the name *simanje-manje* or *maqshiyo*. They sing about traditional societies, their moral values, the tranquility of a countryside long ago abandoned by thousands of men who joined families crammed in brick "matchbox" houses in the sad urban ghettos. In its hypnotic rhythm, its chorus, its dance, mbaqanga expresses the culture gap internalized by an uprooted black population.

With the barriers imposed by petty apartheid[5] designed to divide ethnic groups from each other, break alliances, and weaken any homegrown

---

[4] Marabi, born in the *shebeens,* is a mix of Dixieland, ragtime, and the music of black mine workers; kwela ("climb, go up" in Zulu), played on pennywhistles (of which Spokes Mashiyané, Lemmy Mabasso, and Elias and Aaron Lerolé are the masters), combines marabi, traditional music, and American swing jazz. Sax-jive will add the saxophone and piano to the instruments of the kwela.

[5] *Translator's note:* "Petty apartheid" refers to the system of restrictions on residence and movement imposed on nonwhites within South Africa, in contrast to "grand apartheid," the government's plan to allocate specific lands to specific ethnic groups and spin those "homelands" off as independent countries.

organizations, artists had more and more difficulty producing their works. Symbolic of this was the bulldozing in the 1950s of the township of Sophiatown, close to downtown Johannesburg, which was replaced by a white-only residential area, while its former residents were dumped in a semi-desert area that would become the ghetto of Soweto. Sophiatown had been the symbol of the vitality of an urban music inspired by the big bands of Duke Ellington, Count Basie, Jimmie Lunceford, and, later, bebop. The Dorkay House in Sophiatown was a legendary place where musical theater shared the stage with the beautiful voices of Miriam Makeba, Dolly Rathebe, and Dorothy Masuka, and performances by Kippie Moekesti, Ntemi Pilisquo, Hugh Masekela, Jonas Gwangwa, Zakes Nkosie, Dollar Brand, and others. The destruction of Sophiatown forced many artists into exile or retirement, but Mahlathini and the Makgona Tschole Band, among other favorites of the black population, would continue to perform until bubblegum pop and soothing American disco, played constantly on the air, created unfair competition. After that the "Queens"decided to go back to a family life and raising children.

By a curious twist of history, though, the South African "Howlin' Wolf" and his accomplices made a comeback in the mid-1980s. With amplification, mbaqanga had worked up a new head of steam. The radical teenagers of the Black Consciousness Movement, after the Soweto uprising in 1976, identified with the music's energy. And the international anti-apartheid movement focused its searchlights on the South African scene, revealing to foreign ears a formidable wealth of kwela, mbaqanga, and mbube, not to mention jazz, soul, and reggae. This new environment allowed the three "Queens," now wealthy forty-somethings, to put their scarlet costumes, diadems, and pearl belts back on and rejoin the "groaner," in his panther skin and ostrich feathers, onstage to perform mesmerizing shows in front of stunned European crowds, backed by the brassy, hopeful sounds of a band led by producer and saxophonist West Nkosi.[6]

---

[6] In France, Mahlathini made himself known through the success of "Kazet" (recorded originally by Obed Ngobeni and the Kurhula Sisters under the title "Ku Hluvukile Eka Zets"), a song that recounts the destruction of a township with

The fame of South African groups abroad owes much to Nkosi. A kind of local Quincy Jones, he was artistic director at the Gallo label. When Paul Simon decided in 1985 to make an album protesting apartheid, it was Nkosi who suggested he check out Ladysmith Black Mambazo. Nkosi had discovered this vocal group, led by Joseph Shabalala, in 1970 in Natal. They sang in the *isicathamiya*[7] style, an a cappella method of incredible precision enlivened by breaks in rhythm, changes of tempo, and contrasting timbres, not without some resemblance to gospel, but originating in Zulu and Swazi collective songs. Paul Simon was hooked, and worked with them on the *Graceland* album, which went on to sell seven million copies. In the wake of the album's success, Simon toured with Ladysmith (as well as Miriam Makeba and jazzman Hugh Masekela) and helped create a formidable demand for South African music. Slowly, the Western public was discovering the hidden depths of the South African musical iceberg.

❖

> There's a township mongrel on the scrounge
> A tribal feud in a municipal pound
> A squatter with an ox but no land to plough
> A shipment of AKs on the underground
> A throw of the dice on a Soweto train
> A waiting knife if you should win the game
> A human rights lawyer with a torture claim
> A union activist never ever seen again
> (Chorus:)
> Phendula wendoda

---

bulldozers. Lizzy Mercier Descloux later made a French version called "Où sont passées les gazelles?" (Where Have the Gazelles Gone?).

[7] *Isicathamiya,* a descendant of the Zulu and Swazi vocal traditions, was formalized as mbube in the 1930s after absorbing some elements of European Christian choral singing. This style of unison singing was popularized worldwide by the song "Wimoweh" (1939), which became "The Lion Sleeps Tonight." In the 1940s, mbube changed into the very gripping *isiklhwela jo* (bombardment) before returning to softer tones a decade later.

Lendlela sizofika kanjani
(Answer, Mister,
This way, how will we arrive?)[8]

In the midst of this phenomenon, one man came to embody, to the youth of the North, the dream of a South Africa rid of the cancer of apartheid—unquestionably because he was white. His name is Johnny Clegg. He sings in Zulu and dances the Indlamu war dances with his partners. His career reads like a humanist allegory. Illegally immersing himself in the ghetto environment at the age of fourteen, he befriended and grew up with Sipho Mchunu, a young Zulu with whom he founded the group Juluka (Sweat), which lasted until 1985, when Sipho left to return to his native Zululand. Clegg then formed a more rock-oriented group, Savuka (We Are Standing). He studied anthropology and wrote a thesis on *Ishihamani*, a Zulu system of dances, gestures, and symbols. His music, Zulu inspired but spiked with rock, connected with what the North was listening to. Johnny Clegg became living proof that in the country of "separate development," a fertile multiethnic dialogue was possible.

It probably also didn't hurt his music's political cred any that it had been praised by one Nelson Rolihlahla ("troublemaker") Mandela, "the longest held political prisoner in the world." At the time of his release in 1990, Mandela's liberation was preceded by negotiations for a peaceful transition to shared power—and followed by his election as president of the republic in April 1994. On the night of December 31, 1999, Mandela joined five hundred guests, among them many musicians, at the prison of Robben Island to "reflect on the power of forgiveness" and begin the long process of moving on from the nightmare of apartheid. Mahlathini had already moved on. Five months earlier, after thirty-five years of good and loyal service, the "Lion of Soweto" had ceased his roar. He died at the age of sixty-one.

---

[8] "Talk to the People," from Johnny Clegg and Savuka, *Shadow Man*, EMI Records Ltd., 1988.

ROOTS

Granmoun Lélé and Danyel Waro:
The Pulse of Réunionese Maloya

The Memory of the Maroons and
the Return of Identity

Danyel Waro, second from left, along with his drummers,
warming his drum skins, 1985.

You have to shoot the Creole!

—A PRIMARY SCHOOL SUPERVISOR,
RÉUNION, 1970

S ince at snack time his mother always called, "*Julien, lé lait!*" (Réunionese French Creole for "Julien, milk!"), Julien Philéas—born February 28, 1930, at Saint-Benoît on the east coast of the island of Réunion—was nicknamed "Lélé." His father was descended from Tamil-speaking workers from India and African slaves; his mother's ancestors were Bata (from the African mainland) and Malagasy; and he had four brothers and four sisters. Following in his father's footsteps, he went to work in the Beaufonds sugar plantation and mill, first as a daily laborer, then as a fitter, and finally as chief cooker, until he retired "after fifty-six years, three months, and several medals." The rough environment of sugar-cane workers was interrupted every Saturday by payday, which made it possible to buy rum and party until daybreak. At these *kabarés,*[1] forbidden to children, Lélé, as an adolescent, started singing, inspired by his uncle Arsène Madia. Catching the music bug, he went so far as to buy an accordion "from Lyon." With his friend Tonga Lafa, he gradually started to spread around his *maloya foutan,*[2] until, in December 1977, he registered his group at the police department and recorded four songs on a 45-rpm record that, along with one by Firmin Viry from St. Pierre, would be the first of its kind.

---

[1] From the Malagasy word *kabary* (assembly) from which stemmed the neologism *kabar* (informal concerts, a specifically Réunionese sort of party).

[2] The word *maloya* comes from the Malagasy *maloy,* "to spout words." Another type of the island's music, the primitive sega, had much in common with maloya before the freedmen combined it with European music. In Mozambique, *chega* refers to a dance similar to the Spanish fandango; in Swahili, *sega* means to roll up one's clothes, a typical gesture of dancers in the sega-ravanne of Mauritius, the sega-tambour of the Rodriguez Islands, and the moutia of the Seychelles.

To understand maloya's place within Réunionese culture, one has to remember that the island (970 square miles for 600,000 inhabitants), inhabited only for the last 350 years, has become an astonishing ethnic patchwork[3] marked by one major fact: slavery, abolished in 1848 (there were then 58,000 slaves, about 60 percent of the population). That reality was swept under the rug both by the descendants of the "nouveaux libres," eager to rid themselves of that accursed portion of history, and by the local "elites," who considered any reference to the painful past to be "obscurantist." When Réunion was made a French overseas department in 1946, the Jacobin vision of assimilation reinforced this endemic denial and helped to marginalize the local culture: disparaging for instance the Creole language, which had long been presented as an exotic wonder or a rural patois. The persistence of this negation explains why maloya, "the Cafres' dance," has always been at the heart of the quest for linguistic and social identity.

Thus it is not by chance that, when maloya was banned by Governor Perreau-Pradier from 1956 to 1962, it survived surreptitiously among the sugar-cane workers and those left to fend for themselves in the mountains. Long before the battle to legitimize Creole writing took form, "the music of the ancestors" was the privileged vehicle of what anthropologists call the "unsaid" on Réunion.

The political history confirms this. The PCR (*Parti Communiste Réunionnais*) popularized maloya at its festivals and in its newspaper, *Temoignages* (Testimonies), in keeping with its struggle for autonomy. The

---

[3] Réunion Island has 180,000 people of mixed African, European, and Indian ancestry, who are agricultural workers or small landowners; 120,000 "Malabars," or Tamils who came from southern India, workers at the sugar factories or government workers; 100,000 whites born on the island, either "Gro-Blan" (from the land-owning families) or "Ti-Blan" (poor agricultural and other workers); 40,000 "Cafres," descendants of slaves imported from the African coast via Madagascar; 15,000 Chinese from Guangzhou, who have a monopoly on the food market; 10,000 "Zarabs," Muslim Indians from Gujarat, who dominate the textile and appliance markets; not to mention the 10,000 "Zoreys," metropolitan French. Except for the Zarabs, who are strict Muslims, the population of Réunion is Catholic, although many Malabars continue to practice certain rituals (fire walking, animal sacrifices, abstinence, and magic) from the Tamil religion, a derivative of Hinduism, and the Cafres still observe rituals from Madagascar and Africa called "services" (*sevis malgas* or *sevis kabars*).

first records of Firmin Viry and Granmoun Lélé were produced at its request at a time when maloya musicians were taken to concert venues in covered trucks as if they were hazardous substances. However, the strength of maloya largely transcended political struggle for autonomy of the island. Its aims go much farther than that, as Julien Philéas explains: "On the one hand, a heavy heart; on the other, a happy heart; you have to balance them. When we think about how our ancestors were, we have a heavy heart; but we have a happy heart when we think about how we became free." The spirit of maloya is situated somewhere between nostalgia and hope, blues and anger, stolen humanity and possible happiness. Its words and its minor-key melodies are like the shards of a broken mirror. Its poetry is characterized by piercing voices that are supported by rural instruments: the rouleur ("roller," a drum whose player sits astride it as if on horseback), the bobre (musical bow), and the kayamb, which contains seeds and is shaken back and forth to give rise to the 6/8 signature beat of maloya. The original maloya roulé was only for rituals (unlike maloya pilé, which can be played by all). Linked to Lenten times, when families invite friends to share in the offerings to the gods, it also frames legends, stories, *sirandanes* (traditional riddles), and prayers, during which some people "enter into communication with the other world" through trance.

Familiar from an early age with Malagasy and Tamil rituals, Granmoun Lélé was known on the island as a sculptor-renovator of the *bondiés* (images of gods), which worshippers would install in little shrines, and of the masks worn during the Malabar dances. These activities have strict rules ranging from the choice of wood (only lilac, neem, or camphor) to a mandatory abstinence from meat and sexual relations during the work: there is a fast of eight to ten days before the sculpting. Thus Granmoun Lélé performed maloya as naturally as breathing. In his cabin in Bras-Fusil he came up with most of his repertoire of more than two hundred compositions, songs that speak of his daily life and his dreams, inspired by the rhythms of his environment, particularly the Indian Ocean (because "the little confusions of the sea are, for me, like songs"). His family joined him later to enrich his rhythmic constructions. The ambition of the Lélé clan is to make the maloya like a *zambrokal,* that Creole dish of rice, smoked meat, dry or fresh grains, and spices in which each element infuses the others while keeping its individuality.

Since the beginning of the 1980s, maloya in various flavors (pure or hybridized with elements from sega, jazz, reggae, and rock), courtesy of Rwa Kaff, Granmoun Baba, Firmin Viry, Ti Fock, Zizkakan, and Baster, has been stirring up echoes abroad. The most impressive and innovative agent of this growing acclaim has been Danyel Waro, winner of the *Prix de l'Académie Charles Cros* in 1999.

As an adolescent, he was exposed to and became fascinated with maloya's underground legacy of themes, syntaxes, and rhythmic pulses—a fascination that would reinforce his radical "nationalist" fervor. He eventually spent two years in prison in Rennes, France, for insurrection, an experience he described in a book-pamphlet called *Romans ékri dans le zol an Frans* (Novel Written on French Soil). On his return in 1975, he joined the Troup Flamboyan and became one of the leading proponents of maloya sec, with Creole as its "weapon to fight against oppression." As time went by, while others were edging toward "world music," Waro was seeking legitimacy in the *kabarés*—an immersion that was equally stylistic and philosophical, with the aim of "protecting the depth of our music." An immersion that would bear fruit after long effort. Although rigorous about the traditions he is reviving, this working-class white man nevertheless enriches his music with his predilection for jazzy inflections and the colors unique to the Mascarene Islands. His is an open orthodoxy: "Maloya is not just about Cafres. In reality that's not it at all. It has been a mestizo music from the beginning, since it was created by slaves who were very different from each other. In my singing style there's a little bit of Malabar, of Cafre, and so on. This grand mixture is our wealth. In our palate, there is a taste of masala, chop suey, biryani, and so on."[4]

For a long time now, Danyel Waro has taken the maloya to higher latitudes. With discrimination and determination (he stubbornly refuses offers from show business), he has become the cultural ambassador of a Réunion Island that is breaking away from its touristy, postcard image. His high, soft voice—"*dous'ment, dous'ment*" (softly, softly)—has become a poetic manifesto. His rebel song has taken on new accents. Once an island phenomenon, maloya has found its universality with him.

---

[4] From an interview with the author.

Doudou N'Diaye Rose: The Messiaen of the Dakar Medina

Africa and the Return to Rhythm

Doudou N'Diaye Rose dreaming among his djembes, 1990.

Fifteen or twenty billion years ago the blank page of the universe exploded and the beat began.

— MICKEY HART, DRUMMER FOR THE GRATEFUL DEAD[1]

Born in Dakar's Plateau District (Kaye Findive) in 1930, Doudou N'Diaye Rose, the lead drummer of the National Ballets, with three wives and some forty children, is a living legend in the Senegalese capital. At Street 1, corner 22, drums can regularly be heard booming in his yard, like a heart beating through the whole medina. The drums are those of his children, all percussionists; of his dozens of students; of his friends who come, sometimes from long distances, to visit him. "This is serious business!" says he. This charismatic bandleader just has to be seen, directing his fascinating symphonies of skins and wood with grace and virtuosity, precision and wildness, like a martial-arts master.

Doudou N'Diaye Rose admits it with a smile: "It's hard to match me when it comes to Senegalese rhythm." In fact, he doesn't play—he *lives* the rhythm, which he perceives in everything: the bleating of lean-flanked sheep in the poor shade awaiting the next *tabaski* (feast celebrating Abraham's sacrifice); the fleet of mopeds revving their engines on the dusty avenue; the babble of the multicolored markets...

He has expressed this intoxication with the world of sound since his early childhood, beginning by beating on recycled champagne bottles. "In those days, it was rare to have wood. We would pack a bottle tightly with sand, break it, then surround it with cow skin." Everything could be used to make sound—from milk cartons to five-kilo cans of tomatoes. His uncle, a tom-tom player, was in charge of his education and tried his best to prevent this inclination from devouring his nephew. But even the whip that would follow whenever he was caught at a ceremony

---

[1] Mickey Hart, *Drumming at the Edge of Magic* (Harper San Francisco, 1990).

instead of at school had no effect; nor did the repeated warning, "Learn a trade, but don't be a drummer!" So the uncle gave up. "One day he said that he couldn't beat me anymore because I was too big." He steered him toward employment as a plumber and made gris-gris charms for him, without which it is risky to play percussion.

From hanging out with well-known drummers such as El-Hadji Mada Saka, who spotted him when he was very young, Doudou N'Diaye Rose learned that in percussion there is a science, an expertise, that has to be enriched and made to last. From this came the idea, which his circle at first thought hare-brained, to create a school of rhythm. From there, progressively, was born the continent's first large orchestra of percussionists, containing more than a hundred pieces. Among them there were boys but also—the audacity!—women, often his daughters or daughters-in-law. "There were women lawyers, police inspectors. Why not women drummers?" As evidence, as far as he is concerned: if indeed there are origins of rhythm, one of them can be found among women grinding millet in mortars.

So this "unknown" entered into the customs of the noisy Senegalese capital. Doudou N'Diaye Rose and his drummers have become an integral part of local life. They are invited to stimulate the bravery of the contestants in the national sport, Senegalese wrestling; they emcee marriages, births, and neighborhood parties; they are therapists who ease the pain of five- to six-hour tattooing sessions.

Of course one of the grounds for Doudou N'Diaye Rose's pride is that he composed the national anthem. But he is also happy to have contributed to the renewal of Dakar's drum majorettes. "One day, after independence, Senghor [the president of the republic] asked me to Africanize the majorettes. So we changed their outfits, eliminated the brass band. But we kept the boots. And I hit upon the rhythm of the parade."

To achieve his ends, Doudou N'Diaye Rose uses an impressionist method of composition. An insomniac, he memorizes the night sounds that he hears: the rain, the wind, a creaking window, the rustling trees. In the morning he harmonizes them on the tom-tom. The result could one day become the theme for the television news. Like Beethoven listening to the seasons, or Olivier Messiaen to the birds, Doudou N'Diaye Rose wants to be the "conductor" of the cosmos. This philosophy, or something like it, is shared by all of the continent's great drummers, because in Africa, sound is thought to have magic powers. It has its own truth. It functions as a metaphysical agent independent of the goodwill of man. Because of this, one doesn't venture into the famous "rhythmic wheel" without caution, memory, or humility, for the tom-tom is, at will, a vehicle, a connecting link, a receptacle, a mouth, a medium. Countless are the legends linked to percussion, and in many regions the steps in making the drums owe so much to ceremony that, for example, one must appease the spirit that lives in the tree that will be used—a tree sometimes chosen because it is near villages and therefore is used to hearing human voices. Each drum has its altar, a place where the player enters into contact with the divinity.

This is why Doudou N'Diaye Rose's essential goal—apart from his countless international requests, from a composition with Maurice Béjart[2] to opening for the Rolling Stones—is to share his second religion (after Islam): rhythm. "The tom-tom is an instrument created by the spirits. All at once, it's no longer Doudou playing. It's Doudou and... (*silence*)... something else!" He, who once encouraged Josephine Baker,[3] knows that he is the trustee of hundreds of rhythmic formulas, each linked to a special event: a funeral procession, a circumcision, a war, a healing, a baptism.... Thus, when someone is possessed, it is a matter of beating the rhythm of the particular "djinn" who dwells in the patient, not a different one. In the same way, there are rhythms that make the rain fall, others linked to families, others to animals, and so forth.

---

[2] He participated in the creation of *Mudra Afrique* with Maurice Béjart, himself born in Saint-Louis in Senegal. In July 1989, Doudou N'Diaye Rose's performance was one of the highlights of the French Revolution bicentennial parade conceived by Jean-Paul Goude. Doudou N'Diaye Rose has also been sought out by a large number of musicians, including Jacques Higelin, Bernard Lavilliers, Michel Jonasz, Dizzy Gillespie, Kenny Clarke, Peter Gabriel, and Eric Serra. One of his oldest partners is Julien Jouga, leader of a Catholic choir of a hundred members in Senegal, with which he covers Catholic, Muslim, classical, and traditional repertoires.

[3] In 1959 Josephine Baker invited him to her castle, les Milandes.

It takes a great deal of time to acquire this rhythmic cartography. In their haste, young people, following the international vogue for djembe,[4] often take shortcuts, losing the true meaning on the way. But Doudou N'Diaye Rose, who has thoroughly traversed the countryside in quest of certain two-hundred-year-old drums and understands their "terrible language," knows well that one can die unless one wins over the spirits of percussion.

---

[4] The djembe, which is played without sticks, has become one of the most played non-European instruments in the West and is part of the tourist's panoply. In Senegal, Guinea, the Ivory Coast, and Mali, a djembe micro-industry (Laobe sculptors, tanners, and so forth) exports the instruments by the truckload throughout the world, leading to an alarming deforestation, particularly of the precious sonorous woods used, such as teak, iroko, and lengue. Today, industrial djembe production from other substances, even synthetic materials, is developing around the world.

The "Strange Niger Blue" of Mali's Ali Farka Toure

The Roots of the Blues

Ali Farka Toure with his jurkel, 1995.

You know you can't reap the fruits unless you first take care of the roots.

—WILLIE DIXON

"I have two more months of touring in Europe ahead of me, and already I am in a hurry to get back, because I have a lot of work waiting for me at home. I grow rice, I raise sheep and goats. I have two wives and eleven children. I am first of all a farmer." Ali Ibrahim "Farka" Toure[1] is in Paris after three days of travel by trail, road, and plane from Mali. In the middle of the rainy season, he left his hometown of Niafunke, situated on the upper bend of the Niger River on the outskirts of the Sahara Desert, to start a tour—a lucrative activity that will enable him to import water pumps and tractors to help make the harsh terrain of his region fertile. The focus of this descendant of the Arma nobility is agriculture and the 750 square acres that he has been farming ever since he returned to the countryside after resigning from a radio-engineer position in Bamako. His focus is not the music, which "came to" him "from above in broad daylight." "Without music, I live very well," he likes to say.

But fame has come to visit him. In the middle of the craze for the more percussive of his fellow African musicians, the quiet Ali Farka Toure and his triptych of guitar, gourd, and njarka (a kind of fiddle) have succeeded beyond all expectation—even in the United States, where the famous guitarist Ry Cooder insisted on playing with him well before they collaborated on the hit album *Talking Timbuktu*.[2] This fame

---

[1] Farka, born in 1939, got this epithet from being the tenth born but the first to survive past infancy: *Farka* means "donkey," the symbol of stubbornness and physical endurance. Ali Farka's father, who enlisted in the French army, was killed during World War II.

[2] The album, recorded in two days, was number one on *Billboard*'s world music charts and was nominated for a Grammy. It would be on all the top ten lists in England, Holland, Switzerland, Australia, and France.

started when some English-speaking media noticed that a hundred miles from Timbuktu there dwelt a man who played the blues as if he had lived on the Mississippi, and they compared him to the most prolific bluesman in history. "When I first heard John Lee Hooker—it was in 1967, when a student friend brought back records from Paris—I thought he was an artist from my country. Then I learned that he was an American, and then I thought that he had stolen our music. In fact what in the West they call 'blues' is pure Tamasheq,[3] but the American musicians do not know that. We have the roots and the trunk, and they have the leaves and the branches."[4]

As it happens, the guitar styles of Ali Farka Toure and John Lee Hooker (though a comparison with Mance Lipscomb would be more apt) have some striking similarities. In 1989, in California, the two men met. The American stated publicly that, if he should die, Ali Farka Toure would be the only one that would replace him. The Malian nevertheless points out their differences: "He sings about whiskey, beer, and women. I sing about pastures, forests, nature, the river, the earth and the sky, work, and education against ignorance and racism."[5]

This Tamasheq blues, played in modes called tangani, diaba, hekkam, dialou, segalare, takamba, and ndondo, is innate to him. He began by playing the Fulani flute, the ngoni (four-stringed lute), the njarka (a fiddle that wives play to hold onto their straying husbands!), and especially the single-stringed jurkel—the instrument of the spirits, which causes a trance during voodoo ceremonies and accompanies the cattle heading to pasture as well as the protective rituals against scorpion stings and snake bites. Then came the tidinît (a North African stringed instrument), and a guitar that a hospital-attendant friend had ordered from a Manufrance catalog. And finally came the accordion and the banjo at a cultural center, while the rest of the kids were flipping for Dario Moreno, Dalida, Enrico Macias, or Richard Anthony.

Between 1954 and 1956, Ali Farka Toure, then an apprentice chauffeur in Guinea, attended concerts by the great guitarists Keita Fodeba and

---

[3] *Translator's note:* The Tamasheq are a subgroup of the Tuareg.
[4] Remarks reported by Eliane Azoulay, *Calao,* July 1992.
[5] Remarks reported by Hélène Lee, *Libération,* June 4, 1994.

Kante Facelli. It was a revelation for him. Beginning in the 1960s, while he was directing Troupe 117, which performed on an ambulance boat, he thought of adapting age-old melodies to a guitar tuned according to traditional instruments. He wasn't able to acquire a guitar of his own until his first trip outside Africa, which was in 1968, to Sofia, Bulgaria, for a traditional-arts festival. Then he became an engineer at Radio Mali and a mainstay of the in-house band, and was able to compose abundantly until the group disbanded.

It was after he had heard Ray Charles and Otis Redding that his obsession with the history of blues started. In his home region, a certain kind of music is also called "blue"—a literal translation of the word *baula,* describing the reflection of the scenery in the river water. In Africa many melodies resemble those of blues since they are composed in thirds (major, minor, neutral) and perfect fourths and fifths, and share the famous "blue note" arising from the flattened third and seventh notes of the major scale. Blues history was also a subject he discussed in depth with writer Amadou Hampate Ba,[6] with whom he traveled during the writer's many trips to collect the griots' musical sources with a Nagra tape recorder.

In fact, one can have a lot of fun establishing connections between Mali and the Mississippi Delta, and in looking for the African cousins of Son House, Charlie Patton, Booker White, and others. An example is singer-guitarist Boubacar Traore, alias "Kar Kar" (Hoodlum), of whom a British journalist wrote: "If Ali Farka Toure is the John Lee Hooker of Mali, Boubacar Traore is the Robert Johnson." After years of anonymity, the man who, in the beginning of the 1960s, had been the "Elvis Presley of Mali," strutting like Vince Taylor[7] with a rough knockoff of a Stratocaster on a strap, made a surprising return to music after he had been supposedly dead. Suddenly, with his fluid melodies, melancholic Saharan

---

[6] Amadou Hampate Ba (1900–1991), heir to a powerful Fulani family, imbued with Sufi Islam, animist belief, colonial culture, and supported by the anthropologist Théodore Monod, was an important figure in the battle to safeguard African oral traditions through his work at UNESCO. The phrase "In Africa, when an old man dies, a library burns down" is attributed to him.

[7] *Translator's note:* Vince Taylor (1939–1991) was a rockabilly singer who, throughout his erratic career, was much more popular in Europe than in the United States.

chant, and superb swing, he achieved international recognition. That was
new confirmation of the permanence of the blues that was born in West
Africa before the slave trade. The latest great public proof of the ebb and
flow between U.S. blues and the Mandingo repertoire was the collaboration of legendary bluesman Taj Mahal[8] and Malian master koraist Toumani Diabate on their album *Kulanjan*.

---

[8] At the beginning of the 1980s, the author proposed to Taj Mahal (an erudite bluesman capable of reciting the names of all the great koraists of West Africa!) that he
do a duet with Ali Farka Toure. His response was enthusiastic: the resultant meeting
was a preview of the "White [sleepless] Nights for Black Music" festival in Marseilles,
where several American bluesmen (among them Buddy Guy, Dr. John, Marva
Wright, and Little Milton) met with the bluesmen from Africa.

Bi Kidude: "The Little Thing," Soul of the
Zanzibar Taarab

East Africa Between Bantu and Arab Colors

Remmy Ongala, 1990.

When one plays the flute in Zanzibar,
Africa dances all the way to the Great Lakes.

— ARAB PROVERB

O ctober 1990. In concert on the prestigious stage of the *Théatre de la Ville* in Paris, accompanied by seventeen musicians, is Fatuma Baraka, alias Bi Kidude (translation: "Madame Little-Thing"): a singer veiled in white, striking and full of energy, who, nearly eighty years old, has come all the way from Zanzibar in the Indian Ocean. This simple lady lives in a house of dirt with a roof made of branches in the heart of Ngambo, a mostly indigent neighborhood in the capital of this eighty-kilometer-long island with five hundred thousand inhabitants, a part of Tanzania. A kind of local Edith Piaf, she has fought, against all odds, for a specific idea of music: in particular, taarab,[1] of which she has made a religion since her youth, when she was entranced by the Omani musicians whom she used to hear playing on their boats anchored in the spice harbor.

This taarab came down from Egypt via the Nile and Sudan and established itself in the bars and ports of the eastern African coast before it took root in Zanzibar thanks to a music-loving sultan, Sa'id Barghash (1870–1888), who decided to invite musicians from Cairo and Istanbul.[2] Thus did the land of cloves acquire its first local band: Ikhwani Safaa,

---

[1] The word *taarab* harks back to an expression that means "emotion, ecstasy." Eastern Africa, thanks to a common language, Kiswahili, displays a certain cultural homogeneity, by virtue of which taarab has been able to plant its influence in all the musical styles of the region, from Somalia to Mozambique. The Kenyan ports of Lamu and Mombasa, the Tanzanian cities of Tanga and Dar es Salaam, and even the cities of Mogadishu (Somalia), Bujumbura (Burundi), Maputo (Mozambique), and Kampala (Uganda) have given life to their own particular *taarabs*.

[2] Secular music in Cairo then consisted of the takht band (solo singer, choir, qanun, oud, ney, violin, and riqq), and its taqtuhah version (short song in Arab dialect, treating sentimental themes) became the pattern for the "classic" taarab of Zanzibar.

who are still playing. The genre is based on an instrumental introduction, poetic stanzas of three or four lines (of twelve or sixteen syllables each) separated by a musical interlude, and short refrains repeated by a chorus. A privilege of nobles, it stirred up a flurry of "musical clubs" for men only. But it would soon experience several revolutions.

The first one was in language, when Arabic was abandoned in favor of Kiswahili.[3] The second took place when women took taarab over, following in the footsteps of the great Siti Binti Saad, who, with her superb voice, singing in Arabic, in Hindi, but above all in Kiswahili, took taarab outside the palace. Her repertory left aside the ethereal themes of Arabic romantic love in favor of others more anchored in the reality of the Zanzibari people.[4] And because she recorded in abundance for "His Master's Voice" and for Columbia (after recording her first 78-rpm records in India for Odeon in the early 1930s), her popularity stirred up rivals and created new forms, in particular kidumbak.[5] Born among the Africans of Ngambo, kidumbak, with its dominant percussion became, from the 1940s and 1950s on, the musical means of expression for the women's associations called *lelemana*. These used the music for indulging in competitions that originally were poetic jousts, but in time became real verbal confrontations, to the point that the government attempted to regulate them. This very syncopated kidumbak, called *mpasho*, based on insult, on exposing the other's private life, and on sexual references, is still quite popular, as is the torrid *unyago*, an exclusively feminine style associated with the initiation of girls in puberty, that includes in particular the *kiuno* dance (or how to wiggle one's hips well to seduce one's future husband).

---

[3] In 1964, a revolution overthrew the sultan and brought to power Abeid Amani Karume, who was assassinated in 1972. He decided that taarab was "revolutionary," and the music groups became annexes of the ruling party. The love song—the essential vein of taarab—was no longer in vogue on the radio, and Bi Kidude was, fatally, judged out of fashion.

[4] As in the song *Muhogo ya Jangombé* (later covered by Bi Kidude), a metaphor built around cassava to evoke colonial oppression.

[5] The kidumbak is a small funnel-shaped drum, copied from the Arab darbouka. These ensembles include two drums, a bass made from a tea chest with sanduku string, a violin, cherewa maracas made out of coconuts, and a pair of mkwassa (sticks struck together).

In fact, women, being the main consumers of taarab, put it through another facelift, this one orchestral. The solemn "classical" taarab with its violins, qanouns, darboukas, neys, and riqqs gave way to groups with fewer members, in which guitar, accordion, and bongos—not to mention cheap synthesizers—had more prominence. The rise of Indian film music and the influence of soukous led to fusion attempts, not always of the best quality. But, taking note of these modifications, borrowing colors from Kenyan benga[6] or Congolese rumba, modern groups, such as the Culture Musical Club, from the 1980s on have worked more from kidumbak than from classical taarab.

In a way, then, Bi Kidude, with her cigarette-roughened voice, was the quintessence of this evolution. Taking up the legacy of Siti Binti Saad, with whom she sang, she advanced it further. Turning her back on the aristocracy of the island, she has taken more inspiration from people of modest means and from the buzz of the street. Her temperamental taarab is wedded to the philosophy of a singer who has never managed to live or create according to convention—a woman who, years ago, on the day of her wedding, fled the altar, realizing at the last minute that she couldn't live with a man who didn't understand how a person could love singing in weddings, drinking with prostitutes, playing the drum, and smoking hashish pipes.

---

[6] The modern music of East Africa, a crossroads area, has always made the most of influences, whether those that came from afar, such as the Cuban music that spread through the whole continent, or those of the Congos. For example, Tanzanian urban sound—encouraged by Julius Nyerere's regime after independence (*uhuru*) in 1961 as part of his campaign of "conscientisation"—put new energy into old styles such as *beni ngoma* (from Bantu *beni,* group, and *ngoma,* music) or *danzi,* by way of an urban neo-jazz (*muziki wa densi*). The most creative artist of this genre in the last few years has been Remmy Ongala and his orchestra Matimila. In neighboring Kenya, it's the *benga* beat, modern dance music based first on Luo percussion and then on Kikuyu percussion, that has predominated these last few decades, exemplified by P. Oluoch Kanindo and Daniel Kamau.

THE
CRISIS
OF
SiGNS

Toure Kunda and the "Dance of the Leaves"

African Immigration and the Vogue for Black Music

The musical family Toure Kunda, 1986.

That's it, the demon of the dance is invading me.... And off it goes to my body language, I'm getting high, I'm taking off, I dance, levitation. It's contagious, the whole room is standing up, shaking their booties.... They're called back, they leave, they're called back, not enough, lights on, the sweat has drenched my tee-shirt, my hair is gummy.... Over, it's over, we're happy. Toure Kunda, it's good, it's very good!

—LETTER TO THE NEWSPAPER *LIBÉRATION*
FROM A WOMAN READER, 1983

On a January day in 1984, arriving from Kaolack by bus on the red laterite road congested with herds of buffalo, after crossing the bridge that straddled the Casamance River, the brothers discovered an impressive crowd waiting with tom-toms and dancers on stilts. In order for everyone to see these heroes, a pickup-truck platform was at the disposition of the crowd. The procession, accompanied by a sublime cacophony, progressed between two human hedges. Thousands of children chanted the brothers' name. Women were dancing and forming human chains to facilitate the progress of the vehicles. The deeper into Ziguinchor they went, the more intense this fantasia became. In front of the seats reserved for family, their mothers waited, dressed in their Sunday best, circled by a swarm of uncles, aunts, cousins, nephews, and childhood friends. Yes, the prodigal sons were back! In this part of the world, no one can come home without bringing presents, as is evidenced by the number of Tati[1] bags in planes from France to Africa. On this trip, though, the Toure brothers chose the best gift: to give back to their native land a bit of the music that had made them famous. They had decided to organize a series of concerts in West Africa under the same technical conditions they would have in the North. That was a

---

[1] *Translator's note:* Tati is a famous French department store.

formidable challenge: for this two-week tour through four countries (Ivory Coast, Mali, Gambia, and Senegal), they had to load a traveling stage with state-of-the-art sound equipment on a thirty-eight-ton truck capable of resisting bad roads, accompanied by twenty technicians and roadies. The stops along the tour were Abidjan, Bamako, Dakar, Kaolack, and Banjul. The final destination was Ziguinchor, four hundred fifty kilometers south of Dakar. It is the capital of the Casamance, a "Senegalese Florida" known for its beaches, its water mazes, its mangroves, its animist mysteries... and its irredentist movement. It is also the land where the brothers' history and that of the Elephant clan (Toure Kunda in the local Soninke language) have been rooted ever since the day an ancestor, born in Mali, moved to the river's banks because of the crocodiles whose skin he needed for his job as a traveling shoemaker.

In Ziguinchor, the bright yellow semi truck set up its thirteen-hundred-square-foot stage and its high-tech sound equipment. For two nights, the whole town was invited to the brothers' recitals. In places of honor, next to the authorities, were seated their mothers and dear friends, such as Foularo Yama Nene, their childhood griot, who had come from Gambia. The second night, Yaya, the uncle who had taken charge of the clan when their father died, was there. Despite his skepticism, he had been forced to surrender to the evidence—the solemn mobilization of the city—that "this wasn't bullshit." In fact, as the vox populi reported, "this thing was serious." The brothers' professionalism was impressive, and everyone could hear with their own ears that these songs and themes, composed far from the country, did not betray the essence of Casamance philosophy.

Popular recognition of an artist is always a slow and complex process. In Africa, the importance of the past always comes into play, no matter how famous the artist. For Toure Kunda, local recognition was even more decisive, because their music was fertilized by rites of passage. If, as children, they grew up in a family with a griot lineage,[2] always asked to

---

[2] "Our mothers taught us to build our own drums; they didn't want us touching the ritual instruments, for fear that we would fall into a trance, that we would turn into dingos" (in Frank Tenaille, *Touré Kunda,* Seghers, 1987, the source of all quotes in this chapter).

enliven weddings, parties, or funerals, their musical base came down to, more than anything else, the rhythms and songs linked to circumcision and the initiations that mark a child's entrance into the adult world. In particular, they took their inspiration from the djambaadong, the "dance of the leaves," that for six months used to accompany initiates along their path.[3]

This djambaadong, "revised and corrected" by funk, rock, and jazz, first had to prove its pertinence far from the land of kapok and royal poinciana. In 1975, Ismael arrived in Paris. Like his brothers Amadou, Sixu, and Ousmane, he had lived through various musical experiences. But now he wanted to discover Europe, to make himself heard. It was a rude shock. It was an immersion into a cold, gray, and sour world. It was the discovery of fragments of exiled Africa. It was a time of university restaurants, small jobs, and halls for immigrants, where he gave reading classes in the unhealthy places where manual laborers lived, employed in the mechanical industries of the Parisian area, where solitude, accidents, sicknesses, and job losses accumulated. All this would appear later in certain of his songs. At night, Ismael played wherever he was invited. He composed advertising jingles for African stores, participated in a Senegal-style jazz-rock band called the West African Cosmos, worked on a demo record, and invited Sixu (then employed in Africa by a nongovernmental organization that instructed farmers in new agricultural methods) to come join him.

This duo, in 1977, recorded an album under the name *Frères griots,* an album that prefigured their "Afro-Manding Sound." It included eight songs: "On Verra Ça" (We'll See About That), which evoked the plight of the immigrant; "Samala," about the migrant workers of Casamance; "Baouane," about a drought and the favorable spirits implored to help

---

[3] In the past, these essentially animist initiations linked to circumcision included a long period of preparation in the sacred forest, far from the families, under the direction of "elders" who gave teachings suitable to a collective life and its environment. During this period the child lost his old name (and initiation name) to acquire a new identity through a series of ordeals that tested his endurance and permitted him to access the secrets and myths of his collectivity. Afterward, having left the universe of childhood, he was admitted to participate in the life of the group, his return being punctuated with a celebration marked by the stamp of djambaadong.

defeat it; "Manso" (God); "Kambé," in which an old woman who has just one tooth remaining remembers her childhood; "Africa Lelly," an exhortation to perseverance; "Soyé" and "Touty Yollé," two songs in memory of a dead sister; and "Emm'Ma" (Mama), which later became their signature song. At the time the record came out, African music, which already had a strong community of listeners in Africa (and the West Indies), was searching for its white audience. A few producers felt the need to bring them together. One of these was Gilbert Castro, whose Celluloid label distributed the record. "Africans have feeling, ideas, and talent. It's up to us to provide them with the technical ability to record in good conditions. This is what we have tried to bring to a band such as Toure Kunda. At a time when many other musical streams are drying up, Africans offer an almost inexhaustible mine of rhythms and melodies." The media— from *Actuel* to *Libération*—were also watching, and made themselves proponents of the idea of a multicultural society. And above all, a few venues kept up with the rise to power of this music, breaking away from the more comfortable kind. Three of these would launch Toure Kunda's career: the Dunois, La Chapelle des Lombards, and Le Palais des Glaces. The Dunois, located at number twenty-eight on the street of the same name in the Thirteenth Arrondissement, was a remodeled old mail-relay station. Since 1977, all the geniuses of folk, free jazz, improvised music, and the most iconoclastic sound concepts had passed through this breeding ground of heterodoxy, whose slogan was "An Impregnable View of the Future." It was altogether natural, in other words, that the place should get hip to African music. After two weekends that saw the whole hundred-seat house sold out, Sylvain Torikian, the director of the club, decided to book Toure Kunda for a month. With the help of word of mouth and the press, not to mention the Africans of the diaspora, an audience of discoverers made the trip.

In the evolution of any musical group, the first limited circle of fans is decisive. By its fidelity and by spreading the word, it strengthens the uncertain steps of a venture until a more significant audience picks up the torch. In the 1980s, an audience sensitive to African music began to multiply in just that way. Toure Kunda were the first to prove the audience was there, enticing the European music industry's investment and foreshadowing what would later be called world music. This network of knowledgeable amateurs also existed in the provinces, where the Toure Kunda brothers (having become a trio since the arrival of Amadou in 1979) toured, accompanied by excellent French or West Indian musicians. This was a brand-new combo, all fire and flame, as was demonstrated by a second album, *Turu* (plural of Toure), whose cover showed for the first time an elephant logo.[4] The themes of the new repertoire drew on social chronicles, humor, rural elegy, and legend, hewing to a dialectic of past and present, of tale and myth, in accordance with the Manding tradition that what is spoken and sung is precious to the collective African unconscious. It did not matter if the *toubab* (white) audience did not grasp all the metaphors. Beyond their music, Toure Kunda, through their show, offered an image of the Other, which resonated with a youth that aspired to take part in a society open to the world. After the Dunois, they set up in January 1983 at La Chapelle des Lombards, directed by Jean-Luc Fraisse, in the rue de Lappe—where musette[5] had been born, one of the earliest varieties of crossbred French music (Auvergne mixed with Italy mixed with manouche[6]). Every night at the Chapelle, a temple of Caribbean music, their ornate voices with guttural accents would joyfully sing sweet or percussive pieces, accompanied by saourabas, congas, djembes, and sabars. But this engagement was plunged into mourning by a tragedy: Amadou collapsed on stage and later died at the nearby Hôpital Saint-Antoine.

The loss affected the entire equilibrium of the group, and they had to wait until the arrival of Ousmane, a former physical education teacher, to reestablish their vocal cohesion.

It is said that it takes ten years for an artist or group to establish itself; Toure Kunda confirmed the adage. It was when they moved to the Palais

---

[4] The album includes, among other cuts, "Kalo Kalo" (a Dyoula war song that calls for the rebuilding of a village destroyed by the enemy); "Waar" (a song that suggests preaching rather than making war); "Guedj" (which teaches about the solid ties between the sky, the earth, the ocean, and man); and "Yaya Bah" (a parable of a shepherd who, instead of giving milk every day, prefers to offer his cow).

[5] *Translator's note:* Musette is a form of French jazz dating back to the 1930s, with heavy emphasis on accordion and guitar.

[6] *Translator's note:* Manouche is Alsatian Gypsy jazz, whose best-known exponent was Django Reinhardt.

des Glaces, another venue keen on world music, that they began to encounter a wider audience. Their first television appearances amplified the phenomenon. Clearly, with eleven musicians, the lineup was red hot. They mixed together African voices, Jamaican rock-steady, griot accents, brass riffs, rhythm and blues, and the rattle of percussion; and they invited guest performers every night, from Manu Dibango to kora players from the diaspora.

From there everything came together. The Ministry of Culture financed their video *Labrador;* they were invited to play at a summit meeting of the heads of French and African states in Vittel; and they went on tour, notably in the West Indies. However, Africa remained their obsession. The title of their fourth album, *Casamance au clair de lune,* sounds very much like a confession. Like a return to the source, a rural deviation, this album was full of deep country: its fauna, its flora, its nocturnal rumors, the exuberance of its celebrations, its aromas of *mafe* (stew with a peanut gravy), and ripe fruits. From there, all that was left was to take the step, to accept the family dare. "In memory of Amadou, we had to go and offer our music to our brothers in Africa, who have followed our history for a long time, thanks to cassettes [often bootlegs] that circulate by the tens of thousands in West Africa." And that was how the epic journey to Ziguinchor took place. The approval of Uncle Yaya, of their mothers, and of a whole country reassured them, and prepared these ambassadors for an international career that would soon pass just as successfully through Japan and the United States.

Salif Keita: The Treason of the Albino

The Contradictions of the Modern Griot

Salif Keita amazed by a guitar solo, 1985.

We are bags of words, we are the bags that enclose secrets several centuries old.

—DJIBRIL TAMSIR NIANE[1]

March 1985. The concert-hall audience is disturbed by a high, anguished voice that could compete with the cry of the saxophone, the hypnotic sonority of the kora, and the pointed arabesques of the electric guitar. This head voice with epic accents, preserving the ancestral rhythmic tradition and bending "modernity" to its tempo, is that of Salif Keita, thirty-five years old. This event has brought out the boubous,[2] the "wax,"[3] and the jewelry, because this is Montreuil-sous-Bois, on the outskirts of Paris, the city with the second largest Malian population in the world, after Bamako. A few specialty reporters are also in attendance; they know that for several months "the Domino of Malian song"[4] has been living in Paris. Without a manager or a recording house, the man was a little lost. Needing to send some money back home to Djoliba, he put on these two concerts. Salif Keita was on the eve of a great career in the West, but he did not know it. A few seasons later, in the stride of his sublime first made-in-Europe album, *Soro,* he would be standing on the largest stages, and fawned over in the United States as well as Australia.

For the moment, though, it is the community audience that comes to see him, seduced as much by his iconoclastic personality as by his voice and songs. In West Africa, pronouncing his name is already an

---

[1] *Soundjata ou l'Epopée mandingue* (*Présence Africaine,* 1960).
[2] *Translator's note:* Traditional robes worn by men and women in Islamic West Africa.
[3] *Translator's note:* Batik fabric, introduced by the Dutch in the nineteenth century, but now a favorite material for traditional clothing. "Wax" generally means the most valued brand of this fabric, actually made in the Netherlands.
[4] "Domino" in reference to the other, soccer-playing Salif Keita, glory of the French clubs Saint-Étienne and Olympique de Marseille.

undertaking. In a caste society, the Keitas, in effect, are the nobles. Not only that, they are descendants of Soundjata Keita, the legendary figure who, in the thirteenth century, established what was to become the Manding Empire—an empire that, at its peak, extended from the banks of the Senegal and Gambia rivers to the Guinea forest and present-day Mali and Niger.[5] This immense collection of lands gave birth to a rich culture transmitted from generation to generation by the persons called griots (from the Portuguese *criado,* troubadour). The griot can be at the same time a storyteller, a diplomat, a historian, a chronicler, a commissioner, a messenger, and an interpreter—functions that often go side by side with singing or playing an instrument. As a result, among the "men of caste," the griot musicians were called *djeli* in the Mande languages (such as Bambara, Maninka, and Dyula), the same as the word for blood— that is, the one who saves the lineage from being forgotten is like a fluid that nourishes the branches of the generations with knowledge and memory. Through the centuries, the griots, dreaded as much as sought after, benefiting often from a status of impunity, have developed an impressive capacity for adaptation. If formerly they praised the courage of warriors and served the interests of the great families or professional groups (such as the butchers in the Hausa country), they have now become middlemen for marriages, masters of ceremonies, and sometimes intercessors of first importance—such as when Kouyate Sory Kandia, at the request of President Sekou Toure of Guinea, reconciled Sangoule Lamizana, president of Upper Volta, and Moussa Traore, president of Mali, who had been on the brink of a war. Modernity has not relativized the cartography of the castes. Every West African knows that the Kouyates, Diabates, Kantes, Sakos, and Diawaras go back to the lineage of the griots, whereas the Keitas do not.

To this social transgression, Salif Keita added two other particularities: he was an albino, and he had an unusual voice. In Africa, depending

---

[5] In West Africa, the Ghana Empire [*translator's note:* located in modern Mauritania, Mali, and Senegal, not modern Ghana] developed from the fourth century until the middle of the thirteenth around gold deposits. It was succeeded by the Mali Empire from the second half of the thirteenth century through the fifteenth century, which added to the gold and salt trade the control of navigation on the Niger River. The Songhai Empire of Gao succeeded it, until its fall in 1591.

on the ethnic group, being albino means ostracism or fetishization. So he had grown up with the equivocal status of a "white black," taunted if weak, feared if strong.[6] As for his high-pitched voice (resulting from his vocal cords hardening in childhood because he used to scream to scare away monkeys that were plundering the gardens), it very soon became the delight of the *grins* (tea clubs where Malians like to meet to converse about the way things are going in the world). If this vocal gift won his mother's support, it did not have his father's, because a Keita is not supposed to sing—he's supposed to have his own griots to sing for him. For this betrayal of the family name, Salif Keita would never totally be forgiven. At best he would win the clemency of the elders. "We accept that Salif makes records and sings elsewhere, but he wouldn't be tolerated doing it in his village.... Salif's father, like the rest of his family, likes what he does, because Salif has broken only the rule that forbids a noble to sing. He respects all the others," his uncle summarized one day. To which, Salif Keita, who at the age of thirteen ran away from his village to Bamako and slept under the stars on the sidewalks, had already replied: "When I go into a village, I sing what I want and it's up to them to discuss it. I have chosen a path, and I'm following it. For me, it's our actions that should determine our status. History doesn't define nobility!"

Originally, Salif Keita dreamed of becoming a teacher, but the national education system declared him unfit because of his poor vision, so he turned to music, singing and playing guitar in the *maquis,* the small bareateries where people check things out.

He made his real professional debut in the Rail Band of the Buffet de la Gare in the capital in 1970. The band was at least original, being financed by the national railroad for entertaining travelers waiting for their train on the only line linking Bamako and Dakar. But when Aly Diallo, the head of the station, commissioned Tidiane Kone, a jazz lover and a griot, to form an orchestra capable of "restoring the strength of the cultural patrimony," the tone changed, and the Rail Band became a first-class band, surpassing every other group every night at the hour of cold beer and bats.

---

[6] In 1995, Salif Keita illustrated the album *Folon* with a young albino girl from his family and created an association for support "of albino people."

Until 1973, Salif Keita was the lead vocalist of this group, which recruited some important people, including a certain Mory Kante, who was then a balafonist.

Tired of being an employee of the railroad, however, he decided to put together Les Ambassadeurs du Motel. This hotel, on the bank of the Niger, where traveling foreigners stayed, was managed by Tiekoro Bakayoko, a police official, and a man of expeditious methods and two reigning passions: soccer and music. This transfer between two establishments owned by the state provoked a national debate that had repercussions all the way up to the Council of Ministers. At Le Motel, Salif had carte blanche to compete against the Rail Band. And with his Ambassadeurs (so named because they were of different nationalities), he was able to realize his ambition of shaping a "modernized folklore," aided in this quest by the collaboration of famous Guinean composer-guitarist Kante Manfila.

This tandem effort made for beautiful nights of music in Bamako until 1978, when the two friends decided to go to Abidjan, Ivory Coast. Thanks to an economic boom fueled by rising sales of cocoa and coffee, Abidjan was the city where a music industry was forming. There Keita and Kante formed Les Ambassadeurs Internationaux and recorded the album *Mandjou,* whose title track, glorifying President Ahmed Sekou Toure of Guinea-Conakry, echoed loudly throughout West Africa. Then, sustained by a Malian businessman, the group left for a stay of a few months in the United States, where they recorded *Primpin* and *Toukan,* two albums equally appreciated in Africa.

It was France, however, that attracted Salif Keita; he felt that this was where African music was taking off internationally. When he was invited to the *Festival des Musiques Métisses* (Festival of Mestizo Musics) of Angoulême, he realized his impact on the audience and decided to move to the suburbs of Paris: to Montreuil.

His concerts in this city, his participation in the "Tam-tam pour l'Éthiopie" project, and his album *Soro* (recorded in 1987, under Senegalese producer Ibrahima Sylla) were essential steps in his recent consecration. In fact, during the next few years, for the media, Salif Keita incarnated the emergence of a new generation. As proof of his recognition, in July 1987 he was invited to England (with Youssou N'Dour and

Ray Lema) to participate in the gigantic concert at Wembley celebrating the seventieth birthday of the still-imprisoned Nelson Mandela. And he signed with the prestigious record company Island, the late Bob Marley's label, directed by Chris Blackwell.

Working out the evolution of a Manding rock empowered by the technology of upscale studios, Salif Keita drew on his musical and philosophical tradition as the opportunities arose. With the song "Nou pas bougé" (We Unmoved), he declared himself on the side of the immigrants a few years before the vast *sans-papiers* movement.[7] A little later, he disregarded the pressures of Malian president Moussa Traore (ultimately overthrown), who had asked him not to record songs about the absence of democracy in his country. With the album *Amen* he could be found collaborating with jazz stars such as Joe Zawinul, Wayne Shorter, Carlos Santana, and Cheikh Tidiane Seck. In the track "Africa" he recalled the virtues of Pan-Africanism—a dream that, it saddened him to see, lies fallow. Covering Gainsbourg, Higelin, Le Forestier, and others in a time of quotas in favor of French song, he paid homage to this French music enjoyed so much in Africa. He also made the soundtrack to the movie *L'Enfant lion* (in which he played a griot) and went to Cannes to defend the only African film in competition—and to deplore the fact that the seventh art was not a concern of his continent. Alongside his very sophisticated arrangements, a deep fidelity to Manding blues continued to pervade his albums, a fidelity obvious in his album *Papa,* titled in reference to his numerous offspring... and to his father, who had passed away in 1985.

What a surprising trajectory for this child from Djoliba, who, in private, confesses to wishing to dedicate himself to agriculture one day, and who, in the meantime, has decided to produce, in his country, young artists he respects, such as the beautiful performers Rokia Traore and Fantani Toure. It is a strange paradox that this descendant of the greatest

---

[7] *Translator's note:* Three hundred Africans started the *sans-papiers* (without papers) movement when they invaded a Paris church in March 1996 in protest against government reforms aimed at diminishing the number of foreigners moving to France. The reforms made it harder for foreigners to obtain work permits and residency and, in some cases, even revoked existing papers. As of this date, the struggle is still going on.

resister to colonization should today embody more than his own land of Mali: Africa of course, but also that legacy of Western history, the Francophone world—so much that he is viewed in Sydney, Los Angeles, and Tokyo as one of the leading practitioners of "the French touch" in world music. But his consecration as such has not made him forget his mission to be a modern griot, whatever the ambiguity of the environments, in the North as well as the South:

"The first motivation of my music was never to sell, to please this one or that one. That is why I refused to join in the race to the Top Fifty, to follow a commercial path. I have still had difficulties following the route.... Showbiz in the West is hyperorganized. Thousands of people make a living from it. It's an industry. When you arrive from Africa, you misconceive this reality. You think that having a good voice, moving well on stage, and being a good musician is enough to make a living immediately from music. Not at all! You can be a very good singer-musician-dancer, but if you don't penetrate this showbiz, if you don't know the codes, you risk doing no better than just getting by. It's what happened to me. I discovered the Western world. In front of me was a wall that took years to break down. This said, I only managed to break half of it, because I didn't want to abandon in this face-off the elements of my culture, my Africanness. In sum, I learned that behind a specific idea of culture in the North, politics was hiding too. You had to belong to a group. You had to keep quiet, accepting some things so as not to compromise your career. But I'm a very spontaneous person. I often talk even when it will hurt me. Therefore it has been difficult for me to keep quiet in the face of some situations—when it's a question of Africa, oppressed people, injustice. This freedom of speech made life difficult for me, it's obvious.... But for me, the only true wealth is my original audience. I could be a billionaire, but if I were far from that audience, I would in reality be the poorest man on earth. I don't want to do anything that clashes with my roots.... The same goes for politics. I am always with the oppressed masses. The most powerful African politicians that I have been able to get along with were departmental managers. I prefer that it stay that way. I am of the lowest caste and that is how I want it.... I have never wanted to forsake this status, because I have always wanted to know the problems of the poor people. People whose only means are, often, their mouths, because a poor guy has only his mouth to speak with. I feel close to those people.... I counsel young musicians not to move to the West. The culture isn't welcoming. There is a politics of protectionism in play. After all, when we come here, it is just to get by, no matter how much experience we have! If you raise your head, you're made to lower it! I tell the youth, 'Stay in the country!' Paris is only a six-hour flight away. They should stay where they are, organize to make themselves heard, create, build networks on the continent, make their creations travel. They will have fewer problems and as many perspectives."[8]

[8] Remarks recorded by the author in 1986.

M'Pongo Love: The Feminist Who "Tickles" Men

African Diversity's Unspoken Matter

M'Pongo Love, 1986.

I have become a businesswoman
And I have sold my soul to the Kasai River
To look for money
In order to feed my children.
What suffering for the unhappy woman I've become!
(chorus)
Don't whine!
Search for a way to help your children!
Because children are your security.

—"FEMME COMMERÇANTE,"
HIT BY M'PONGO LOVE[1]

L eaning on the microphone stand, immobile, eyes closed, in a big boubou
with blue ribbons, she sang in Lingala, in a slightly nasal voice, one
of the songs that made her famous.

> *Love is as fragile as an egg.*
> *Wrap it with all precaution*
> *For fear that it will break*
> *If it falls.*[2]

At her feet, like a field of dried leaves, is an impressive carpet of
bank notes that the spectators have thrown, as an obvious sign of pleasure, along with carefully signed checks and pieces of jewelry. The
great hall of the Mutualité in Paris, usually a setting for important political meetings, was full and radiant with happiness. There was at first,
due to questions of prestige, a social rift between the balcony, where
the embassy staff showed their rank in well-cut suits from expensive

[1] M'Pongo Love, "Femme commerçante" (Toulemonde).
[2] M'Pongo Love, "Motayo," (Toulemonde).

tailors, and the community audience in bright colors below. But during
the concert everything mixed together. The Cameroonian *groto*[3] and the
Senegalese street sweeper, the imposing Zairean *mama-Benz* and the
young Malian coquette, communed together, under the approving eye of
Manu Dibango, who had come, like many other musicians from the
diaspora, to render homage to the lady backstage. The Zairean M'Pongo
Love is one of the most adulated of singers; her public loves her "like a
sister."

   If she holds herself so stiff, it's because since the age of four she has
been scarred by polio, ravager of children in Africa. A shot of penicillin
left her paralyzed, and she spent her first years crawling around on all
fours. Treated "European style," she came out of the ordeal with a lasting
handicap and a prosthesis forcing her to hold herself up on the side of
the stage, while her dancers accompany with their suggestive curves the
soukous rumbas that alternate with her sentimental songs. What concerns Aimée M'Pongo Landu, alias M'Pongo Love—daughter of a director of a social center for the education of girls, former switchboard
operator trained in church-choir style (back when she was called Nana
Mouskroum)—is feminist song. "Yes, I am very feminist," she told a
reporter once, laughing. "I sing about women's problems, I try to give
them courage . . . and I will stop singing when the relations between men
and women in Africa become problem free. But what African man
doesn't have a mistress? In addition to a hard life, women have a lot to
endure. I have a feminist duty to see they fight, that they defend themselves, that they hold their heads high, that they take independent
women as examples." And she added: "We must know how to stay what
we are, we African women, without fearing all the modernism that we
need to assimilate."[4] Of course, what with polygamy, being feminist in
Africa has a strange sound. To convince yourself, it is enough to observe
the language of the wrappers that the women wear—those wraparound

---

[3] A *groto* is a man with an appreciable social status. The term *nanas-Benz* (or
mamas-Benz), designating women who have made it in the business world, has been
in existence since the 1960s, when the first women who succeeded in the fabric trade,
especially in Togo, bought themselves Mercedes-Benzes for their comfort and air
conditioning—Togo having once been a German protectorate.
[4] Remarks recorded by Kidi Bebey, *Afrique élite*, 1989.

bolts of wax cloth, of fancy, or of batik[5]. The designs have names like "My Rival's Eye" (all red from crying or anger); "My Foot, Your Foot" (drawings of steps that warn the husband that his wife will follow him); "Mistress, Let Me Have My Husband." But alongside "Jealousy," "Apple of Divorce," and "My Husband's Pack Animal," the fabric designs also refer to housework, money, the disappointments of the city, the difficulties of childbearing, and the ordinary life of the African woman. In her songs, M'Pongo Love evokes all of this: women who have a hard time making ends meet, mothers who devote their imagination to teaching their children, women who fight to keep their families together.[6] The diversity she embodies can be understood only by observing the land grants, fields, and markets of Africa. Everywhere, from the hoe to the oven, from the *tontine* (neighborhood credit union) to the care of children and elders, women are on the front line. No wonder, therefore, that "mamas," women in their forties, appreciated for their experience and tact, were the first to contribute to the success of M'Pongo Love—a success that's symptomatic of the vogue for female African singers since the mid-1970s. In the past, female griots had tasted fame in their own countries, but from this time on, one saw a number of "queens" of modern music command attention in a Pan-African way.

Starting in Zaire, along with M'Pongo Love and Mbilia Bel, Abeti "The Tigress" and her "perfumed soukous" fought for public favor against Tshala Muana, "Ms. 100,000 Volts," and her torrid shows. From Abidjan, Queen Pélagie, "Lady of Iron and Fire"; Aicha Kone, "The Empress"; Nayanka Bell, "The Princess"; and Monique Seka were the feminine expressions of the Ivory Coast's "economic miracle." In Mali, Nahawa Doumbia,[7] Oumou Sangare, Amy Koita, Oumou Kouyate,

---

[5] *Translator's note:* These are all grades of cloth dyed by the batik process. The most expensive and highest quality fabric is *véritable wax hollandais* made by Vlisco in the Netherlands; *fancy* and *batik* are less expensive local products.

[6] "Ndaya" (The Two Women) claims through the heroine's mouth: "I am sure of my husband. / Nobody can separate me from him. / I don't know the name of my rival." "Bansongueur" (Whore Tongue) calls out people who gossip and tell women the supposed escapades of their husbands. The chorus proclaims: "When we loved each other / there weren't any witnesses. / You won't succeed bringing discord into our home."

[7] Nahawa Doumbia, a daughter of the caste of blacksmiths (therefore in principle not permitted to sing), is one of the many destroyers of taboos in Mali. This queen

Coumba Sidibe, and others overthrew the codes of the ancient griot, and some of them questioned the practices of prearranged marriages, female genital mutilation, and polygamy.

In the past few years, a new crop of African women—many of whom have left the continent for various reasons (sometimes for their own survival)—have joined in this ongoing critique of ideological and musical conventions and are tenaciously making new viewpoints heard. Among them are Angélique Kidjo (Benin), Sally Nyolo (Cameroon), Rokia Traore (Mali), Khadja Nin (Burundi), Maryam Mursal (Somalia), Chiwoniso (Zimbabwe), and Aster Aweke (Ethiopia).

Angélique Kidjo—baptized "voodoo girl" in New York, where she now lives—is currently prowling the terrain of funk, soul, and hip-hop. When interviewers ask her whether she's still making African music, she bursts out in her great ferocious laugh. The tradition—she knows it. She grew up in Ouida, nerve center of the slave trade; she sings in Fon, Mina, and Yoruba; she injects the adarra, fuji, and juju rhythms of her native milieu into Western dance; she lives the tolerant philosophy of vodou and knows the Fâ divination practices of Benin and the luxurious imagination linked to the cults of the old gods. This faithful reader of *Le Monde diplomatique,* for whom Jimi Hendrix's "Voodoo Child" was an epiphany, likes to recall that her paternal grandmother, who died at the age of 101, was a pioneer in the wrapper business, which helps many women to acquire their autonomy. Kidjo's desire to cross over drove her to France (first as a member in several groups, and then solo) and finally to the United States. Her four albums of Afro-funk in search of a universal groove and her brilliance onstage have earned her the favor of European, Australian, and American audiences. She makes no apologies for her work or herself, declaring her cosmopolitan music "open to the world" and embracing her image as a provocateuse, known to take strong positions ("an idealist," she says) and not shy about speaking her mind. One of her first hits, "We-We" (The Torturers), is a prime example.

---

of Bambara didadi (a rhythm built on three drums), with a sensual voice and spellbinding lyrics, tends to comment on the news. The title track of one of her albums refers, for example, to the expulsion of seventy-seven Malians "in irregular situations" on a charter plane, which was plundered on arrival in Bamako.

"In 'We-We,' the beginning is completely Yoruba. It's Shango. My maternal grandmother was from Nigeria and I learned this stuff when I was a kid. It's the type of song performed only by women, when they have had it up to here with men's stupidity. It means, 'The fire is burning in our hearts, our houses, our fields! Beware, the fire will come back to you too!' So, to denounce torture I borrowed this gimmick because it was my feeling of 'sick of it' about this problem. Because, for me, singing is a vital way of expression. The unhappy person starts singing. The sad person sings her sadness. I have always known that. I have an aunt who knows how to sing in every situation. For example, if she wants to insult you in singing, then it's very serious. Because singing, to us, is a way to exorcise violence. Instead of physically harming someone, we sing him. It's more acceptable, and paradoxically, it does more damage. The song is also used in polygamous marriages. It's when these couples start fighting that you hear the most beautiful songs there are."[8]

---

[8] Remarks recorded by the author in March 1992. Often asked to give her opinion on the situation of music in French-speaking countries, Angélique Kidjo has never stopped denouncing the "totally tragic" problems of distribution, bootlegging, and authors' rights, and has proposed the creation of a French-speaking multinational record firm.

Zao: "Mr. Corpse"

The Spices of Humorous Music

Zao and his crown of feathers, 1991.

I call for the saving laugh. I demand that tragic courage chuckle in knowing why.

—SONEY LABOU TANSI[1]

O n November 10, 1998, in the small village of Thiowor, Senegal (1,500 inhabitants, four water faucets, and no electricity), Abdoulaye Ndiaye died at the age of 104. He was the last survivor of the battalions of Senegalese riflemen who fought in the trenches of *quato'ze–dix-huit* (1914–1918, or World War I). Of the 600,000 soldiers recruited from the French colonies, sometimes forcibly, 81,000 did not return ("black force to be consumed before the winter," one general calculated). In an ironic twist, a few days later Abdoulaye Ndiaye was to have received the Legion of Honor medal, but Africa had had the magnanimity to prevent that. So the Congolese singer Zao, in his own way, paid homage to these black *poilus* who died on the slopes of Verdun with a ferocious anthem: "Ancien Combattant" (War Veteran)[2], a song a French friend and a Brazzaville appliance store had helped him record, enabling him to win the Radio France International prize in 1983.[3] He sang this anthem in a military uniform decorated with colored 32nd notes.

> *Count the steps one-two,*
> *War veteran Mundasukiri.*
> *You don't know that I am a war veteran too,*

---

[1] Note to the producer of the play *Moi, veuve de l'Empire,* 1987.
[2] Zao acted in the film *Camp Thiaroye* by Senegalese filmmaker Sembène Ousmane, playing the role of the public entertainer in the midst of soldiers waiting for indemnities they would never receive. Zao also did a tropical version of "Lili Marlene," the most famous song of World War I, sung on both sides of the trenches.
[3] Started by Francoise Ligier, in 1981, the Découvertes (Discoveries) contest by Radio France Internationale gave a leg up to hundreds of artists, some of whom, once primed, went on to great success, such as Habib Koite (Mali), Nahawa Doumbia (Mali), Regis Gizavo (Madagascar), and Sally Nyolo (Cameroon).

I am a war veteran,
I fought in the World War.
In the World War
There is no Wayi friend.
In the World War
There is no pity, my friend.
I've killed French,
I've killed German,
I've killed English,
Me, I've killed Czechoslovakia....[4]

And Zao explained: "A wise man said: 'As long as humanity doesn't kill war, war will kill humanity.' So I stood in the shoes of a veteran who denounces the atrocities he has experienced. I wanted the message to speak to everybody. To all those who believe they can find an answer in the use of weapons, I say they will all end up as corpses. Humor enables us to translate this kind of thing. I wanted a war veteran to talk the same way the Senegalese riflemen did."

When the World War comes,
Everybody is a corpse.
When the bullet whistles, there is no choice.
With the blow of the club,
All at once, bang! Corpses.
Your wife a corpse, your mother a corpse,
Your father a corpse, your children corpses....[5]

Before denouncing neutron bombs, Pershing and SS20 missiles, and other weapons of the time, he stated his hope for brotherhood in dozens of languages:

If you saw French, bonjour,
If you saw English, good morning,

---

[4] Zao, "Ancien Combattant" (FKO).
[5] Ibid.

If you saw Chinese, hihon,
If you saw Senegalese, nagadef,
If you saw Malian, anisokoma...[6]

The future Zao ("*Z* for someone who started from zero, *A* for some-one admitted to the musical scene, *O* for an omnipresent artist"), or Zoba Casimir on his birth certificate, was born in 1953 in Goma-Tsetse, a district of Brazzaville, and grew up in a musical family. His father played the sanza; his uncles, percussion; and he spent his days among the church choirs and traditional-dance groups of his neighborhood and high school. This musical culture, a hybrid of Catholic gospel, African tradition (in particular, that of the region south of the Pool[7]), and the inevitable rumba, led him, in 1968, to join Les Anges, a Congolese music-and-dance ensemble that came to be fairly famous. Because the Congo was proclaiming itself "Marxist-Leninist" at the time,[8] the group was invited to perform in all the "fraternal countries": the USSR, Cuba, East Germany, and Algeria—an experience that, together with the influence of Franklin Boukaka (a politically dedicated singer shot in 1972 by the military), Bourvil, Maxime Le Forestier, and Jacques Dutronc, encouraged him to compose songs that leaned toward social satire.[9] Zao, having become a school teacher, showed a particular devotion to Jean de la Fontaine. And in fact, what he did was to put African society into fable.

---

[6] Ibid.

[7] *Translator's note:* The capitals of the two Congos, Brazzaville and Kinshasa, are on opposite sides of the Pool Malebo (formerly known as the Stanley Pool), a lake on the Congo River: Brazzaville to the northwest, Kinshasa to the southeast.

[8] In December 1968 the Parti Congolais du Travail (the Congolese Labor Party) came into power, and vocal groups with names like Cheveux Crépus (Frizzy Hair), Nez Épatés (Flattened Noses), Mains Velues (Rough Hands), the Walla Players, and Les Gazelles were honored. With them and renowned bands such as Les Bantous de la Capitale, dance, and especially a dance called the boucher, became a way of life. The open-air dance clubs (Cabane Bantoue, La Joie du Congo, Elysée-Bar, Pigalle, and others), were routinely packed with patrons eating *gamoutch* (kabobs) and *makobé* (a freshwater fish) while drinking large amounts of alcohol.

[9] "With theses of universality such as those of Senghor or Aimé Césaire, one can devour oneself. I believe the solution is to work on purely African themes using Western techniques. I imagine Beethoven's *Fifth Symphony* reprised on the mvet with xylophones and drums." (Remarks recorded by the author in May 1989.)

"Soulard" (Lush, a portrait of the *cuveurs,* or drunkards, who desert their families), "Porte-monnaie" (Change Purse, i.e., an empty one: an impossible marriage), TOI (*Tourbillon Odieux International,* the odious international maelstrom; that is, AIDS), "Louvouezo" (a song in Kikongo about a woman ill-treated by her husband), "Pierre de Paris" (a Westernized dandy comes home and renounces his origins), "Sorcier ensorcelé" (Sorcerer Ensorcelled), "Moustique" (Mosquito), and "Patron" (Owner) were some of the many titles that sketched picaresque tales of everyday life in and around the Brazzaville suburb of Poto-Poto—life and death, heart and ass, all on display against a background of funky rumba and wordy humor.

These songs, designed to "tickle the poor and scratch the rich," were always stamped with a generous irony. You only need to listen to another big hit, "Corbillard" (The Hearse): "It's a dark piece, the story of a corpse that doesn't want to go to the cemetery because he has too many debts. So the corpse and the hearse start talking. The corpse doesn't want his estate to be liquidated to pay off his debts. He even tries to bribe the hearse, but the hearse refuses to be paid off."

To conclude that Zao plays the king's jester might seem hasty, except that the play-acting tradition of the griot survives to this day as a constant in popular African satire, as a never-ending game of hide-and-seek between life and parody, History and history. That is what emboldens its theater, in the case of the abrasive works of Sony Labou Tansi, founder of the Rocado Zulu Theatre. It is what one finds in Africa's "crude" pictorial art, typified by the Zairean Chéri Samba. It is what became the hallmark of the ferocious humor of Essindi Mindja,[10] XYZ, and Jean-Michel Kankan, and of the songs of Francis Bebey, such as "Divorce Pygmée," "Si les Gaulois avaient su" (If the Gauls Had Known), and "Agatha."[11]

---

[10] The Cameroonian humorist Essindi Mindja, a history professor, wrote several iconoclastic sketches in his time. In one, an imaginary president said: "In Africa, there are two parties, the civilian party and the military party." A second concerned the disappearance of some monetary funds into Swiss banks. A third described the "Bérékaki," a particular genus of animal, found at all crossroads (beret-khaki). These sketches earned him banishment to a remote region of Cameroon.

[11] Some lines from "Agatha": "Agatha, you think I'm completely crazy, don't you? / Listen, you have the right to pour me some more palm wine / and not to lie to me. /

That satire, in national or vernacular languages, sometimes plays with its limits. The classic case is that of Hilarion Nguema, the Gabonese king of the *ambianceurs* (party animals) in La Gare Routière, the most populous district in Libreville, who, after a most explicit "*Crise Économique*" (Economic Crisis), sang "Sida" (AIDS), a small masterpiece that diverted a dramatic crisis from its medical reality.

Evidently, in situations that create anxiety (unemployment, violence, disease), laughter is a wonderful antidote in Africa, especially when provoked by animist imaginations, naturally magical, funny, and surrealist. That these buffoons so irritate the powerful is also only natural: in changing societies where leaders have often failed, the singer plays the role, if not of an opinion leader, then at least of an oracle. Just remember Zao who, in the shade of a mango tree, prophesied: "The real world is threatened, for example, by the arms race. Today, the youth pays for the carelessness of the older generation. I get sick when I see all these bored young people having to give in to all sorts of vices to forget. They are a sacrificed generation."

More than ten years after these words, in 1997, a terrible civil war, for the sake of petroleum revenues, and waged by teenagers wearing armbands and calling themselves Cobras or Ninjas, destroyed Zao's country and home and lost him his son, proving him sadly right.

This isn't my son, even if he's yours! / Agatha, your son was born more than a month ago / and until now he hasn't decided to take the local color / My mother was right when she told me: / 'Son, I warn you, this woman, / she'll make you see all the colors.' " (Words and music by Francis Bebey.)

Alpha Blondy: "i Am a Rastafoulosophe, You Know!"

The Rooting of Reggae in Africa

Alpha Blondy with his Bible and his Koran, 2000.

Look to Africa for the crowning of a Black king; for the day of deliverance is at hand, and he shall be the Redeemer.

—ATTRIBUTED TO MARCUS GARVEY

n 1985, Alpha Blondy, from the Ivory Coast, put out his third album, *Apartheid Is Nazism.* Over a classic reggae tempo, one song in particular caught the ears of the youth: "Afriki."

> *Sam! Set my ass on fire . . .*
> *Wai ai ai!*
> *We have left black Africa*
> *To go for a spin;*
> *We are in Montego Bay, Kingston, JA.*
> *No matter where I look, everywhere Dyula,*
> *No matter where I look, everywhere Bete,*
> *No matter where I look, everywhere Baoule,*
> *No matter where I look, everywhere Ashanti,*
> *No matter where I look,*
> *Jamaica is Africa!*[1]

This Pan-African anthem diverged from the usual creed. It suggested that the unity of the black world matters not only for Africans in Africa, but also for a community of identity that transcends geography and history. But the rallying cry "Jamaica is Africa" also had a more pointed meaning for the singer, now at the height of his international fame. For years this native of Dimbroko, this *kameleba* (proud and brave one) who wanted to be a "mutant," had been struggling to transplant the music of Jamaica to the land of coffee and cocoa. This record was Alpha Blondy's latest bid to legitimize an African reggae.

---

[1] "Afriki," *Apartheid Is Nazism* (EMI, 1985).

He owed part of his intellectual makeup to his grandmother, who raised him in the country. She taught him the wisdom of the Koran, Dyula morality, and tolerance toward people of mixed ancestry, which made him say later: "There are eighty-seven ethnic groups in the *Côte d'Ivoire;* the eighty-eighth is that of the whites." In high school, which he made his way through chaotically, he liked to be called Elvis, and his musical interests ran to the imported idols: Johnny Halliday and the *yéyés*[2] on the French-speaking side, the groups dear to the hippies (from Deep Purple to Pink Floyd) on the English-speaking side. In those days, in Odienné or Korhogo, where he grew up, clubs specializing in impromptu parties were replacing cultural groups and traditional eateries.

With his friends Jos, Dylan, Négus, and Mao, Alpha Blondy founded the Atomic Vibrations and cultivated such a rebel attitude that his beloved grandmother gave him the name "Blondy," a corruption of the French word *bandit;* he would keep that nickname and later add the more esoteric "Alpha" (symbolic of beginning).

In 1975, after a year of learning English in Liberia, the teenager went to New York. The Immigration and Naturalization Service, not convinced that this boy sporting blue bell-bottom pants, platform shoes, and a shirt displaying all the flags of the world had come here to study, put him briefly in a detention center while they verified his story. He went on to take computer classes at Columbia University, work day jobs, and meet his wife, a woman of Jamaican origin.

Not coincidentally, this trip to America marked the beginning of his involvement with Rastafarianism. "Look to Africa, when a black king shall be crowned, for the day of deliverance is at hand," the Jamaican Marcus Mosiah Garvey had predicted in 1927, sowing the seeds of the Rastafarian philosophy. In the course of the century, Garvey's goal of a physical return of blacks from the diaspora evolved into a spiritual journey, with Ethiopia and its emperor, Haile Selassie,[3] becoming the iconic focus of this redemptive quest. In addition to imbibing these

---

[2] *Translator's note: Yéyé* was a light French rock 'n' roll popular in the 1960s.

[3] The late Haile Selassie, a descendant of Solomon and the Queen of Sheba, was, in Rastafarian eyes, the man destined to unite the members of the diaspora. He was one of the founders of the Organization of African Unity (OAU) in 1963 in Addis Ababa.

Rastafarian doctrines, Alpha Blondy made his first visit to Kingston, the Mecca of reggae. There he could appreciate in situ the reggae idiom, the art of transmuting the nation's frustration and social violence into hope and a message of peace. On returning to the States, he performed at small New York venues, playing Bob Marley[4] themes adapted into Dyula. "If the Jamaican Africans spent their lives defending Africa, they must have had a good reason. So I wanted to translate the Rastafarian message into an African language."

But Babylon[5]—its misery, its betrayals, its violence, its drugs—got the best of him. After he ingested a hallucinogenic substance he identified as angel dust, a serious mental crisis led him to Bellevue hospital in New York. Labeled a "dangerous element," he was forced to make the transatlantic trip back to the Ivory Coast. Upon his return he was committed for several long months to the Bingerville psychiatric hospital.

Once this obligatory stay at the "university of the gifted" (as he called it) was over, he found a job as an English translator at *Radio-Télévision Ivoirienne* (RTI), where, in 1981, the producer, Roger Fulgence Kassy, noticed him and gave him his first TV gig. For his appearance on *Première Chance,* "ghetto" scenery was designed. In the midst of trash, old tires, crumbling walls, and graffiti, Alpha Blondy appeared singing "Bintou Were," provoking a great outcry from the Ivorian elite and a positive reaction from the local youth. Subsequently, in 1983, another producer pushed him to record, in an eight-track studio with an in-house orchestra, the album *Jah Glory,* which went gold three times over.

Among his compositions, one brought him particular popularity among the *balados* (street kids) of Treichville and Adjame, the ghettos of Abidjan: "Brigadier Sabari." Sung in Dyula, spiced with French words, it broke a taboo by mentioning a beating by the police during a *coup de poing* (fist strike) operation. The Alpha Blondy of myth, mouthpiece of

---

[4] The maternal side of Bob Marley's family was of Akan origin—a major ethnic group in the Gulf of Guinea region. An analysis of trade routes shows that Jamaica welcomed people from this region, who were known for their resistance to domestication. The Akan region is also the heart of the vodou cosmology that informs the Jamaican ritual practices of Myal and Obeah.

[5] *Translator's note:* Babylon, in Rasta speech, means any system of power under which blacks are enslaved.

the poor, the marginal, the rebel youth, was born. In 1984, with the support of the multinational firm EMI, which was interested in the African music wave, he and his band the Solar System produced a second opus, *Cocody Rock*. This time the reggae message was explicit. The topics included Samory Toure, a leading figure in the resistance against colonization in western Africa; the dignity of the poor; the superpowers and the menace they posed to the planet; and, of course, the emerging African Rastafarian movement. The last track was recorded in Kingston with the Wailers, Bob Marley's fiery band—a nod to the legend whose name opens doors throughout Africa, where everyone feels like his spiritual brother.

In Africa, then, reggae had a special place.[6] Although other imported musics—Cuban, rhythm and blues, rock, jazz, even to some extent French *chanson*—had important stylistic repercussions, the reggae influence was on another level: that of identity.

What does reggae have to say at a time when generations have grown up with postcolonial independence? Essentially, it's about affirming a culture's quest to find its place in history—its own history—without ignoring that of others. For many artists, outsiders to reggae style, this self-reliant humanism is a revelation. It reinforces their confidence and their own principles, inspiring them to put them into practice. And Alpha Blondy is a propagandist of this message. Never mind the later escapades of this self-proclaimed *rastafoulosophe*[7] (a name that refers to his psychiatric crises and his conflicted relations with Northern show-biz). He expresses out loud, in his own way, the unspoken things of Africa. That explains why the positions he takes can be surprising.

"I belong to only one ethnic group: God's," he says. "This people is the nation of Abraham, as the Bible and the Koran say." Putting this

---

[6] Communities of reggae fans and artists exist in most African countries, adapting the music to local languages. South African Lucky Dube, of Transvaal origin, is the other African reggae star (500,000 copies of *Slave* sold in 1988). In the new generation, the most creative are Ismael Isaac, Jah Solo Gunt, Waby Spider (in the Ivory Coast); K. K. Kaseko, Kojo Antewi (in Ghana); and Majek Fahek and Ras Kimono (in Nigeria). Important Rasta communities are also found in the Indian Ocean.

[7] *Translator's note:* The word combines not only *Rastafarian* and *philosophe* but also *fou* (crazy).

philosophy onstage, he sometimes stands at the mike holding the Bible and the Koran in his hands. For the Rastaman, fond of symbols, there must be reconciliation. He does not hesitate to provoke, as when he went to sing in Marrakech wearing a Star of David and braving the accusation (printed in some papers) of having "sold out to international Zionism." To those who would listen, he preaches reconciliation in the Middle East, with a noteworthy consistency—as evidenced by all of his titles that refer to Jerusalem, a place where church, mosque, and synagogue exist side by side, or again by his homages both to Egyptian president Anwar al-Sadat, assassinated by zealots, and to Yitzhak Rabin, Israeli prime minister, victim of extremists in his turn. This ecumenism applies to his own country, too. In 1987, he adapted, on one side of the album *Révolution,* ten minutes of a speech by President-for-Life Houphouët-Boigny in which the president mentioned the former RDA (*Rassemblement Démocratique Africain,* African Democratic Union), even though it got him branded as having "sold out" to power. To that charge he answered: "This relative peace that we enjoy in the Ivory Coast costs us much effort. The country has sixty-seven ethnic groups, and if we don't all get behind the chief, there will be anarchy, as in other African countries that move forward only by coups d'état.... I am behind Houphouët because he has held up well.... Money and power are babies in Africa."[8] The recent atrocities in Rwanda and then in Liberia and Sierra Leone haven't exactly proved him wrong. Nevertheless, on the B-side of the same album, the same Alpha Blondy put out "Election Koutcha," an evocation of endemic electoral scheming and corruption.

Reggae, with its sense of narrative, its vocal groups ("the voice of angels that must carry the listener on clouds all the way to heaven," according to Alpha Blondy), its argot, and its use of proverbs, is, like gospel, a particularly effective form for preaching and communion. With time, Alpha Blondy's reggae, enriched with sonorous colors, has become more mystic. It pleads for a dynamic Africanness, asking the continent to overcome its fatalism, born of the force of the past and the seriousness of present problems. This reggae wants to be planet-wide

---

[8] Conversation with the author.

and visionary. "I would say that we are orphans of the universe: we are the only ones who can measure it, we are the basic measure; time would be blind without us. And when you have *Voyager* that keeps on showing pictures of the Earth until it totally goes out of the solar system, you see that we are what? Like a pulse, a period, a blip on a cosmic computer. Increase this to the universe, the universe is a blip, we are the beats of this blip, and in our microscopism, we see ourselves as giants when we are really just atoms.... And I believe that it's this spiritual, mathematical, scientific, physical, and biophysical complexity that the wise men of old called God, and formulated using poetry: the Bible, the Koran.... The equation in front of which we are placed right now, as humanoids, what is it? It's reaching our own dimension that will make gods out of us—these gods that we are in reality."[9]

In this way, the children of an immense ghetto, Alpha's African listeners, youths for the most part, have been invited to imagine solutions within their reach, from nutritional self-sufficiency ("the greatest gift of God is the Earth, where you can plant a bit of manioc or a banana tree") to new philosophies ("these young people are traumatized by all the *-isms* offered to them and that don't have anything to do with African reality: capitalism, communism, socialism").

Years later, a new reggae generation is following in his footsteps; examples in the Ivory Coast include Ismael Isaac, Serge Kassy, and Tiken Jah Fakoly. In 1997, Fakoly put out a cassette, *Mangercratie* (Eatocracy), with unambiguous lyrics:

> *We have seen all the -cracies.*
> *Now we want eatocracy or nothing.*
> *Go tell the politicians*
> *To take our names off their business:*
> *We understand it all.*
> *They use us as camels*
> *In conditions we deplore.*
> *They often take us for a ride*
> *In unknown directions.*

---

[9] Conversation with Hélène Lee, *L'Affiche,* June 1994.

> *They light the fire, they activate it,*
> *Then they come and play firefighter.*[10]

This song had an immediate resonance. In the Ivory Coast alone, three hundred thousand copies were sold. Two hundred thousand others were distributed in neighboring countries—not to mention the probably equally large volume of bootlegged cassette copies.

---

[10] Tiken Jah Fakoly, *Mangercratie* (Globe Music, 1997). On December 23, 1999, Ivorian president Henri Konan Bedié was deposed by a military coup directed by General Robert Gueï, who announced his intentions over the radio after a track by Alpha Blondy was broadcast! The principal accusation against the overturned president, besides his economic ineptitude, was his propensity for exploiting ethnic prejudice, which the reggaemen, who greeted his ouster, have never ceased to denounce. A week before the putsch, Alpha Blondy's album *Elohim* had come out, on which two titles, "Voleurs de la république" (Thieves of the Republic) and "Dictature," were the most explicit. The track "Journalistes en danger" (Journalists in Danger) described the assassination of a journalist from Burkina Faso.

Mamadou Konte's Little Hat

The Activists of Black Showbiz

Mamadou Konte, 1993.

Mamadou told me, Mamadou told me,
We pressed the lemons, we can throw away the skins
(repeat)
The lemons, they are the Negroes,
All of the tanned of Africa,
Senegal, Mauritania,
Upper Volta, Togo, Mali,
Ivory Coast and Guinea,
Benin, Morocco, Algeria,
Cameroon and all the others . . .

—"MAMADOU,"
FRANÇOIS BÉRANGER

A t 29 rue Wagane-Diouf in Dakar, behind Independence Place, the elders remember the comings and goings of European celebrities who used to turn up for a good time away from the public eye. This old colonial house with a pool was taken care of by a well-known madam, and served as a trysting place for members of the 1960s jet set. Today it is mainly musicians who have made it their headquarters: Wolof rappers like Positive Black Soul, neofolk performers with Fulani sauce like the Frères Guissé or the Kassé Stars, whose wild tamas (armpit drums) make the girls' rumps shake. Concerts are held in one hall, six evenings a week. Upstairs, ten rooms are regularly rented to traveling artists or foreign managers. For modest prices one can eat a *tiéboudienne* (a rice dish with fish and vegetables) on the premises, or drink a beer. If the house has become a focal point for the African musical world, that's all because of the new tenant, impresario Mamadou Konte, who rebaptized the place "Tringa" in reference to his native region. A picaresque personality who represents all the principal figures in African music,[1] Mamadou Konte, behind the scenes, has also contributed to its promotion abroad. This tall, thin man, gentle and placid, who always wears a little soft felt hat, knows how to read, but does not write. He is also an agitator to whom we owe the adventure of Africa Fête, tool of promotion for African culture.

At the outset, Mamadou Konte could never have imagined that he would one day consort with pop stars. In August 1965, having left his native Tambacouda (a region of Senegal), he landed in Marseille in the baggage hold of a steamship. He was illiterate. In the outskirts of Paris, he became an illegal worker. He spent ten years in factories as a vaguely specialized laborer. One day, as he took the Métro to work at an assembly plant in Strasbourg-Saint-Denis, he searched for the Laughing Cow cheese ad that had served him as a landmark, but it had disappeared. He became lost, wandered around in vain, and lost his job.

Having made the acquaintance of militant unionists, Mamadou Konte joined the CGT (*Confédération Générale du Travail,* a major French labor union, aligned with the Communist Party), He went on to mobilize against the "sleep merchants" of the Sonacotra (*Société Nationale de Construction pour les Travailleurs,* a semigovernmental organization for providing lodgings to migrant workers), to found the Trotskyist organization *Révolution Afrique* in 1973, and then to create a federation of immigrant tenants in the Paris region. It was through this last group that he made the connection with music. In 1976, the singer François Béranger agreed to give a concert to pay for this federation's posters. He was joined by Pierre Akendengue and the Ballets Lemba. The experiment succeeded and was continued. New artists who volunteered included Bernard Lavilliers, Claude Nougaro, Djamel Allam, and Toto Bissainthe. In 1978,

---

[1] African music has suffered from the absence of any real national music industries (except in the case of South Africa). Artists whose creative potential was sold off are innumerable, this waste being another face of the infamous unequal development. In the last decade, though, following the example of Mamadou Konte, some professionals in charge of management, record labels (for example, Ibrahima Sylla, head of a Francophone catalog of 4,000 titles), and studios have been changing a playing field occupied for too long by pirates, corrupt bureaucrats (with government mandates), and other swindlers. Some of these newcomers have joined together to form the association *La Transafricaine des Arts.*

in reaction to the "return aid" fund (an anti-immigrant proposal offering ten thousand francs each to foreigners who agreed to go back where they came from) planned by government minister Lionel Stoléru, Mamadou Konte created the *Association d'Aide au Retour Créateur des Travailleurs Africains* (Aid Association for the Creative Return of African Workers). To finance his projects (such as a library at Thiès in Senegal and agricultural apprenticeships) he organized Africa Fête. In the coming years, he would be glad he did: his other projects for his country may have met with mixed results, but Africa Fête turned out to be an unqualified success. At the same time, in 1981, the left's rise to power in France permitted African culture an unprecedented institutional opportunity, matching the vogue for black musics. In addition to Manu Dibango, Toure Kunda, Xalam, Salif Keita, Francis Bebey, André-Marie Tala, Jacques Higelin, Cheb Khaled, Djamel Allam, Mouloudji, Baaba Maal, Princesse Erika, Donké, Zao, and Dédé Saint-Prix, others outside the French-speaking area also took part in the enterprise, artists such as Osibisa, Malopoets, Dollar Brand, Aswad, Tony Allen, and the Mahotella Queens. Newspapers, radio, and record companies endorsed the venture. Mamadou Konte directed the saga from a little office set in a street not far from Pigalle. He continued to live in spartan style, his landlord giving him occasional credit, and the post offices of the Thirteenth Arrondissement displaying his telephone bills.

An unrepentant idealist, Mamadou Konte continued to dream of a Black Culture Foundation, of intrepid cultural cross-bracing...and gradually set up an artist management firm whose first client was Salif Keita. Years later, his management network would cross the Atlantic as a result of agreements with Chris Blackwell, the man who, with his firm, Island Records, had helped make reggae an international phenomenon. And Africa Fête[2] would organize tours of artists—from Baaba Maal to Angélique Kidjo—in the United States.

---

[2] Beside Africa Fête and the now defunct *Nuits Blanches pour la Musique Noire* ("White [or Sleepless] Nights for Black Music") in Marseille, several African musical gatherings have persisted in France, the most notable being the Musiques Métisses festival of Angoulême (directed by Christian Mousset) and the Africolorfestival in Paris (directed by Phillipe Conrath). In 1999, Africa Fête, equipped with a digital studio and funded by the Africa Fête record label, modernized its Dakar headquarters.

With the 1980s the economic and cultural data changed. Globalization and the major record labels no longer embraced the notions of live performance, of authors' rights to profit from copyright, or of cosmopolitanism. Mamadou Konte told himself that it was time to go home to his country. Later he remarked: "I saw many films of Indians when they were colonized by the English and Spanish. In the battles they withdrew in order to come back stronger. I withdrew to Dakar to deploy African culture better in Europe." In this way "Tringa" was born: a base of support, resources, professionalism, and concerts.[3] There, Mamadou Konte, spreading out his large arms and citing Cendrars, Fanon, Leiris, or Picasso as proofs of his interest in fertile dialogue, setting up the framework for a new venture: that of a real African record industry, with Motown as a model, so that "an artist is no longer forced to expatriate whenever he wants to make a record, a clip, concerts"; and, even more utopian, that of African unity, for as he says, "African integration will not happen without cultures and without solidarity with them."

---

[3] On June 2, 1993, as the dawn ripened on Demba Diop stadium and the crowd of 30,000 spectators slowly dispersed, Omar Pene closed the ten hours of Africa Fête de la Musique. On the program had been no less than Finaçon, the princes of Cape Verde funana; Guinea's Sekouba Bambino; Mali's Nahawa Doumbia (1984 winner of the pan-African Découvertes-RFI competition); the rap-ragga idol MC Solaar, a Chadian who grew up in Dakar; Lemzo Diamono (a breakaway from Omar Pene's Super Diamano), adepts of the style xhatbi, "dance of the pissing dog"; Ismael Lo, the "Senegalese Dylan"; Youssou N'Dour, who lent his soundboard; the Tukolor Baaba Maal; and of course Omar Pene, the idol of Pikine, the neighborhood of the capital's rejects. This Fête had been planned by Mamadou Konte, organized with the logistical support of the Centre Cultural Français of Dakar, which was then directed by François Bélorgey.

The Eskista of Mahmoud Ahmed

The Case of Ethio-Jazz

Mahmoud Ahmed in a trance, 1999.

Jazz was born in America but its deepest roots are in Africa. African musicians are therefore in a good position to play jazz taking off from their local music.

—MULATI ASTATQE,
FATHER OF ETHIO-JAZZ

From Ethiopia, all we have known are images of famine, the military conflict with Eritrea that was the longest war of the continent, and the clichés of Rasta mythology around "Negus" Haile Selassie.[1] How could we imagine, then, that this country has, in its strange and secret isolation, created over several decades an astonishing music that combines the furies of Afrobeat, the indolence of Latin swing, and the voluptuous subtleties of neighboring Arabia? Ethiopian music astonishes with a palette that ranges from a danceable and brassy jazz to a melancholic desert blues, and in between, haunting, inexplicably modern melodies sung by heartrending crooners with thin voices.

Yes, there is an Ethiopian paradox, and a capital—Addis Ababa, 7,500 feet above sea level—crazy about music. Whether at *tedj bet* (bars where the national beverage *tedj*, a kind of mead, is consumed), dance halls, weddings, community parties, or stadiums, the venues are taken by storm whenever a local star happens to show up.

Flashback. As in most underdeveloped countries, the arrival of Western band instruments (brass and guitars) meant that new musical cards

---

[1] Ethiopia, which, contrary to cliché, is two-thirds high green temperate plateau, and is the only country of Africa that was never colonized (despite a superficial Italian presence), presents passionate cultural particularities. Converted in the fourth century, it was one of the first Christian countries. The bagana (a large lyre with ten strings), descended from King David's harp, prohibited during the two decades of the socialist Derg regime because of its association with orthodox Christianity (Haile Selassie played it), paid dearly for its prestigious past. With its classic poetry, religious music, and tradition of itinerant bards, Ethiopia captivates by the variety of its

were being dealt. After Mussolini's brief occupation (October 1935 to April 1941), large bands were formed under the aegis of military or cultural institutions.[2] The training was often directed by true music lovers like Tsege Dibu, chief of police, who recruited numerous foreign teachers, trained countless hand-picked applicants as young as fourteen, and, in love with strings, even pursued the dream of a symphony orchestra. Beyond their formal functions, these groups worked as big bands and were the crucible of careers such as those of the great modern singers (Alemayehu Eshete, Talahoun Gessesse, Bzunesh Bekele, and Hirut Bekele). Numerous independent groups drew their inspiration from these bands as well: the All Star Band, the Girmas Band, Soul Echo, Wallias, Venus, Ethio Stars, Black Lion, and others. And, until the middle of the 1970s, these were the official groups (following the example of the Imperial Body Guard Band, the Army Band, and the Police Orchestra), which accompanied the majority of the icons of native song, onstage or on record.

Ethiopia was ruled at the time (and since 1930) by Haile Selassie, the 225th descendant of King Solomon, to whom the divine right was guaranteed by the ancient Book of Kings. He was a monarch before whom one bowed down whenever he crossed the capital in his green Rolls-Royce, but who contributed to the birth of the Organization for African Unity in 1963, and, after a failed coup d'état, understood the urgency of engaging his country in progressive change. Thus Addis Ababa, as capital of the nonaligned countries, was brought into tune with the world. Young men strolled about in bell-bottom pants; young women sported miniskirts and Afro and beehive hairdos. The stars of soul music and the gods of the electric guitar brought forth scores of local emulators. As

---

music, which also includes a beautiful tradition of vocal polyphonies among the Dorzé, Deri, Ghimira, and others, who, like the Pygmies and the Bushmen, prove (as if it were necessary) that polyphony is not only a Western invention.

[2] It was Haile Selassie, passing through Jerusalem, who booked the Arba Lidjotch, a band composed of young people displaced by the Armenian genocide, to make their music the official music of the kingdom; their leader, Kevork Nalbandian, became the first musical instructor of the Ethiopians and composer of the national anthem. With his nephew Nerses, he would be a decisive actor in the modernization of Ethiopian music from the 1950s to 1974.

evidence of this effervescence, the essentials of Ethiopia's discography (five hundred 45-rpm singles, thirty 33-rpm albums) were produced between 1969 and 1978. The label Amha Records alone recorded 250 titles in six years.[3] Brilliant and sophisticated arrangers worked on this contemporary music. And, although it incorporated Western (curiously, in contrast to other African countries, Latin American influence is practically nonexistent) or Arab elements, on a melodic or rhythmic level it took its inspiration directly from traditional music, which gave it its inimitable grain. It integrated into its sound, for example, the tradition of the *azmari*,[4] the minstrel who crisscrosses the Christian countryside with his instrument in search of paying gigs. It also reexamined many Abyssinian rhythms through jazz lenses. But this "golden age" came to an end with the seizure of power in April 1974 by a Stalinist military junta (the Derg), which imposed on the country a regimen of Spartan harshness—and banned its official art.

In this chaotic process, Mahmoud Ahmed, by virtue of his longevity, represented the archetype of the "classic" singer. Born in 1942 in the heart of the labyrinth of the Mercato, the swarming and permanent market of Addis Ababa, he was of very modest origins and, with his studies cut short, entered the working life as a shoe shine boy. Going from one small job to another, he found himself, at twenty years old, a jack of all trades at the Arizona, one of those clubs where the stars of official orchestras came to earn extra money, notwithstanding the military ban and obligatory arrests. There he unexpectedly replaced someone at the last minute

---

[3] Amha Eshete took refuge in the United States and did not return until 1993. We owe the unearthing of these treasures to the passion of Francis Falceto, who compiled them in the invaluable Ethiopiques series of CDs released by Buda Records and directed by Gilles Frucheaux.

[4] The *azmari* accompanies himself on the kraar (a six-string lyre, "the devil's instrument"), the masinqo (one-stringed fiddle), or the accordion. Like the Manding griot, he assumes a mongrel status, between praise and mockery, leading to both respect and mistrust. Thus it was at one time considered bad for a girl to marry an *azmari*. Guardian of collective memory, musical standards, and the art of double meaning, the *azmari* is completely at home in the city. The tradition, embodied in the past by Yirga Doubale and Bahrou Qenié, was followed, fixed, or "modernized" by the artists of the new generation such as Betsat Seyoum and Abebe Fekade; the latter opened a nightclub in Addis Ababa that was extremely popular.

and found himself invited, thanks to his remarkable skills, to be a part of the Imperial Body Guard, the premier band of the day, in which he would remain until 1974.

> *I am from Addis Ababa and you from Harar.*
> *You, the mandarin tree of Harar and the enkoy tree of Godjam,*
> *Tell the wind to bring me your perfume,*
> *I have to gallop to find you again.*[5]

The songs of Mahmoud Ahmed, largely consecrated to love, earned him great fame. He surrounded himself with the best musicians; his recordings were distributed on cassettes produced by music shops. These shops constituted the only pleasure in the ice years of the Derg regime,[6] a period in which cultural life was chloroformed, the clubs had to close down, and promising careers were shattered. It was out of the question to perform outside the country, the rare authorizations being granted only to artists who had pledged allegiance (Mahmoud Ahmed's first trip abroad, after several fruitless attempts, took place in 1994). But though many groups had to put away their instruments, some resisted, such as the Roha Band (formerly the Ibex Band), with which Ahmed continued to perform in the numerous grand hotels of the capital, from the Hilton to the Ghion, where foreign diplomats, members of non-governmental organizations, prostitutes, and all the beautiful people lived, cut off from the world while the weekend curfew was in effect.

When he could appear in front of the general public, Mahmoud Ahmed was also appreciated for his talents as a showman, because he had no equal in letting loose the famous eskista, with the heaving quiver of the torso and shoulders, of which Ethiopians are so fond. Eskista is *the* dance of the Amharas, enhancing amorous repartee and expressing collective jubilation. Its origins among the Gurage, a population famous for the exuberance of their dance, explains its atmospheric qualities.

---

[5] Mahmoud Ahmed, "Asha Gedawo," *Almaz* (CRC Edition–Buda, 1973).
[6] During the "Derg time," hits that under Haile Selassie had sold 5,000 copies sold over 100,000.

With the fall of the Mengistu regime in May 1991,[7] paired with an economic frenzy shared by the businessmen of the music industry, cultural life in Ethiopia rediscovered its colors: witness the opening of numerous *azmari bet* (houses of *azmaris*), where the new-look *azmaris,* rebellious, farcical, and unconcerned with caste, invented *bolel* (literally, automobile exhaust)—a genre between gossip and the absurd that feeds on satellite images as much as on tradition—and played with repertoires and allusions in the evident desire to fully assume their role as the bad conscience of Ethiopia.

And it is in this context of upheaval that Mahmoud Ahmed, with his powerful, throaty, undulating voice that ranged from a growl to a cry, revealed the tip of the Ethiopian musical iceberg to the world. Revealed it, indeed, even before the fall of the Derg made it safe for Ethiopian music to come out of hiding. In 1986 the eight brilliant minutes of Ahmed's "Ere Mela Mela," a scorching groove released in 1975 in Ethiopia, was a roaring success on the specialty radio stations of Europe and the United States. His music opened the door to that of a new generation—more pop, less brassy, and more electric—which boasts a respectable number of women: for example, Netsanet Mellesse (and her Wallias Band) and the exiled Aster Aweke, heiress to the great Bzunesh Bekele ("the First Lady of Ethiopian popular music"), who died too soon, in June 1990, at the age of fifty-four.

---

[7] Precipitated by the union of the Tigrean and the Eritrean guerrilla armies, which had been fighting a war of liberation against successive Ethiopian governments since Eritrea was annexed in 1962. Eritrea became independent in 1993.

WORLD
SOUND

Mory Kante: The Electric Griot

The Mutations of the Instrument

Mory Kante and his kora, 1995.

I would like to use the kora in a completely electronic music, a breakdance Smurf style!

—MORY KANTE, AT THE TIME OF *COUROUGNENE,* 1981

One cannot climb into the mango tree and leave the bag at the bottom.

—MORY KANTE, AFTER "YEKE YEKE," 1988

n West Africa, one often sees a kora player replacing the carrying strap of his instrument with his wife's head kerchief. This detail expresses the attachment a musician has for his wife during his journeys, but it also signifies the place the kora has in his life—a place that can make him admit that it is his "second wife."

This wonderful kora, with a rich past, full of symbolism, and also a surprising organological complexity, is one of the cardinal instruments of Africa (along with the balafon, the pluriarc, the djembe, and a few others), on which the progress of many contemporary styles is based. This is the one, in any case, that reveals best the modal character of African music.

Over several centuries, this harp-lute, native to the five Mande countries (Guinea-Conakry, Guinea-Bissau, Gambia, Mali, and Senegal), has been, par excellence, the instrument for praise and entertainment of kings and the rich, already playing that role at least as long ago as 1799, when the explorer Mungo Park mentioned it in his travel diary.[1] But it goes much farther back—to origins even the experts can't determine with any certainty. With a neck a meter or more long, and using a half-calabash

---

[1] Mungo Park, *Travels in the Interior Districts of Africa,* ed. Kate Ferguson Marsters, (Chapel Hill, NC: Duke University Press, 2000).

covered with a tanned goatskin as a resonator, the kora can have from nineteen strings (as in the Guinean seron) up to thirty-six. It usually has twenty-one strings, corresponding in the collective Manding psyche to the steps of life that lead to maturity, symbolized by the persistence of the sound of the drone (bass note). The musician plays the instrument with the thumbs and index fingers and must use the middle, ring, and pinky fingers to grip a handle on each side of the strings. It is played using three types of musical scales,[2] among which a vast array of musical pieces and improvisations are distributed.

If the kora has achieved a degree of fame outside of Africa, it owes this to Mory Kante, even though some great players made the journey decades earlier. The man was born in 1950 in Albadaria, a village of Guinea nestled at the sources of the Niger River, of a Malian mother, Fatouma Kassimoko, and a Guinean father, El-Hadj Djelifode Kante. In Africa, the prefix *djeli-* carries a message. Mory Kante says, "I am a *djeli,* which means 'blood' in Manding and is equivalent to 'griot.' The griot is an artist before the Eternal, the storehouse of the people's memory, its conscience. He is wisdom. The griots were the ones who demanded a constitution from the Manding emperor. The griot tradition is transmitted from father to son. It's that of the exemplary man who must reveal the truth and in turn is protected by society and taken care of all his life."[3]

Mory Kante's family tree really runs the length of seven generations. His maternal grandfather never went anywhere without at least sixty musicians, from the singer to the balafonist. His father, a veteran among Guinean griots, had twenty-eight children, all artists. His brother, Kante Facelli, was the famous guitarist for the Ballets Keita Fodeba. Mory Kante himself was initiated into the secrets of the *nyamakala*[4] at an aunt's house in Mali. Later, as balafonist and guitarist, he played with a

---

[2] The tomora scale (i.e. mode of great men, heroes, but also of love, nostalgia, and solace) resembles the Aeolian or Dorian (minor) mode; the sauta (used for epic praise) corresponds to the Lydian or Aeolian (major) mode; the silaba (mode of entertainment) to the Mixolydian.

[3] Interview with the author.

[4] The word *nyamakala* can have a meaning close to "griot." In fact, it goes back to the beginning of the eighteenth century, when, implementing a theocratic state in

band called the Apollos, before being recruited by the famous Rail Band of the Buffet de la Gare in Bamako by its founder, Tidiane Kone. There he met an albino singer on his way to a great career, Salif Keita. During his stay with the Rail Band, whose musicians were civil servants working for the national railroad, Mory discovered the Cuban music that numerous musicians brought back from their terms of study in Fidel Castro's country, as well as contemporary rhythms brought from France. He picked the kora as his favorite (a transgression for a descendant of balafonists) because it seemed to him to be the tool best suited to his desires for "modernity." He was able to realize these desires beginning in 1978, when he moved to Abidjan, in the Ivory Coast, and formed a big band consisting of traditional instruments, which found plenty of work in the terrain plowed by the soul and salsa hits of the day. In 1981, Mory Kante recorded, in Lomé, Togo, a well-crafted album, *Courougnene,* and had it mixed in Los Angeles by a young Senegalese Manding producer whom Stevie Wonder noticed soon after. This album, which sold very well in West Africa, attested to his ambition and his talents as a composer and arranger.

In 1984, in Paris, a city that had become the international hub of African musics, Mory Kante decided to start from scratch. In a room at the Mutualité, rented thanks to some friends, he recorded an album as a kind of calling card, *Mory Kanté à Paris.* At about the same time, Jacques Higelin, whom he had met during a visit to Africa, invited him to perform with him on the huge stage of the Palais Omnisports de Bercy, along with Youssou N'Dour. Then he met Philippe Constantin, former critic for the paper *Rock and Folk* and devotee of black music, who had become an agent for the Barclay label. After *Ten Cola Nuts,* much admired by the specialty press, *Akwaba Beach* (whose title track referred to a beach in Abidjan where he liked to go to meditate) was a hit. The album evoked God, love, universality, and the reconciliation of Africa, and included a

---

Manding country, the Muslim Fulani tried to replace the the fetishists' music with the reading of the Koran. But the blending of the musics of all the regions' captives gave birth to a new music ultimately tolerated (though some religious people still consider the *nyamakala* to be nonbelievers). Under colonization and since independence, the *nyamakala* (who often answer to an individual calling) have been key agents of musical innovation.

song that would revolutionize the music biz. Originally, "Yeke Yeke" (Feeling-Feeling) was a Manding melody sung during the millet harvest, but on the record, while the melody conserves the string of crystalline notes played on the kora, it benefits from an intoxicating beat and a catchy chorus, and is galvanized by a pack of brass and drum machines. That technological facelift was the work of Nick Patrick, a British producer with rock tendencies.[5] In fact, with this song leading the way, *Akwaba Beach* became the "best Francophone[6] album of 1988" (that is, best-selling). This success made the major labels' mouths water for years. Its total sales, it was rumored, equaled the gross national product of Burkina Faso! Thereafter, the profession (and major media) would live under the influence of " 'Yeke Yeke' syndrome." If in the past a few Pan-African hits had generated large international sales (such as "Pata-Pata" by Miriam Makeba, "Mario" by Franco, and "Soul Makossa" by Manu Dibango), "Yeke Yeke" rode a genuine international wave, leaving behind it a trail of gold records in France, Germany, Switzerland, Spain, Belgium, Israel, and elsewhere. Versions of "Yeke Yeke" were produced in Hebrew, Arabic, Chinese, Hindi, Portuguese, Spanish, and English. The title was on all the charts for months, whatever the age group of the listeners.

This success also had a psychological impact among African musicians. Many wondered about the incredible alchemy that had transformed a ballad written many years ago into a worldwide success. Some of them were driven to take the plunge (often losing body and soul) into this miraculous studio technology they thought could make gold.

---

[5] During recording of the next album, *Touma,* with a budget over one million francs, Nick Patrick characterized his contribution as follows: "My work is to make sure that Mory's music is accessible to Western ears. If we recorded all the percussion in only one take, as the Africans do, it would be a mess. This is why we used the computers and the studio technology." (*Le Monde,* September 26, 1990).

[6] *Translator's note: Akwaba Beach,* however, is not in French; "meilleur album francophone" means the best album from a French-speaking country.

Papa Wemba: The Elegant Rumba

The Third Congolese Wave

The elegant Papa Wemba with his dog, 1986.

Europeans who find cultural alibis in Manding or Dogon music have trouble appreciating African pop, the highest degree of pleasure.

—KANDA BONGO MAN[1]

I f we owe the first phase of Zairean music to Joseph Kabasele and the second to Franco, Tabu-Ley Rochereau, and Dr. Nico, the third one must reckon with Papa Wemba. Born Jules Shungu Wembadio Pené Kikumba in 1949 in the village of Lubefu in the Kasai River region, and growing up in Kinshasa, he had his real debut in 1969, when, influenced by Anglo-American music (he took the name Jules Presley for a while), he participated in the birth of Zaiko Langa-Langa, a band that would overturn the codes of the old rumba and impose a "new wave." In an environment rich in personalities, his voice, with its melancholic accents, charmed the people of Kinshasa. It was a voice based on minor harmonies whose timbre, he says, he shaped by listening to his mother, a professional mourner at wakes. The whole neighborhood would come to listen to that voice when he served as cantor of the eight o'clock Mass at the Catholic parish church.

With Zaiko Langa-Langa, Papa Wemba pushed the modern-traditional syncretism peculiar to Congo-Zairean music still further. Wind instruments were replaced by drums. The old rumba tempo, slow and rolling, was accelerated with electric guitars.

To pursue his goal better, Papa Wemba left Zaiko and started his own ensemble, which he called Isifi-Lokole. *Isifi* is an acronym for the French translation of "Institute of Ideological Knowledge for the Formation of Idols," and *lokole* refers to Kasai percussion. The rhythmic texture of his songs was based on the ondole, griot drum, used for the pulse of celebration dances in the manner of the *nyaka-nyaka* or *yucca,* which has the function of representing the cosmic harmony between man and

---

[1] *Le Monde,* November 6, 1992.

nature. Through various mutations, his famous group, Viva la Musica, came to birth (that name was chosen in reference to the rallying cry of one of his favorite musicians, Cuban Johnny Pacheco, founder of the legendary Fania All Stars). With Viva la Musica, Papa Wemba obtained Pan-African recognition, sealed with several hits, such as "Analengo."

He owed his fame also to his special social status as "Pope of the *Sapeurs.*" In 1977, Papa Wemba decided to change the name of his housing tract, in the outskirts of Kinshasa, to Village Molokai,[2] of which he declared himself traditional chief. Then, within this perimeter, he advocated a clothing style that featured, among its distinctions, a beret, and that went along with a way of walking, talking, and behaving toward others. This initiative gave birth to an urban movement, the *Société des Ambianceurs et Personnes Élégantes* (Society of Tonesetters and Elegant Persons), or SAPE: a way of expressing an identity that was antipoverty, antidepression, and antipower (because it opposed the *abas-cost,* the uniform imposed by Mobutu) for thousands of young Kinshasans, as well as for Brazzavillians on the other side of the Congo River. For these *sapeurs,* the essential thing was to dress elegantly, with name-brand clothes made by famous designers if possible. In the absence of Versace, Venturi, Cerutti, Capobianco, Kenzo, Cardin, Gauthier, or Yamamoto, one could, thanks to imported patterns, have the local tailor make similar models, onto which one would painstakingly sew the distinctive label.[3] These tropical dandies could not adopt such measures without privation, but it was the price to be paid to distinguish oneself, to keep from slipping into a world left adrift. Papa Wemba made himself the movement's chief pedagogue and specified that one must not be a slave to fashion, but rather must take part in some kind of resistance to the

---

[2] *Translator's note:* Catholic missionaries had once shown a film in the neighborhood about Father Damien (1840–1889), who served lepers banished to Molokai Island in Hawaii until he died of leprosy himself. The same kind of effort was needed to restore hope to Village Molokai, it was felt.

[3] Instead of a suit from Paris, one could have the large linen pants, the silk handkerchief (which emerged casually), and the BCBG blazer made by a "maker." Because Paris was the alpha and omega of fashion for the *sapeur,* not having been to Paris was something of a sin, and he had to be familiar with the Métro timetable or at least have in his pocket the famous little yellow ticket then in use.

crisis and to the skepticism engendered by an Africa preyed on by its demons. One of his anthems exclaimed: "Work! Take the trouble! Work's the asset we lack the least."

At the beginning of the 1980s, when he moved to France part-time and signed a contract with a major recording house, his career took a sharp turn. Through a series of albums made with arrangers who were on the lookout for new sounds and digital possibilities (from Hector Zazou to Martin Meissonnier), his "new wave soukous" seduced the North. The constituency of new listeners interested in world music broadened his audience.

His fame led to some curious cultural cross-fertilizations. In Japan, the Yamamoto-clad singer stirred up a singular fanaticism—so much so that Japanese charter flights traveled all the way to Kinshasa, while in Tokyo, clone bands skilled at his kind of soukous multiplied.

Papa Wemba adapted easily to this North-South duality. For example, he set up two groups to accompany him: one with an international mission and the other more "roots" in its sound, since African ears, on the continent or in the diaspora, demanded a "down-home" sound with more "dirty" rhythms, better fit for dancing, more in accord with their conviviality.

Thus, with the passing years, Papa Wemba, a hardworking and intro-verted man, has come to embody "African pop," forming a triptych with Youssou N'Dour and Salif Keita. He was seen on tour with Peter Gabriel (who had become the producer of his albums) in huge halls such as the Paris-Bercy (16,000 seats), in humanitarian campaigns (from the cam-paign against antipersonnel mines to another encouraging ethnic toler-ance),[4] collaborating on the soundtrack of a Bernardo Bertolucci movie, and covering "Fa Fa Fa Fa," a hit by his idol Otis Redding.

The most illuminating step of his progress is the realization of how this intuitive man unites the perception of globalization with fidelity to

---

[4] "So Why?" ("Why... so much hatred? Let's stop the massacre of our brothers") was the slogan of a campaign conducted in 1999 by Youssou N'Dour, Papa Wemba, Lag-baja (Nigeria), Jabu Khanyilé of Bayeté, and Lourdes Van Dunem (South Africa) to denounce ethnic violence. Emblematically, these five musicians went to Angola, Liberia, Sudan, and Kwazulu-Natal. This campaign gave birth to a book of large pho-tographs, a video, a documentary, and a compact disc for the benefit of the Red Cross.

his origins without an unnecessarily wide gap. Conscious that the American and European ears are not totally the same, his arrangements take note of the differences. And if he flirts with different styles (soul, zouk, salsa, rap), he has never given up his Kasai River musical trajectory and has always shown more concern for melody than his soukous peers, whether Koffi Olomide, Pepe Kalle, or Kanda Bongo Man. Thus, with the album *M'Zée fulagengé* (The Wise Man Who Breathes Happiness) he tried to create an Afropop attuned to the new millennium and called his new band Nouvelle Ecriture (New Writing).

He chose to celebrate that album in Kinshasa, the town where he has always reconnected with the child he once was, a young peanut vendor waiting at the door of the Vis-à-Vis, a musical club with a cult following where the singers of his dreams performed. For his return, during a huge concert at the stadium of Les Martyrs, in the presence of seven chiefs of Papa Wemba's tribe, the Tetela, the city witnessed his enthronement as Ambassador of the Anamongo to the World.[5]

---

[5] This title was previously awarded to only two people: Miriam Makeba and Charles Aznavour. Kinshasa and its picaresque life were in the Franco-Zairean movie *La vie est belle* (Life Is Beautiful), filmed in 1984, in which Papa Wemba played the lead role. Papa Wemba has always paid attention to the *chegués* (street kids) and *balados* (idle youth who live by thefts) and has often expressed himself on the subject.

Geoffrey Oryema, or the Sorrow of the Great Lakes

What Music After Rwanda?

Geoffrey Oryema with his lukeme, 1983.

The true brotherhood is not that of the blood, it's that of sharing.

No one hates himself more than the one who hates others.

—RWANDAN PROVERBS

n Burundi and Rwanda there is a mystical link between men and sacred drums. Each year, a ritual task consists of finding and then felling a tree (which may yield four or five drums) called *umubugan-goma*, "tree that makes the drums talk." The rest of the world first discovered the ingoma drums made from these trees when cinema served them up as folklore in movies such as *King Solomon's Mines*, and international tours subsequently revealed the spectacular court art they serviced. With electric guitars, synthesizers, brass, and drum kits, one might think that these drums, increasingly cut off from traditional rural inspiration, are falling into disuse. Nothing of the sort has happened. Ingomas, democratizing themselves, have reappeared in contemporary recordings, just like the musical bows, flutes, sanzas, and zithers of the Great Lakes region (Burundi, Rwanda, Uganda). How else could it be? These instruments' age-long history has been their password for admission to the satellite era. Consider the harp, present in Africa for thousands of years, companion to the storyteller, the healer, the seer, vehicle of its own speech, which formerly made the harpist within the royal courts and chiefdoms a person of great importance.[1] We find that harp today, pentatonic, played in bars in central Africa, its strings of yesteryear (vegetable fibers or braided snake skins) replaced by fishing line or brake cable, and played together with cowbells to obtain a less reflective, more vulgar music. The heart of Africa, still not very urbanized, is starting

---

[1] The harp is often considered the harp player's "double," a notion reflected in the anthropomorphism of the instrument as shaped by the luthier-sculptor. See *La Parole du fleuve, harpes d'Afrique centrale* (Cité de la musique, 1999).

to take up these mutations of instruments and musical practices in a singular fashion, once its bands' understandable imitations of Zairean rumba, Cameroonian makossa, or taarab from the East Coast have been transcended.

When local artists imagine adapting a style and a repertoire without betraying their own cultural identity, many of them think of Geoffrey Oryema. Born in 1953 to parents belonging to the nobility of the Acholi people, he grew up in Kampala, capital of Uganda and was raised in a rather strict fashion according to Anglican precepts. His family included many storytellers, poets, and musicians, so he was immersed very early in traditional culture. His father, an English professor, taught him the nanga, a seven-stringed harp that is said to be able to drive one mad or to suicide. His mother traveled through the country at the head of a prestigious dance company, the Heartbeat of Africa. As a teenager, he learned to play flute, lamellaphone (or lukeme, as it is known locally), and guitar, and participated in the Uganda School of Dramatic Art, because his first ambition was theater. Crazy about Brecht, he would also be inspired by techniques dear to Stanislavsky and Grotowski to write avant-garde plays. It was the theater of the absurd, marked with tribal sounds and improvisations, infused with allegories, fed by rumors and onomatopoeia. Those influences would be found in his songs later on.

Theater was a way for him to put into words his deadly environment. Since 1971 his country had been ruled by Idi Amin Dada: a six-foot-three, 220 pound, psychopathic tyrant. A former member of the British army (therefore protected for a while by the ex-colonial power) and a boxing champion, he forced the *habaka* (king) of the Baganda, who had been head of state since independence, into exile, and seized power. He progressively turned into a dictator, machine-gunning his own soldiers, chasing out foreigners (Israelis, Indians, Pakistanis), and showing the world how he fed his opponents to crocodiles or chatted with the severed heads of his enemies. "We had to survive from one day to the next, with what was happening in the street under our eyes," Oryema later recalled. "In sight and with the knowledge of everyone, people were shot or stuffed into car trunks."

In 1977, Geoffrey Oryema's father, who had become Minister of Water and Resources, paid the price for the paranoia of the black Ubu.[2] He died in a "car accident"—the local euphemism for a covert assassination. Geoffrey Oryema understood the message. He got past the border in the trunk of a car en route to Kenya, where the French cultural center also hosted a production of his latest play, *Le Règne de la Terreur,* which got him investigated by the Ugandan regime. Then, because of his love for Sartre, Hugo, and the French language—"one of the most beautiful in the world"—he went to France, which had by then become a focal point for African musics.

With the influence of English pop on one side, and the Acholi tradition on the other, between day jobs and shows at the local MJC,[3] he perfected his introspective music of exile. At that time his demo tapes found few attentive ears, and it was the British team behind WOMAD (World of Music, Arts and Dance, a world-music festival launched by Peter Gabriel) who contacted him and recorded his first album. *Exile,* which alternated between guitar-based tracks and others accompanied by nanga, lukeme, and nyamulere (a type of flute), was an immediate hit. In France, it climbed to the top of the charts and sold more than fifty thousand copies at the time of its release. This success was certainly due in part to media promotion by Brian Eno and Peter Gabriel, songwriters who assisted in the gestation of these tracks, but above all it was because the European audience was discovering a kind of African music that had nothing in common with the kinds usually heard.[4] The stripped-down melody replaced the abundant beats of the tom-tom, the arpeggios were

---

[2] In 1974, Idi Amin Dada, with 200,000 dead on his conscience, was the star of a film by Barbet Schroeder, a self-portrait that served the purpose of keeping the myth of the "Negro king" alive by presenting a caricatured image of Africa, just as Bakossa of Central Africa and Mobutu of Zaire did for the French-speaking zone. These three characters benefited throughout their reigns from the self-interested tolerance of the former colonial powers and their African allies. [*Translator's note:* Ubu is a grotesque antihero created by French playwright Alfred Jarry.]

[3] *Translator's note: Maison des Jeunes et de la Culture* (Youth and Culture House), a youth club somewhat like the YMCA but with a secular and humanistic philosophy.

[4] In France, a track by the "African Leonard Cohen" (he had adapted the latter's "Suzanne") was chosen as the main title music for the popular television show *Le Cercle de minuit.*

fluid, the folk-blues was sober and had none of the Oriental ornaments of Manding pieces. Between mystery and shyness, a voice ranging over three octaves recounted exile and solitude via a sort of ballad, and denounced the divisions of the continent.

This was a songwriting style appropriate to the Great Lakes region, where, paradoxically, under the malediction of a terrible *jok* (malignant spirit), calming and peaceful landscapes were backgrounds to dark dramas of history. How can one reconcile the beauty of Uganda's countryside with its having been for so long the playground of a man whose favorite saying was "A man never runs faster than a bullet"? How can one comprehend that neighboring Rwanda was the setting both for massacre after massacre and for the sublime and ethereal songs of Cécile Kayirebwa and Florida Uwera, two exiled women, carriers of a whispered music enhanced by the peaceable plucked notes of the zither and lamellaphone? How can one reckon all the musicians and songmakers who were among the victims of the machete, more than a million all told, during the last terrible genocide.

In 1989, Geoffrey moved into a modest house in the small town of Lillebonne in Normandy and got married. Since then, his long braids have become part of the landscape. With its green dells, Normandy reminds him of the west and south of his country, formerly called the "African Switzerland" (though, to be sure, Ugandan cows have more impressive horns). But when he strolls, he hears music. And he swears that sometimes, sitting in a meadow or on a tree trunk, playing his harp, he disappears. He is conversing with his ancestors.

From Kodé di Dona to Cesaria Evora:
Sodade in A Major

The Music of Cape Verde

*Cesaria Evora on stage with her table, her alcohol,
and her lamp, 1995.*

World, you play blind man's bluff with me while constantly
   pursuing me.
With each of your tricks
A new pain
Brings me a little closer to God.

—MORNA BY B. LEZA

I n a lunar corner of São Tiago Island, in Cape Verde, lives Gregório Vaz, known as Kodé di Dona (*le cadet de la dame;* the lady's youngest— that is, the youngest child of his grandmother, who raised him). By trade he was a forest ranger charged with keeping the goats away from acres of American dwarf pines planted in pits lined with pebbles. His basalt house, surrounded by black pigs, was spartan. The only touch of color was some plastic flowers—the only kind the arid climate permitted. After coming home from work barefoot at sundown along the red dirt trails, he liked to play his *gaita* (accordion)—a diatonic Hohner with eight basses, some of whose moving parts had been replaced with bits of photographic film or internal parts from an alarm clock. For that accordion he had traded some forty-five gallons of corn, packed in a barrel that, like most of the items on the archipelago, dated to the time of the Boston whalers, when they used to come to recruit crews around Fogo or Brava. Beside him, scraping with a chipped knife his reco-reco (made from a piece of metal fence), José Ferreira Vaz, called "Zezito," accompanied him with a metronomic beat. Between two pinches of snuff tobacco, Kodé di Dona, with an absent look, played pieces with rough beauty, strong as the *grogue* (local cane moonshine) that he makes himself. His abrasive voice reminds one that his Creole is accented with Bantu and Yoruba syntax.

It was in 1947, it hadn't rained much.
Discouraged by life,
I went to sign up for São Tomé,
To register on the list, number 37.
I bowed my head and I sat down
To think about my life,
Then I picked up my things,
I put them in a bag
And I climbed in the boat
That took me to the ship...[1]

Kodé di Dona composed this magical piece, "Famine of '47," based on a neighbor's account. In his other litanies he evokes the toughness of the days, the passage of time, disappointed love, and his many children.

It was under the influence of the musician Antão Barreto that this native of São Nicolau Tolentino switched to the accordion and then composed dozens of pieces that became "classics," often looted by the musicians of newer generations—he himself encouraging the borrowing, because it never occurred to him to claim title to his compositions. Studying the musical affiliations of the archipelago proves that he was one of the essential proponents of this São Tiago Island funaná style, upon which many groups (Os Tubarões, Bulimundo, Finaçon) built their work of renovation.

Funaná—an echo of the days of slavery and the triangular trade between Europe, Africa, and America—is a link connecting proto- and post-blues, reminding us that the Cape Verde Islands, an archipelago of stones and wind five hundred kilometers west of Senegal, served as a warehouse of "black ivory,"[2] before the end of the trade and the plunder of natural resources let the islands fall back into solitude. A remnant of African expression, the song of the *badiu* (runaway slaves) has survived on the sly.

---

[1] "Fomi 47," *Kodé di Dona* (Ocora, 1996).
[2] *Translator's note:* Literally, "ebony wood," a euphemism for slaves.

The other end of the Cape Verdean rainbow of sound is farther upwind,[3] on the island where the town of Mindelo sprawls. It is symbolized by a Lusophone Billie Holiday: Cesaria Evora, high priestess of morna,[4] a nostalgic song form whose origin is lost in the waves, its basic elements borrowed maybe from the mulattos of the West Indies or from the Portuguese modinha of the eighteenth century. Morna takes its sustenance from betrayed love, solitude, and, of course, parting (always inexorable)—a key theme of any island's metaphysics and, in Cape Verde's case, so closely linked with the great mysteries of existence that some mornas do double duty as an accompaniment both to the port and to the grave. Morna chose as its birthplace the harbor of Mindelo, a notable port of trade at the beginning of the twentieth century, where fifteen hundred ships on their way to the Cape stopped every year to restock with water and coal, leaving behind sounds from the West Indies, Brazil, or Europe.

Cesaria Evora, whose violinist father succumbed to alcohol when she was seven years old, and whose cook mother gave her to an orphanage so that she could learn to read and sew, spent her adolescence singing in the bars, encouraged by a guitar-playing sailor who would remain the sole love of her life. She became the great voice of the soil, putting all the best composers to work. But except for the colony radio station that employed her at twenty-five *escudos* per title, she had no prospects on this tiny island. It took a trip abroad for her life to take a new turn. In 1987, Bana, the greatest singer of the Cape Verde Islands, took her with

---

[3] *Translator's note:* The two chains of the Cape Verde Islands are named in reference to the continuous trade winds from the northeast. Cesaria Evora comes from São Vicente in the northern or upwind chain, whereas Kodé di Dona lives on São Tiago in the southern or downwind chain.

[4] Two or three violas (viols with five double strings) or guitars, a cavaquinho [*translator's note:* a small four-stringed guitar], and a violin (rabeca) give life to the plaintive song of morna (perhaps from the English word "mourn"). Since the 1960s, along with the coladeira, it went from four beats (compas) to two. The struggle for national liberation of the Portuguese colonies (Guinea-Bissau, Cape Verde, Angola, Mozambique) exercised its effects. Coladeira engages in a different discourse than morna does: its irony and mockery became means of political expression. Certain coladeiras called the people to rebel against the colonial power. Although coladeira

him to the United States and to Portugal. In Lisbon, in Bana's restaurant, a Frenchman of Cape Verdean origin, José da Silva, a switchman at the SNCF,[5] heard Cesaria.

In came the lonely anguish called *sodade*...

> *Oh sea, tell me about my love*
> *Who one day left for abroad*...
> *Leaving me to cry on the beach,*
> *Scarf in hand.*

...and impishness too:

> *The too frivolous woman dances the cha-cha-cha,*
> *Her husband corrects her with the belt.*
> *She continues to dance the cha-cha-cha:*
> *Does the belt taste like honey?*[6]

He decided then to try everything to popularize this incredible talent. Having considered recording an album for the French, he invited Cesaria Evora to come to France. Then, with a series of records, each of which hewed more closely to her expressiveness, "Cize's" charm did its work—despite the efforts of the TV networks to commercialize what they labeled "hot music," such as zouk, lambada, and soca. At last *Miss Perfumado* was released, selling three hundred thousand copies, and presaging several more gold records. Beyond languages and borders, the

---

is played with the same instruments as morna, its rhythm is jerkier, inviting couples to dance as if stuck together, and it favors synthesizers and electric guitars. Other local specialties include the batuque, in which women dance to polyrhythms that they beat on tightly rolled-up loin cloths held between their legs; the finaçons of São Tiago Island, improvised with help from the audience; the festa do pilão, on the feast of the saints, when everyone grinds the corn; the tabanka, which designates secret societies and parades like those of the Brazilians; and the drumming of Fogo Island.
[5] *Translator's note:* SNCF (*Société Nationale des Chemins de Fer*) is the French national railroad company.
[6] "Derrière l'horizon" (Behind the Horizon), morna by B. Leza (translated into French by Luis Silva), *La Diva aux pieds nus* (Lusafrica-Buda); and "Cinturão Tem Mele" (Belt Like Honey), morna by Luis Morais (*Mar azul*, Lusafrica-Buda).

public adored the "barefoot diva,"—so much so that she was nominated for a Grammy award.

She, who in her life has been on intimate terms with the destructive-
ness of alcohol, the fickleness of lovers, the rudeness of the bourgeois,
and the arrogance of the powerful, looks on her fame with amusement:
"I don't believe in dreams. You fall asleep rich and wake up poor. I don't
believe in destiny. Morna took me and I don't know anything else. Finally,
I'm now living how I should have lived young."[7] Her loyalties go to her
family, her friends, those musicians who understood her: Gregório "Ti
Goy" Gonçalves, Morgadinho, Frank "Cavaquinho" Cavaquim, clarinetist
Luis Moraes, and especially her uncle, the sublime songwriter Xavier
Francisco da Cruz, nicknamed B. Leza (pronounced *beleza,* "beauty" in
Portuguese), who, by introducing the Brazilian "half tone" into the morna,
gave it the inimitable color that makes perfume of its *sodade;* and who,
as Cesaria Evora has never forgotten, died of polio, alone, and as desti-
tute as could be.

Kodé di Dona and Cesaria Evora: two sexagenarian emblems of one
musical identity—that of a collection of scattered bits of volcanic rock
as big as half of Corsica.

Today, the inexorable chanteuse is making up for lost time as she
treads the world's stages. With her royalties, she has built a "house of
happiness" on the street of her childhood, open to friends and paupers,
where it feels good to share the *catchupa* (a local dish). "In Cape Verde
we say that it is better to drink the gall first, and the honey last. But a life
of honey doesn't change the way we sing: the sadness of morna is always
the same," she says, looking at the bay where carcasses of wrecked ships
rust. Further south, Kodé di Dona attends to his occupations. A few
stays abroad, a few recordings, a brand new accordion,[8] and his large
family are enough to sustain his frugal happiness.

---

[7] Remarks recorded by the author in 1990.

[8] In September 1993, Kodé di Dona traveled to La Nuit de Nacre (Mother-of-Pearl
Night) in Tulle, France, a festival dedicated to the accordion, then directed by
Richard Galliano. In partnership with the Maugein factory, located in the city for a
century, a group of friends decided to have a custom accordion made for him, which
the author of these lines delivered to him the following year.

Anne-Marie Nzie: "The Golden Voice of Cameroon"

When "Country" Music Is Invited into World Music

Anne-Marie Nzie and Wendo Kolosoy, 1999.

All my life I have looked for paternal warmth,
I have looked for maternal warmth,
I have only traveled like a bird,
And today I feel like a robin
Who sings unhappiness from pasture to pasture.

—"MA SANGUONG,"
ANNE-MARIE NZIE[1]

Every region in the world has some singers who, through their voices, express the anthropological reality of a people and draw its collective landscape. Anne-Marie Nzie is one of these few chosen ones. All it takes for a Cameroonian is to hear her, and he can see the red laterite soil, hunger for fish *ndolé*,[2] or imagine himself languid in the warm night, sitting in a *maquis* (dive bar) while drinking a cool *jobajo* (local beer).

It's just that they've been dealing with Anne-Marie Nzie for no less than four decades of song. Her professional debut was back in 1954, when she recorded her own compositions for the Belgian Congolese label Opika, accompanying herself on the Hawaiian guitar.

Her vocal and instrumental aptitude was revealed in her childhood. Her father, who played the mvet (a harp-zither intimately linked to the interpretation of epic chant), awakened her musical sense.[3] An evangelist preacher, he also made her actively participate in the congregation's choir. Ultimately, one of her brothers, Moise, who had a musical career

---

[1] *Anne-Marie Nzié* (Indigo-Label Bleu).
[2] *Translator's note:* The national dish of Cameroon, a soup made from a leaf that is very bitter in its natural state.
[3] The mvet is a zither of ancient origin with one to five strings. Among the Fang, who live between Gabon and Cameroon, the term denotes both the instrument and the epic genre it serves. The mvet has a wonderful richness, which is literary, historical, initiatory, and prophetic all at once.

under the name Cromwell, played a key role in charting her course. He taught her to play guitar when, at the age of twelve, she was immobilized in the hospital because of an infected sore resistant to treatment. He encouraged her to play in the widely exported Hawaiian style (played in glissandos, the guitar flat on the knees) popular in the Congo area since the 1940s. He later hired her as a backup singer on his albums.

After winning a guitar contest promoted by the ministry of information and organized by German guitarist Siegfried Behrend, this native of Bibia in southern Cameroon decided to perform onstage, always accompanying herself on the Hawaiian guitar, first in a duo with the banjo player Bignouan, and later with guitarist Emmanuel Ntonga, younger brother of her future husband, Franck Denis Nziou, whom she would marry in 1958.

From that point on, her stage activities and radio appearances earned her such incredible success that, starting in 1967, she became the only woman to record on the Africambiance label, created in Douala by Joseph Tamla and Samuel Mpoual, which had also been home to such national glories as Manu Dibango and Francis Bebey.

Of course, Anne-Marie Nzie owed this fame principally to her generous voice, but she also had the advantage of her proven ability to adapt to styles in fashion (from biguine to Congolese rumba), to modernize local idioms (from bikutsi to assiko), and to use the multiple languages of the country (Ewondo, Douala, English, Ngumba, Fulani, French, and so on).

President Ahmadou Ahidjo's government pampered her. "The Golden Voice of Cameroon" became an ambassador of national culture. She performed in many countries, including France (at the beginning of the events of May 1968, she sang for the UN's Food and Agriculture Organization and signed with French label Pathé-Marconi, who would produce three of her albums), Algeria (at the famous Panafrican Festival of Algiers in 1969), and Nigeria (at FESTAC in Lagos in 1977). This international activity motivated her to equip herself with a real band capable of energizing her appearances.

But, as in many African countries, Cameroon's musical industry was corrupt. Artists there were, more than elsewhere, victims of swindlers (the directors of the associations supposed to be defending the rights of authors and composers) who crippled every project in the long run and condemned performers to semiprofessional status at local or township festivals. This explains the outflow of many talented musicians (especially Cameroonian) to Europe and the United States.[4] Remaining in the country, Anne-Marie Nzie paid the price, even though in 1979 she was recruited to pep up the National Ensemble (with limited means). Now in her fifties, she had decided to retire when, in 1984, the launch of an album, *Liberté!* (released by a producer who was a fan of hers), resulted in a comeback. All of Cameroon was excited about the title track, a remake of a song composed in the 1960s that exalted post-independence Africa. Here was proof, once more, that Anne-Marie Nzie, named deaconess of the Presbyterian church of Kamkana in the same year, was serving as a living national memory.

With the phenomenal success of world music, many of the planet's musician-singers, formerly too hybrid to interest the venues that specialized in "ethnic" or "scholarly" music, but too "roots" according to the pasteurized criteria then in vogue, would benefit from a new state of things. Anne-Marie Nzie was one of them. "Who is this stunning singer?" wondered the public that discovered her in spring 1998 at the *Festival d'Angoulême* and then at the New Morning in Paris. At the age of sixty-seven she had not only a voice of stunning youthfulness, but also the groove of the tireless women who dance all night, night after night, in the vigorous bikutsi rituals of Cameroon's Beti people. Proof of Mize's energy lies in the recordings she made in France, which not coincidentally are steeped in the bikutsi rhythm, a style that has come to the forefront of Cameroonian musical culture—and brought with it Nzie herself, perhaps its oldest trustee, followed closely by her sixty-year-old lead guitarist, Marcelin Ohandja, formerly of the Veterans, one of the bands that first got the bikutsi craze rolling.

---

[4] Cameroon is a musical hotbed teeming with styles and rhythms, yet to date only makossa and bikutsi have known a convincing modern adaptation. Other crucibles are also rich with possibilities, such as assiko, personified by Jean Bikoko, who has the distinction of using beer bottle tops as bottlenecks; or bol (pidgin for French *bal*, "dance"), laced with waltz and mazurka rhythms and played with the accordion, brought to Cameroon by settlers from Wilhelm II's Prussia; or ka, from which Sally Nyolo (Découvertes-RFI winner, 1997) takes her inspiration, a rhythm of the Eton people and a musical form that historically precedes bikutsi.

What is the bikutsi sound? It has a very ancient Cameroonian musical history, especially compared to that of makossa, popularized worldwide by Manu Dibango not long after its invention as an urban fusion of essewe and rumba. At the outset, bikutsi was a war dance that involved striking the ground (from *biku*, "strike," and *tsi*, "ground"). Then it became a women's dance, and its raging tempo would not be tamed by the balafon and tom-tom. For a long time Cameroonian artists played this bikutsi in a Zairean mode, overpowered by the influence of Franco, Rochereau, and Dr. Nico.[5] Eventually Ndo Clément, founder of the Veterans, offered a new interpretation, still in "Zaire style," but singing in Ewondo. Then Messi Martin (head of the cult band Los Camaroes) came up with the trick of putting a piece of sponge on the bridge of an electric guitar to make it sound like a balafon—the decisive mutation.

For a long time the hegemony of makossa, Congolese soukous, and Nigerian highlife marginalized bikutsi. Of course, in the south and the center of Cameroon one couldn't have a decent wedding without a local bikutsi orchestra set up on a Peugeot station wagon. Nevertheless, at the professional level—and with the exception of the Veterans (first with their founder, then shepherded by Ambroise Meyong), who maintained the bikutsi spirit in their temple-club l'Escalier-Bar—no bikutsi artists were able to break through the prejudice that "outside of makossa there is no salvation!" And then came George Seba's 1981 hit "Abakuya." And after that: Mbanga Mbarga, Dieu Ngolfé, Ange Ebogo Emerent, Marc Knodo, Mbala Rogers, Maurice Elanga, and others—until Les Têtes Brûlées,[6] punks with a tropical sound, led by the exceptional guitarist Epé Théodore, a.k.a. "Zanzibar," made bikutsi sound young and urban. Its beat, with its rage, its virulence, needed nothing from funk, from Senegalese mbalax, or from South African mbaqanga.

To look back over this long process of recognition is to recognize Anne-Marie Nzie (along with the late Oncle Medjo Me Nsom) as the keeper

---

[5] The main French-speaking radio stations, installed by the colonial powers, broadcast from Léopoldville (later Kinshasa) and Brazzaville, whence the influence of Congolese rumba throughout French West Africa and French Equatorial Africa.
[6] In 1984, Les Têtes Brûlées were the subject of a movie by Claire Denis, *Man No Run*.

of the flame, as much at the level of tempo as of a very specific blues-like approach.

Her repertory of over a hundred titles marries social critique with intimate chronicle, moving easily from the plight of women, orphans, and the uneducated to the evocation of loneliness or of a happiness always hard to attain. This is what every non-Cameroonian listener, without understanding the words, feels from this woman who has warned for a long time: "The day I die, bury me with a microphone in my left hand!"

LEAViNG

THE

TWENTiETH

CENTURY

Manu "Papa Groove" Dibango: The Pastor and His Flock

From Sidney Bechet to Techno

*At the piano, from left to right,
Lapiro de Mbanga, Ray Lema,
and Manu Dibango, 1990.*

Today, the body, we take care of it by giving it clothes, refrigerator, air conditioning, a car.... But the price for one minute of soul per day, I don't know how much that costs.

— MANU DIBANGO[1]

In January 1985, at Korem, Ethiopia, at an altitude of ten thousand feet, tents were lined up in a refugee camp housing more than thirty thousand people whom a handful of physicians from *Médecins sans Frontières* (Doctors Without Borders, or MSF) and some Ethiopian nurses were attempting to treat. There were mothers who had no milk left, men who could not eat anything because their muscles were too weak, children on intravenous feeding who would soon be dead. These were victims of one of the worst droughts that sub-Saharan Africa had ever known. And this was the camp that Manu Dibango and Mory Kante visited, arriving from Addis Ababa in a borrowed pickup truck.

The two musicians made this voyage despite the administrative headaches and the lack of cooperation from the authorities because they were the founders of the "Tam-Tam pour l'Éthiopie" project: a single featuring many African artists, proceeds from the sales of which went entirely to MSF in order to help the victims of the famine.

"We are not politicians, but we wanted to show that with our voices, with our instruments, maybe we could be of some use." Starting from that concept, Manu Dibango first mobilized all the top-drawer African artists he could round up; then a series of professionals, from publishing to distribution; and finally the media, including the primary French television network.

The famine that affected a part of Africa that year had no precedent. Throughout the world, the stark news images stirred up acts of solidarity. As usual, the artists were the first to act. In England, the collective

---

[1] Before performing at the Olympia, in Paris, 1991.

"Band Aid" united the biggest names in pop (from Culture Club to David Bowie) and recorded a single entitled "Do They Know It's Christmas?" In the United States, Quincy Jones brought together some fifty of the most famous rock, pop, jazz, and country artists for "We Are the World." In France, backing up Renaud (a French artist), thirty-five singers and comedians got together for the big "Éthiopie."

"Tam-Tam pour l'Éthiopie" was above all an initiative of African artists, radiating the kind of Pan-Africanism the youth of Africa have long looked to for a solution to the problems that plague the continent. But the continent is a big one, and diverse. To marry talking drums from Nigeria, Manding blues, Swahili song, makossa tempos, and kora harmonies, and to bring so many rhythmic and melodic worlds together for the recording sessions in the Davout and Acousti studios, a unifier was needed.

Manu Dibango was the right man for the job.[2] For all the musicians of the continent, the "Kojak of Sax," alias "the Great One," alias "the Old One," embodies an authority based as much on a longevity that Africa still appreciates as on his status as a "Negropolitan" (a term he likes to use). More than anyone else, he has lived and breathed the ambiguous relationships between Africa and its musicians, between the West and Africa, and between tradition and modernity. His long career, a saga proving that music is anything but a peaceful river, has ended up making our sax blower into the wise man of the French-speaking village, or at least a sort of pastor (considering his Protestant upbringing) who has always indicated what road to follow.

What has he not seen, this son of the Yabassi (by his father) and of the Douala (by his mother), who lived all the imagery of French West Africa and French Equatorial Africa, listened to Tino Rossi on the record player and sewed with a Singer machine, learned to read and write from *Mamadou et Bineta*,[3] and saluted the tricolor? This Douala teenager

---

[2] The project ultimately brought together over the course of several days some forty artists, among them Mory Kante, Bovick, Souzy Kasseya, musicians from M'Bamina and Ghetto Blaster, Ray Lema, Salif Keita, Toure Kunda, and King Sunny Ade, and producers involved in African music, such as Martin Meissonnier.

[3] *Translator's note:* A French primary-school book, published in the Ivory Coast and known throughout French-speaking Africa.

grew up between Protestant hymns and Glenn Miller imitators in sailor bars before making the long voyage to France in the spring of 1949, in a cabin aboard the steamer Hoggar.[4] As a student he caught the jazz virus via Sidney Bechet and Saint-Germain-des-Prés. He would go on to ride every musical wave, from clubs in Belgium to African *maquis*, from *yéyé* to world music.

The career of Emmanuel Njoke Dibango (born in 1933) resembles a game of "identity Ping-Pong." *Ping*, when, employed in Belgium—where he met the Belgian model Coco, who married him—by the great Congolese bandleader Joseph Kabasele, he left for Léopoldville and found himself faced with what he calls "an exceptional historical configuration": independence. *Pong*, when, after starting a club in the "Quartier Mozart" in Douala, he had to give it up because of local harassment (ranging from slander to a snake left in his room), having learned that Africa can be "as hard as a stone." *Ping*, when, as a sideman, first with Dick Rivers and later with Nino Ferrer, he embodied the "token Afro"—identified with movements across the Atlantic claiming that, actually, "black is beautiful." *Pong*, when, influenced by the compositional art of Miles Davis, he composed "Soul Makossa"[5]—a mix of a traditional makossa rhythm and U.S. soul, a title that was very popular in 1972 America. Years later, Michael Jackson would pick up a few measures of it for the bridge of "Wanna Be Starting Something," one of the hits on his album *Thriller*, which became for a while the best-selling record of all time.

Because of his bipolar culture, and the will he has always had to compose the music of his era, "Papa Groove" would assume the role of

---

[4] In memory of his host family in Saint-Calais, a small village in the Sarthe, Manu Dibango has been organizing a festival named *Soirs au Village* (Evenings in the Village) since 1998, dedicated to African musics.

[5] "Soul Makossa" was the flip side of an anthem Manu Dibango composed for the eighth African Cup of Nations [*translator's note:* a biennial soccer tournament; the eighth was held in his native Cameroon in 1972]. The record took off by surprise while he was still playing nights at an underground club in the Rue Vieille du Temple in Paris. "All of a sudden I become a star at the Apollo in New York. Cinderella! In New York, people, Blacks, got in touch with me to ask whether I lived with crocodiles and elephants. It's the typical story of the ambiguous adventure that I still live today. Fortunately it happened to me when I was forty—I'd already been living a dog's life" (*Libération*, 1991).

pioneer and catalyst throughout a career that's been nothing short of
stunning (so stunning, in fact, that it's generated its share of jealous back-
biters). True, you can't teach an old dog new tricks, but in retrospect, his
zigzag trajectory doesn't look like the slick moves of a quick-change artist
so much as a musician's adaptation to a changing and sometimes hostile
milieu. In Africa, bad intentions are often ascribed to the chameleon
because of its ability to change. But is the animal not there for a purpose?
The protractile tongue that shoots out of its mouth to catch insects, its
curled and powerful tail, its helmet head, its eyes independent from each
other that look in every direction, and especially its capacity to change
color until it blends into its environment, testify to the reflexes of survival and the skills of adaptation for this most peaceful and distinctive animal. The African musician is in a similar situation. He must be a gifted
social animal. He also personifies an occult power, that of music—a power
that one must either conciliate or control.

Many African musicians, including Manu Dibango occasionally during his stays in Africa, have been accused of having a direct association
with the spirits. President Houphouët-Boigny of the Ivory Coast stressed
"hospitality" to the point of making Manu Dibango the artistic director
of the Ivorian television orchestra. President Ahidjo of Cameroon had a
car ready for him.[6] But until the 1970s, was civil society free enough for
artists to live without participating in this perverse game, as tough as the
old griot traditions were?

Manu recounted his journey in 1989 in his book *Trois kilos de café*.
There are two ways to read his testimony. One of them shows the steps
of a career punctuated by twenty albums conforming to each aesthetic

---

[6] The fact is that Manu Dibango has always used the crossover possibilities of the
moment, creating *Afromusique* (the first French magazine about African music, under
the direction of Jean-Jacques Dufayet), a TV program, and a collection of orchestral
scores. In Cameroon, he artistically coordinated one of the rare anthologies of African
music produced in Africa, titled *Fleurs musicales du Cameroun* (Musical Flowers of
Cameroon), which brought together the cream of the crop (including Eboa Lottin,
Mama Ohandja, Oncle Medjo, Missé Ngoh, André-Maria Tala, Anne-Marie Nzié, and
Francis Ngallé Jojo). Also, Manu Dibango has often involved himself in the interests
of the French-speaking community, the fight for the defense of author's rights, broadcasting, North-South and South-South cooperation, and the emergence of a specifically African jazz.

period, labeled makossa, soul, reggae, funk, juju, jazz, rap, and so on, tallying up his greatest hits onstage (from Madison Square Garden in New York to the Olympia in Paris) and his honorific distinctions. The other, more discreet and personal, shows how his musical ambitions clashed with local contingencies more often than usual.

In any case, two albums express the terms of his musical humanism. *Négropolitaines* reprises reorchestrated, superb pieces from the 1950s to the 1970s (including "Indépendance cha-cha" by Kabasele, "Scoubidou merengué" by Dr. Nico, "Diana Lama" by the prolific Samé Lottin, "Pata Pata" by Miriam Makeba, and so forth) as a reminder of the richness of a contemporary heritage and its creators. *Wakafrika* proposes a musical safari, employing not only artists immersed in the grand bazaar of world sound (Angélique Kidjo, Salif Keita, Ladysmith Black Mambazo, King Sunny Ade, Papa Wemba, Youssou N'Dour, Ray Phiri, Ray Lema, Kaissa Doumbe), but also musicians more committed to the traditional aesthetic, with both groups remaking "classics" of contemporary African music. This album was intended as a metaphor for the reunification of southern and northern Africa, and its cover represents the silhouette of Manu Dibango posing in the shape of the continent. In the process of its making, this album was an attempt to provide the start of an answer to an old question: "When different aesthetics meet, when traditional and contemporary Africa mix, who must take the first step? I like arranging, I'm in love with timbres, with mixing them, in love with the language of these local musics. It's a language of initiation into a culture, a part of Africa, but not the whole world. The sonorous beauty of this language is so alive that it needs to be rerouted to widen it for a larger audience. That is what I have tried to do with this album, made up of a strong group of singers and a more secret alliance of sound."[7]

What conclusion does "Papa Groove" make of all his "periods" (as we say about painters)? This most youthful of African artists—who likes nothing better than the atmosphere of jazz clubs, the festivals with human faces, the endless discussions, or reading the newspaper—breaks out in his thunderous laugh. He thinks about it later on: "At first you make music because you like music, and it's a love story. Then time goes by

---

[7] Manu Dibango, *Trois kilos de café* (Lieu commun, 1989).

and it's the other generations that listen.... The miracle of this alchemy takes place over time: for one reason or another, you and your era are friends for a while. From then on, you feel responsible, not to the music, but to the people who love music. For what exactly? Would it be only to tell the newcomers to avoid the mistakes you made as much as possible? So you feel that you have to leave a mark, not in the music, but in the process. That's when we can talk about the 'elder,' the 'sage.'... You haven't thought about being that, it's the others who think you are."[8]

---

[8] Interview with Rémi Bouton, *Le Bulletin*, 1990.

Abidjan–Dakar–Johannesburg: What's All This Gnama-Gnama?

Rap, Zouglou, Kwaito: The New Generation

*Positive Black Soul, 1998;
Busi Mhlongo of the
kwaito group Legkoa, 1995.*

We can't stand that the term "black" is still constantly associated with a negative or sinister idea, as in the expressions "black humor," "black cat." The color black absorbs light, so for us it is light.

— POSITIVE BLACK SOUL[1]

January 1989, Abidjan. The news traveled like a burning fuse: "Ful' is dead!" It was a real shock for the kids of Treichville, Abomey, and Port-Bouët. For a week they came one after another to the base of the Tramontane tower, in the 220 Logements district, under a giant portrait of their idol painted on the wall. Throughout this wake all the glorious musicians of the Ivory Coast took turns at a podium, and in the warm night thousands of candles were lit. This strange mini-Woodstock, African style, in honor of Roger Fulgence Kassy, host of the television programs *Tremplin, RFK Show, Première Chance, Nandjelet,* and *Podium,* was followed by the most impressive funeral in all the years since independence (not counting the one for ziglibithy singer Ernesto Djedje in 1983). Thousands of youth rallied for a somber march from the morgue in Treichville to the television station in Cocody, where, as soon as the hearse pulled into the parking lot, the most violent storm seen in many dry seasons started, a development the Ivorians immediately interpreted as a sign of destiny.

It's not every TV host that inspires such devotion. But keep in mind that in addition to using his programs to promote the emergence of a new generation of artists (including Alpha Blondy), RFK had engaged his young audience perhaps more directly than anybody on television ever had, bumping up against industry standards with an impertinence that had gotten him fired countless times. On the set, RFK talked *nouchi* (ghetto slang), appeared in jeans and sneakers, and didn't hesitate to end his show with a sly dismissal of the older generation: "Guys, now that

---

[1] Positive Black Soul, cassette, Abidjan, 1986.

we're through, the old folks can go to sleep and we'll *djoh* (meet) in Treich-
town, OK?" He seemed to speak with both feet firmly planted—not in
the world of the *grotos* (the comfortable set), but on the hard surface of
the street, where the majority lived their lives. He was the echo of the
dreams of a generation plugged into international television and radio,
and for that reason he'd ended up a kind of big brother to them.

This Africa "of the third kind," born of the contradictions of an
economic globalization ever more destabilizing in the South, could be
encountered in zouglou, the most popular musical style among Ivorian
urban youth, a sort of hip-hop that wasn't. In fact it was a Bete rhythm,
called *alloucou,* minced into a cocktail of synthesizers and fighting
lyrics:

> *We're tired of your pretty speeches,*
> *Tired of the unemployment rate,*
> *Tired of all these untouchables,*
> *Tired of your hospitals,*
> *Tired of insecurity,*
> *Tired of all these hold-ups.*[2]

It was at the beginning of the 1980s that zouglou appeared—along
with student protests. The university was obsolete; it didn't anticipate
the student boom. Lecture rooms and student residences were totally
unrenovated, and the financial system was in crisis. Nevertheless, President Houphouët-Boigny was at the same time building a "new capital"
in Yamoussoukro, the village where he was born: a sumptuous plan whose
crown jewel was a basilica identical to that of the Pope in Rome, but a few
meters shorter, so as not to offend the Holy See!

Bands like Les Parents du Campus put this type of contradiction to
music while the situation got worse. The forces of "disorder" were not
completely paralyzed—many students were severely reprimanded, others expelled from the university. But the zouglou movement was here to
stay, much to the establishment's despair. A style of dress, a dance, and a
"relaxed French" were the specific signs, not to mention sometimes-suicidal

---

[2] Words of a song by Digbeu.

practices such as *boro d'enjaillement* (from *boro,* "bag" in Dyula, and *enjoy-ment,* an English word imported by prostitutes from Ghana). This consisted of riding—despite the fatal accidents that routinely resulted—on the roofs or bumpers of city buses.

Amid an economic crisis that made plain the worthlessness of the CFA[3] franc, the bands kept multiplying. The most well-known were Sur-Choc (Supershock), Poussins chocs (Shock Chicks), CRS Danger public (*Compagnie Républicaine de Sécurité* [one of the police forces] Public Danger), Shuke Pat, Didier Bilé, and Système Gazeur (Gas System). Speaking for the dangerous neighborhood of Yopougon, Les Salopards pushed the sarcasm further. One of their tapes had a most explicit title: *Génération sacrifiée* (Sacrificed Generation). In the manner of Public Enemy, who wanted to be "the CNN of ghetto youth," and after whom they patterned themselves, the Salopards tried to inform their audience about everything that was happening in Africa, beyond the lies and confusion. In contrast with nearly all other artists on the Ivorian stage, the zouglou crowd always made it clear they wanted no alliances with the powers that be.

Meanwhile, up in Senegal, this same chaotic mood, this *gnama-gnama* (brothel, traffic, mixup) that was as pervasive in the neighborhoods of Dakar as on the streets of Abidjan, had latched onto a different vehicle of expression: rap.

> *At the start, independence the great illusion!*
> *When you talk capital, man, you talk confusion!*
> *From all the little villages, they arrive in trucks,*
> *Trying to get themselves a day job.*
> *Now it's all the fashion to go there in the dry season.*
> *Workers, peasants, these guys live in poverty,*
> *For the lack of a little courage, a little energy.*
> *Look, the clouds are gathering. It means winter's coming.*

---

[3] *Translator's note:* the CFA franc is the common currency of thirteen African countries (in West Africa: Benin, Burkina Faso, Ivory Coast, Mali, Niger, Senegal, and Togo; in Central Africa: Cameroon, the Central African Republic, Chad, the Congo, Equatorial Guinea, and Gabon. CFA in West Africa stands for *Communauté Financière Africaine,* and in Central Africa for *Coopération Financière en Afrique Centrale*).

You get it right away, so you get back to your crib.
You lie down, you see your mother crying,
You see your father dying.
Look at the tears of your sister crying...[4]

In the mid-1980s, in Dakar's suburbs, free-style tournaments were organized. And thus it was that one day Didier J. Awadi, alias "D. J. Awadi," a member of the Amitié 2 (Friendship 2) neighborhood syndicate, met Amadou Barry, alias "Doug E. Tee," of the Liberté 6 (Freedom 6), a key member of the King MCs. The two young men who would found Positive Black Soul (PBS), one of them Muslim, the other Christian, discovered a common ideal—nothing less than the "rehabilitation of the black soul." They revered the same heroes, in particular two pinnacles of African culture: the writer Amadou Hampâté Bâ, who played a major role in the preservation and recognition of oral tradition, and the Senegalese historian Cheikh Anta Diop, a passionate advocate of the idea of a United States of Africa, who above all served as a proponent for the antiquity of Negro civilizations, especially Egypt.

In invoking these two intellectuals right from the start, PBS weren't just throwing big names around: what they wanted was to give their rap an African stamp (while their counterparts elsewhere on the continent tried to imitate the American style) and a philosophy of dignity: "We are fighting for people to recognize the colossal part that Africa has played in how this world has worked out."

Rap, it is true, has several reasons to thrive in Senegalese soil.[5] The oral tradition remains important there. Between the griot, master of speech, and the rap MC, master of ceremonies, there is only a difference in surroundings. The art of discussion, of social communication, is a constant in African life, and the rapper speaks to this collective need. Africa has

---

[4] Positive Black Soul, "Exodus."
[5] Thanks to a bit of help (from, among others, *Le Centre Cultural Français*, Africa Fête, the French rapper MC Solaar, Radio France International, and the *Revue noire*), Senegalese rap (Daara-J, Kanthioli, Jant-Bi, Pee Froiss, and others) is starting to be heard around the world. Top export: Dakar's own PBS, whose growing international reach has won them an audience with President Abdou Diouf and official recognition as ambassadors of their country. Also worth noting is the number of rappers from

always been fond of "commentators" who take up and speak what is socially unspoken, who on their own level are rappers. And then of course there's the protomusical character of rap, founded on rhythm and tone, which suits the sensitivity of African tastes precisely with those two elements.

In 1990, PBS recorded its first album, *Boul'falé* (Don't Worry). This record announced the arrival of a movement animated at the bottom by hundreds of penniless bands whose tapes (bootlegged or not) sold like hotcakes at the markets of Sandaga and Thiaroye-Gare. This rap was created with whatever means were available. Without vinyl, sophisticated drum machines, or sound banks—too expensive—and without a thought of scratching or sampling, they created their own recipes. The colorful and rugged Wolof language, traditional instruments (Fulani flute, balafon, kora, sabar, tama, riti), and griot meters (such as *tassou,* improvised patter used by women in wedding ceremonies [*tax-ourane*]) were employed to transmit pamphlet-style texts or to react to African pessimism. For if on TV screens America was omnipresent (via satellite dishes and imported videos), real life modified the trajectory of local rap. Thus, in contrast with its American counterpart, Senegalese rap fights violence, exalts companionship, preaches harmony, respects tradition, does not regard women as "ho's," and wants to be a "new way of wisdom." This constructive, community-centered outlook is found in the self-organization of thousands of youths through their fan "posses."[6] And PBS are no different: these "messengers of familial happiness" (according to one of their posters), the first African rap group to have signed with a multinational label (Mango, a branch of Island), have aimed above all to open people's eyes and "responsibilize" them.

Francophone African countries who have looked to France for their primary models, soaking up style and attitude on the rare occasions when French rappers like Imhotep, Les Sages Poètes de la Rue, Zoxea, and Kool Shen have performed in their countries. Nor does the road only run North. With their 1999 album *Racines* (Roots), French rappers Bissa Na Bisso, of Congolese origin, marked a return to their origins and evoked a "black international" of the second generation.

[6] A survey by the nongovernmental organization Enda Tiers Monde counts 3,000 rap groups in Senegal.

One of their theme songs, "Loto-PetMU" (*pet* meaning "bilked" in Wolof),[7] denounces the Senegalese mania for imported gambling games as "the road to disappointment, because it aims to put all objections to sleep." Another, "Ataya," takes on the ritual of tea, which, though favorable to conversation, "puts people to sleep." A third evokes the devaluation of the CFA franc; a fourth, the endemic poverty of some, and the undue wealth of others.

Will this musical radicalism of the new African generation last? Farther south are signs that other tendencies are at work. In Johannesburg, out went the mbaqanga popularized by Johnny Clegg, and in came kwaito, the dance of the townships—those big tin shantytowns. Kwaito merges American house music with the rich sonic traditions of the ghettos. Leading figures of this music are Arthur (150,000 copies of his records were sold in 1995), Boom Shaka, Abashanté, Brenda Fassie, Washmen, and Iyaya, who, in spreading, concentric waves, softly conquered the dance floors of all southern Africa.

To understand the eruption of kwaito (the word fuses *kwai*, "anger," and *to*, short for "township"), one must understand the South African context and the transition from a smothering system of apartheid to a democracy under the leadership of Nobel Prize–winner Nelson Mandela, who, before handing the reins to his successor, Thabo Mbeki, applied himself to negotiating a peaceful transition with the white power, to healing the wounds of a racist regime, and to reinforcing civic peace. But if, after decades of oppression, many democratic steps were taken, the task still revealed itself to be too big for the results, at the level of everyday life, to meet the high expectations of the people. So, in contrast to the preceding "generation of fighters," the kwaito generation that grew up under Mandela started expressing its resentment openly. These black, Indian, and mixed-race teenagers, who had believed that the "rainbow nation" would know how to respond to the crying needs of work, housing, and education, now brutally affirmed that things weren't going as planned. The numbers, unfortunately, agreed with them: one-fourth of

---

[7] *Translator's note:* PMU (*Pari Mutuel Urbain*) is an off-track betting company. In addition to its meaning in Wolof, *pet,* pronounced like the French name for the letter *P* ("peh"), is also the French word for "fart."

the population lived in shantytowns, 42 percent of blacks were unemployed, 37 percent did not have electricity, 65 percent were illiterate, and 20 percent lived without running water. Violence was endemic, with a thousand police officers killed in five years, seven times more homicides than in the United States, a rape every thirty minutes, and four million illegal weapons in the country.

In this status quo, kwaito vocalists have found their vocation as social critics. Singing in *iscamtho*—a slang mixing all the languages of the country, including the Afrikaans of the white former oppressor—they denounce hypocrisy in an aggressive and sexually suggestive tone that's especially effective for needling a country steeped in puritan Protestantism. The girls of Boom Shaka went so far as to transform the national anthem into a lewd tune, to Mandela's great displeasure.

Paradoxically, the same kwaito, hitching a ride on the grooves of hiphop, jungle, drum-and-bass, and ragga, has accompanied the opening of South Africa to the world. Although watched closely by local record-industry mavens, this opening has generated its own studios and stables of artists—and its own high-tension environment, complete with struggles over influence and settling of old scores that have very little relation to distant connections with the music.

The Youssou N'Dour Connection

The Prototype of the African Artist of the Future?

Youssou N'Dour and his talking drum, 1992.

Music is our petroleum.

—MANU DIBANGO

U p to the age of thirteen, young Youssou N'Dour had expressed himself only at *kassak* (circumcision ceremonies) or *ngente* (baptism
parties), but at this age he paid homage to the recently deceased
famous saxophone player Papa Samba Diop, called "M'Ba," in a song, and
his family had no choice but to recognize that this boy really had a talent
for music. They enrolled him at the Institute of Arts in Dakar. He had, it
was true, some big shoes to fill: his mother and two of his grandparents
were *gawlos* (Tukolor for griots), local praise singers.

The first band he was in was the Diamono; then he created L'Étoile
de Dakar, which was followed by the Super Étoile in 1981. Rapidly, his
slightly breaking head voice became the favorite of the Senegalese. With
his group, Youssou "You" N'Dour stepped forward as a major craftsman
of the rebirth of modern Senegalese music, which had already known
some hours of glory after the war, thanks to the neo-jazz of Saint-Louis,
then the capital.[1]

Youssou N'Dour's recipe had a name: *mbalax.*[2] Until the mid 1970s, Senegalese urban music was a broad blend of traditionally spiced Afro-Cuban

[1] At the end of a large lagoon isolated from the ocean by a sand ribbon, Saint-Louis,
the first French establishment on the African coast, grew from commerce (gum from
Mauritania, gold and slaves from the upper Senegal River, ambergris from the sperm
whale, ivory, and leather) and was fed on French colonial expansion before giving up
its status of capital to Dakar. About the time of World War II, after the American ships
put in at the Senegal River, leaving behind banjos, trumpets, record players, and
records, the youth launched themselves headlong into a new kind of music. From 1945
to 1957, Saint-Louis, then an intellectual crossroads of Africa, was the place of hot nights
par excellence, animated by a constellation of quicksilver groups (such as Sor Jazz,
Saint-Louisien Jazz, Amicale Jazz, Star Jazz, and Quintet Baby), performers of great talent (such as Aminata Fall), and prestigious instrumentalists (such as Abou Sy, Ady
Seck, Baraud N'Diaye, Dioury, Gana M'Bow, and, of course, Papa Samba Diop).
[2] *Translator's note: x* in Wolof is pronounced like the *ch* in German *Bach.*

rhythms. Baobab, Labah Soseh, the Star Band, Number One, Super Diamono, and Xalam[3] played with these mixes, each with its own proportions.
With You, the proportions changed; it was the local rhythms that sustained the music. The sensual tama (arm drum) and the ecstatic *mbalax,*
percussion instruments that, solo, led Wolof dances, came to the forefront. The rhythms of the Serer, Dyula, Tukolor, Fulani, and other ethnic
groups of Senegal progressively enriched the sound palette and set it
apart from jazz, rock, and reggae tendencies. The lyrics and the guttural
sounds of Wolof did the rest, especially among the female audience who
made up the majority of the public for the inventor of the "ventilator
dance."[4]

But beyond his vocal gifts and the appeal of his compositions, he also
owed his success to his talents as an organizer, his capacity to learn from
his experiences, and his will to leave his mark on his times—qualities that
make him the prototype of the African musician of the twenty-first century, turning his back on a culture of "almost" from which his musical
world suffered so much. "In Africa, it has been problems of organization
that have held music back the most. Musicians aren't respected. The
groups get together and split up. With me, the musicians don't have any
money troubles. They are among the best paid, they have staff salaries."
As soon as he was able, You called upon himself to stabilize his team. First
there were the concerts at the Thiossane in Dakar, a concert club that he
owned. Then he created SAPROM (Société Africaine de Production Musicale, the African Musical Production Society), of which he was the main
stockholder: an enterprise of several dozen people who managed his business, his African tours, and his productions, and rented sound equip-

---

[3] Among the key groups of the Senegalese musical renewal, Xalam is particularly noteworthy. Performing since 1974, Xalam jammed with Dizzy Gillespie, Stan Getz, and
the Rolling Stones, and was seen as a groundbreaking fusion group, mixing percussion, *mbalax,* lamb, goumbe, and so forth with funk, jazz, or zouk at the instigation
of its leader, drummer Abdulaye Prosper Niang, who died of cancer on April 29,
1988, after recording the album *Xarit.*
[4] The *ventilateur* showcases the rumps of the women dancers and the motion of the
arms. [*Translator's note:* The women lift their robes, much to the outrage of those
concerned about public decency.] The corresponding dance for men is the *hoti chaya,*
which calls for pants with wide hips and was inspired by a postcircumcision dance
that signaled that the teenager can think about girls again.

ment to other artists. Piracy was an endemic plague, nourished by big producers who flooded the informal market with truckloads shipped from Southeast Asia and bribed the customs officers. You decided to gain a speed advantage over them by issuing tapes on his own, two titles at a time as soon as he composed them, marketing them through a network of small dealers.

His French debut came in 1983 thanks to an invitation from the *Association des Chauffeurs de Taxi Sénégalais* (Senegalese Taxi Drivers' Union), when his hit of the hour was "Immigrés" (Immigrants). Two years later he could be found first at the Printemps de Bourges, then in Paris in the vast Bercy hall (where Jacques Higelin hooked him up to his mega-spectacle along with another unknown, Mory Kante), and at the Théatre de la Ville. Supported by Peter Gabriel, participating in "Tam-Tam pour l'Éthiopie," he released albums acclaimed by European critics. It was, however, his participation in 1988 in the Amnesty International tours for human rights that made him undeniably a star. Together with Sting, Bruce Springsteen, Tracy Chapman, and Peter Gabriel, he went on a tour that attracted much media attention in twenty of the world's largest cities. This experience had a profound effect on his evolution. "Thanks to this tour, I understood that I could go further. I became familiar with the concept of mélange, and I learned to lean toward a universal music. Furthermore, with Amnesty, I learned to do something else beside music: to lead humanitarian quests, promoting the Declaration of Human Rights, which I didn't know existed and that I want, now, to popularize in Africa." He used this perception of cultural contrasts in his recordings. In 1989, if the Senegalese version of the album *The Lion* (*Gaïndé* in Wolof) gave percussion its proper place, the version made in London married rhythms to synthesizers and dosed the original with all the possibilities of a forty-eight-track studio. *Set,* his next opus, came out first on tape in Senegal and then, about a year later, as an album in the North.[5]

---

[5] The production of *Set* (meaning "Clean"), whose title track stressed "cleanliness in your spirit, cleanliness in your acts, cleanliness in your soul, cleanliness in your body," corresponded with a large spontaneous salubrity movement started by the youth in Dakar, who used brooms and brushes to transform walls and sidewalks. Thousands of frescos invited youth to join the fight against trash, drugs, and AIDS.

Was this an enrichment or a dilution of musical detail? At the beginning of the 1990s, the record industry was infatuated with world music, which it hoped would bring to the uninspired pop scene of the day a new aesthetic perspective (and, of course, a lot more of those sweet profits it was already starting to generate). There was much blurring of the line between the notion of a true mélange of ingredients and the neocolonialist scam of taking a few exotic rhythmic or melodic elements and subjecting them to the same old studio formulas. For a considerable price, a few studio big shots were in demand in Los Angeles, Miami, or London. In this confrontation, African musicians, who had learned much (to the point of furnishing a respectable number of "studio sharks" of the French and foreign variety), did not always have the means to impose their views once their contracts were signed.

Youssou N'Dour had such an experience. His contract was not renewed because his label estimated that his sales would not be enough to recoup the studio expenses run up by the production technocrats. This led him to produce his own work in his own country, starting with the release in 1994 of *Wommat* (The Guide), his eighteenth album. "It's a matter of pride for me to have produced this album from A to Z in my own studio," he declared. He came to a distribution agreement with Spike Lee, maker of the movie *Malcolm X*. From then on, working from his African base, Youssou N'Dour organized his web with regularity and rigor, conscious that, for export, African music needed symbolic acts that strike the imagination. "Africa Remembers" was a song dedicated to the black diaspora; the video was directed by Spike Lee. *Africa Opera,* a production (with Angélique Kidjo, Aicha Kone, and Djanka Diabate) at the Opera Garnier in Paris, a temple of lyric art, unfolded as a fresco about African identity. *So Why,* a collective effort for the Red Cross, denounced the criminal ethnic divisions of a continent in the footsteps of the tragic events in Rwanda, Liberia, and Sierra Leone. As he met various artists, from Ryuichi Sakamoto to Neneh Cherry, he multiplied his collaborations. Then he was chosen by Michel Platini,[6] a sports idol on a continent where soccer is the primary religion, to compose the anthem for the 1998 World Cup,

---

[6] *Translator's note:* A French soccer star from 1971 to 1988, active in the international governance of the sport since his retirement.

which You performed during the opening ceremony, transmitted to hundreds of millions of viewers.

Always faithful to his motto "to live and work in my country," he gives most of his attention to his Senegalese organization. In more than ten years, SAPROM has become a large enterprise, often in demand for organizing regional music and encouraging, through festivals, the emergence of young talents. Xippi ("open the eye" in Wolof) Studios now has its own catalog of artists (*Jojoli*), such as Cheikh Lo, who carry on international careers. Asked about these many initiatives, a calm Youssou N'Dour answers simply: "I consider myself a modern African. World music? I want to do what I want to do, and what I want is how I live." That does not prevent this ambassador for UNICEF from surprising everyone with his hungry drive. Because of his aura abroad, some amuse themselves by imagining him as a Minister of Foreign Affairs. Afterall, he created a communication group (Com 7 SA), the radio station (7 FM) most heard in Dakar taxicabs, and a "neutral journal of general information" (*7 Week-End*) . . . while the launch of a new, more ambitious daily is expected.

Ray Lema, or the Great World Band

When Music Is Humanism

Ray Lema and "les voix Bulgaires," 1990.

Since I left the Catholic Church, I have searched a lot: among the Rosicrucians, the Buddhists, in the martial arts.... I sunk into anything that pretended to talk about God. Now, I am certain of only one thing: there has to be a supreme "artist" behind all the world's beauty. I am a believer, but I am trying to arrive at a religious music that doesn't speak of God. The word is so debased that it closes doors instead of opening them.

— RAY LEMA, 1989

I f there are premonitory signs, then the birth of Raymond Lema-A-Nzi Nzinga on a train is one. In 1946, on the Kinshasa[1]-Matadi line, his mother started having pains, and she gave birth to him in the Lutu Toto station. Maybe this event explains his propensity for musical nomadism, which has made him one of the most paradoxical African artists.

At eleven, he entered the minor seminary of Mikondo in Kinshasa. Because he was talented, he was taught organ and Gregorian chant, and was educated in the Western style with a syllabus of Bach, Mozart, and Beethoven. After leaving the seminary and adapting his piano techniques to the guitar, he discovered the capital's clubs and the unkempt beauty of urban music. It was a fateful discovery: he abandoned his studies in chemistry at the University of Louvain to join a group, the Yss Boys, with whom he played the big pop-rock hits of the moment: those of the Beatles, Jimi Hendrix, Eric Clapton, and the rest.

His mastery of European music and his intellectual baggage made him a special musician: "I was so much into non-Zairean music that they called me the 'I Know.'" He found himself working as a nightclub pianist playing international requests. In 1972, because of his knowledge, the Zairean government entrusted him with the task of putting together

---

[1] *Translator's note:* Then known as Léopoldville, Belgian Congo.

a national ballet. The *mindele ndombe* (black white) began to research the musical reality of a country with more than 250 ethnic groups, collecting sounds and meeting with hundreds of musicians and dancers, some of whom would help form the famous ballet. This encounter was a revelation for him. During the year-long journey, he experienced in the flesh the richness and complexity of the African "rhythmic wheel." He noticed that every time there was a festivity in a village, the percussions (including the players' bodies), coupled with the other instruments, would form a sort of continuous rhythmical pump in which each, depending on mood, inspiration, and temperament, could join at any moment. This mathematics of sensation always confounds exactness with synchroneity. In fact, because rhythm in Africa refers to cosmic energy and founding myths, everyone knows his or her place. The impetuous, "talkative" young drummer may well strike a hundred blows on the tom-tom while the older one strikes only five. The master drummer, alpha and omega of this collective heartbeat, ultimately keeps the whole group together.

After the second FESTAC (Festival of African Culture) in Lagos, Nigeria, in which he participated with Franco's group, Ray Lema composed with the group Y'A-Tupas (named after the Tupamaros, an urban guerrilla organization operating in Uruguay at the time). And his experimental recordings, listened to by a jury in Paris, earned him the Golden Maracas award in 1978.

In 1979, the Rockefeller Foundation offered him a scholarship, and he went to the United States, where he decided to stay and compose. His rhythmic talents and analytical mind gave birth to two albums: first *Koteja*, then *Kinshasa–Washington DC–Paris*, striking marriages of traditional styles enhanced by modern technology.

In Zaire, his too avant-garde sound and some of his mocking lyrics[2] did not endear him to *La Voix du Zaire*. In the United States, some were beginning to say that he played "African piano." Far from discouraging him, however, these reactions only reinforced his sense of artistic direction, for he was then, above all, seeking to uproot himself from the classical concept of piano. It was becoming something like an obsession,

---

[2] In "Mwan Aiwe," for example, he sang: "Three brothers from Kinshasa: one is a *balado* (a loser, a thief), the next is a businessman, the third one is in politics, which allows him to go to the john in a Mercedes."

and in its grip he dreamt of a "rhythmical piano," and saw himself playing it on its own percussive terms.

It was then that, put off by the violence of the big American cities—and what he considered a spiritual chaos among their inhabitants—he decided to leave for Europe, where, thanks to Jean-François Bizot and the magazine *Actuel*, he could freely pursue his own style. From that point on, his musical crossbreeding became a strength. And he who had sometimes been considered a traitor by other Zaireans, accused of turning his back on his country's music, denied the accusation by insisting that he only wanted to get "the rumba out of its rut." And so he would. The youth of Europe were turning their back on classical music, he realized, while the youth of Africa were turning theirs on tradition. Lema decided to embrace the status of a hybrid musician instead, and turned his back on neither.

Was this ecumenical synthesis just a dream? "In the North," said the singer with a preacher's voice, "everything is based on the verticality of the harmonies. In Africa, everything is horizontal. Everyone has his place with a bit of melody and stays there. In the North, people are taught by the scale. They do not understand the gaps that exist in the African modes, where some notes are purposely avoided. But things change. Yesterday, Arab music sounded out of tune to them, but now many understand the beauty of the quarter tone."

He was soon applying himself in all directions. Stewart Copeland, drummer for the Police, collaborated with him on a solo album, *Rythmatist.* He recorded the album *Medecine* with Martin Meissonnier, on which he transferred the essence of Zairean music into the computer world (CMI keyboards, Prophet, PPG, DX7, Moog), playing, between the bush and the urban jungle, an intense trance. Critics acclaimed it. He composed the music for Thomas Gilou's film *Black Micmac.* A passionate reader, he collaborated on a play about Arthur Rimbaud. He wrote some arrangements for the Cape Verdean group Finaçon. He formed a group with Jacques Higelin, Charlélie Couture, Alain Bashung, Willy N'For, Manu Dibango, and others, and sat them down to cut a record, released with the same name as the group: *Bwana Zoulou Gang.* He coproduced the album *Nangadeef* ("How are you?" in Wolof, a title chosen to show that he felt more African than Zairean), which showcased the vocals of the Mahotella Queens, the saxophone of Courtney Pine, the fretwork of Jesse Johnson (guitarist for Prince), the bass of Étienne M'Bappé, and the drumming of Paco Séry. He put out the strange *Gaïa* (a mystical name for the Earth).

On into the 1990s Lema continued to bridge the gaps between disparate musical cultures: his collaboration with the German jazz pianist Joachim Kühn on *Euro African Suite;* a work with the Bulgarian women's choir Trikia (on the album *Ray Lema, Professor Stefanov et l'Ensemble Pirin*); also a creation with Wereweré Liking, the African Ariane Mnouchkine, for the opera *Un Touareg s'est marié a une Pygmée* (A Tuareg Man Married a Pygmy Woman); and finally he composed a piece for the Swedish orchestra of Sundswall and a string-and-wind quartet, *Le Rêve de la gazelle* (The Gazelle's Dream).

While so many others, dizzy with globalization, were dreaming only of "fusions," Lema, attuned to a less watered-down notion of universality, wanted mostly to establish ties, to break out of cultural yokes, to form bonds between eternal rhythms and sounds, to create a play of mirrors between yesterday and tomorrow. This is the quest of an impenitent, mischievous dreamer on the trail of a conviction: "All musics come from just one music, which has been divided."

Afterword

The Duty of Memory

El Hadj Djeli Sory Kouyate and his balafon, 1993.

They brought us to the Congo
To make the Europeans' railroad
Called the Congo-Ocean.
I am sending you a letter: listen!
I tell you that my kidneys ache.
If you saw the work that I do,
Woman, you'd wait for me in tears.
I am sending you a picture.
I don't know what's to become of me.
The white man says that we're coming home.
Woman! What a life of suffering!
You like only dancing; now dance!
In the Congo, we dance to forget our sorrow.
Understand? Let's dance.

—"WALI, SO GIGI TI PASI!,"
JUDE BONDEZE (CENTRAL AFRICA)[1]

ecause urbanization and the large-scale rural exodus are such recent developments, modern African music,[2] in spite of increasingly obvious breaks in communication, maintains an intimate relationship with traditional music. As the latter has great practical and spiritual value (songs and music of work, hunting, praise, healing, cosmogony, and death), many of its characteristics, linked to the collective unconscious, are found in modern music as well, though deritualized. The geography of the two musics match and are in turn wedded to

[1] Translated from Sango by Pierre Saulnier, in his *Bangui chante* (l'Harmattan, 1993), which analyzes 138 songs from 1960 to 1985, for the most part "slices of everyday life," complaints about the difficulties of life, and celebrations of the loved one.

[2] By "modern music" we mean music that shows a concern for professionalization and industrialization, through discs, concerts in clubs, road tours, publicity, and so forth.

linguistic zones, each language demanding its rhythm, scansion, and melody.

Like traditional music, modern African music is often, to the foreigner, the object of fallacies and truisms. For a long time, it was perceived through dance and judged to be mainly rhythmic, though a closer look reveals the richness of its melodies and the African public's passion for lyrical compositions. It's true, of course, that this entertainment-based modern music gives importance to dance, and all the great musician-singers have distinguished themselves thereby, from Doctor Nico, who "knew how to make even skeletons dance" with his magic guitar, to the *ambianceurs* (mood-setters) such as Koffi Olomide, Pepe Kalle, and Kanda Bongo Man; not to mention torrid Amazons such as Tshala Muana or the young bombshells of Ivorian mapouka or of South African kwaito. Yet though a multitude of dance styles, from the Senegalese *ventilateur* to the Congolese *danse des très fâchés* (dance of the very angry), has turned up the temperature of the clubs and drinking spots on the continent, at the bottom it all goes back to the social role of music, of which dance is only the most spectacular demonstration. Africa has at its disposal a vast panoply of music and songs for listening alone, as attested by the network of the Manding griots; the credibility of the bards, whether Ethiopian, Gabonese, or Malagasy; the importance of religious choirs (Catholic, Protestant, Kibanguist, and so on); and the sophistication of polyphonies, among other things. This, in contrast to African pop's more percussive and brassy tendencies, is what the likes of Ray Lema, Geoffrey Oryema, Lokua Kanza, and Wasis Diop have been expressing in the last few years, in minimalist and intimate registers. All this proves that modern African music covers a wide aesthetic spectrum and harbors, and for those who wish to explore it, a wealth of sonorous potentials.

In this modern music, instruments have pride of place. Evidently, the importation of European instruments (often through the bars or ports) played a fundamental role in the emergence of urban musical languages. The imagination of local musicians gave life to surprising adaptations, whether with sophisticated or rudimentary instruments. The most enlightening example is the fate of a small straight metallic flute, the tinwhistle or pennywhistle, which, after being imported by the German company

Hohner, met wide success because of its modest cost (a penny). Its success is also due in part to the fact that the indigenous player can adapt it to his needs. After widening its lip with a knife to strengthen the sound, he plays it by pushing the mouthpiece deep inside his mouth at an oblique angle in order to use a familiar harmonic technique linked to the musical-bow tradition. The contact with the inside of the cheek, the angle of breath, and the use of the mouth cavity as a resonator enable him to obtain a sound that can be changed at will and reinforced with harmonics. In South Africa, this mutation would give birth to the style known as kwela ("climb" or "reach" in Bantu), a trademark of South African urban music, combining traditional rhythms with American jazz influences. Kwela was popularized by Willard Cele's hit "Pennywhistle Blues" (1950), and later by players as important as Spokes Mashiyane, to the point that the diabolic little flute became the identifying instrument of an entire rebel-youth demographic of the time—the "ducktails" (juvenile delinquents)—and made for a classic band genre, until the arrival of brass rendered the whistle marginal.

For a time, modern African musicians mostly played foreign instruments, adapting them to balafon, kora, sanza, or harp styles (as was the case with the guitar). Thanks to progress in instrument building[3] and to the bounty of the "Electricity Fairy," however, a number of the continent's emblematic instruments (kora, tama, drums, and so forth, "factors and markers of cultural identity," as ethnomusicologists have regularly noted) have returned to the front lines and organized musical genres around their instrumental specificities.

Moreover, if modern music makes a lot of room for dance,[4] it attaches no less importance to words. Furthermore, it is striking to realize that the majority of international or Pan-African hits[5] turn their back on

---

[3] In Senegal, for instance, the monks of Keur Moussa have made the tuning of the kora easier, thanks to a new system of knobs.

[4] Modern African dance—a body language, a locus for articulation of attitudes and political values, particularly for youth—for the most part borrows elements from traditional dances (especially the many varieties of the famous soukous).

[5] In 1990, to celebrate its tenth anniversary, Radio Africa No. 1 released a collection of major hits from the continent from the past thirty years. It includes "Indépendance cha-cha" by Joseph Kabasele; "Gentleman Vikey" by Bobby Benson and G. G. Vikey;

evanescent trifles, choosing instead to evoke reality. Whether the subject is independence, neocolonialism, the status of women, the economic crisis, African unity, racism, respect for memory, or endemic diseases, African song, more often than is usual in popular song, shows a philosophic disposition with pedagogical and even moralistic emphases.

One thing, however, distinguishes modern music from traditional music: although loved by millions, the former has received little bottom-line consideration from institutions in Africa or elsewhere, whereas traditional music has had the attention of ethnomusicologists (both African and European) who have accomplished work essential for saving entire expanses of memory and for passing the baton to new generations. Modern music has had little such solicitude, perhaps because it was thought that commercializing it was enough to legitimize it and ensure its continuity. But because not all artists are in the same boat, and fame is fickle, most of what is considered part of contemporary heritage has gone by the board. (Who, for example, will tell of the lost beauties of the old rumba cavacha, which people shared in the open-air dances on the banks of the Congo?) Poverty, as well, takes its toll: old tapes from a national radio station are erased and reused; discographic treasures become prey to termites or plunderers. This cruel reality suggests, we hope, a future project for the nations of the world, so that due thanks may be given for the multitude of marvelous modern African musicians, singers, composers, and dancers, often forgotten after having given so much happiness to millions of night owls, mothers in their villages, youth in "the hood," immigrants, exiles, and music lovers everywhere.

"Espoir" by Hilarion N'Gueman; "Les Immortels" by the Congolese Franklin Boukaka; "Rockia" by Bella Bellow; "Paquita" by Tabu-Ley Rochereau; "Tu m'as deçu, chou-chou" by Doctor Nico; "Kumbelé Kumbelé" by Les Bantous Jazz; "Soul Makossa" by Manu Dibango; "Africa Obota" by Pierre Akendengue; "Mannequin" by Koffi Olo-mide; "Yeké-Yeké" by Mory Kante; "Mario" by Franco and the TPOK Jazz; "Brigadier Sabari" by Alpha Blondy; "African Music Non Stop" by Elvis Kemayo; "Ancien com-battant" by Zao; and "Pon Moin Paka Bougé" by Pepe Kalle. The song that sold the most in Africa (13 million copies) was "Sweet Mother," sung by Cameroon Prince Nico Mbarga and his Rocafil Jazz Band, recorded in Nigeria. The theme of this song: a tribute to the protective mother!

APPENDIXES

Musical Areas: Africa in Ethnomusicolor

*The Beninese Stan Tohon during
a voodoo concert, 1996.*

When it comes to describing Africa and its music, the plural has to be used. The official "world music" version, for some reasons that ring true and others that merely fumble, has tried to subject African musics to its reductive criteria, but they keep breaking loose. How could it be otherwise with a continent—a Babel of cosmologies—three times the size of Europe, with an extraordinary variety of climates, a panorama of landscapes ranging from the most unforgiving desert to the most implacable forest, hundreds of ethnicities, fifteen hundred spoken languages? Notwithstanding the generations of hasty observers who have pontificated on what must be meant by "African music," all we can do, at best, is demonstrate groupings, flag similarities, designate cultural families, and indicate some paths to the sources of acoustical pleasure.

The Sudanese Area

The savanna, which borders the desert to the north and the tropical forest to the south, is an area with a strong Islamic influence, covering Senegal, Gambia, Mali, Burkina Faso, part of Sudan, and Guinea. It is the territory of the *nyamakala* (Fulani nomadic musicians)[1] and griots, whose status depends on the caste system and the great Manding epic performance (which was a tool for cohesion among sub-Saharan ethnic

---

[1] *Translator's note:* The Mande word *nyamakala* means a person with an inherited talent for handling *nyama,* or world-energy. The *nyamakala* caste includes blacksmiths (who handle the power in inanimate matter), griots or poets (who handle the power of words), and tanners (who handle the animal power that remains in skins after death). See Patrick R. McNaughton, *The Mande Blacksmiths: Knowledge, Power, and Art in West Africa* (Bloomington: Indiana University Press, 1988). In the restricted sense of "griot," the word *nyamakala* was borrowed by the Fulani and reinterpreted in their language as "eating at more than one table" (see Thierno Diallo, *Institutions politiques du Fouta-Djallon au XIXè siècle,* [Dakar: IFAN, 1972], ch. 3.).

groups). That epic concerns the history of the old kingdoms of Ghana, Mali, and the Songhai, and is a rich heritage of pre-Islamic musical traditions, enriched by the contributions of Islam and of dynasties of musicians. Within the vast perimeter of the Manding realm, characteristic instruments are the kora, a harp-lute; the balafon, a kind of xylophone; the riti, a one-stringed fiddle; the one-stringed lute called xalam in Wolof and ngoni in Mande; and the tama, or underarm drum—all instruments that contemporary musicians put at the heart of their sonorous quests.

Since the 1960s, several musical strands have developed, finding inspiration in outside influences (such as European or Cuban), drawing support from the old griot modes, or energizing various elements of regional styles. The cardinal figures of this area are Salif Keita, Mory Kante, the Toure Kunda, and Youssou N'Dour (the foremost name in the Senegalese *mbalax* genre).

The Guinean Area

The forests that extend over part of Guinea, Liberia, and the Ivory Coast have favored the existence of a wonderful range of percussion instruments. Its roots in animism[2] give the tom-tom (generic term) an essential role. Under these circumstances, Guinea, where an International Percussion Center was created, has been a wonderful source of drummers, presided over by "grand masters" Fadouba Olare, Mamady Keita, Famoudou Konate, Soungalo Coulibaly, and Aboubacar Camara. At the other musical pole is the Ivory Coast, whose capital, Abidjan, has been

---

[2] Since the theory of animism as "the first step in the phenomenon of religion" was definitively knocked down by James George Frazer and Marcel Mauss, the definition of the term has remained open, even though the cult of spirits and ancestors (which is different from polytheism) has a place among the religions of the world. In general, initiation has a key function in animist belief systems, but for the most part, animism's only broadly defining features are negatives: it is not based on a revelation; its participants are not missionaries; it does not have founding texts; and the sacred object is not the representation of an idol but the link between nature and sacred, between the clan and the world of the ancestors and spirits.

a meeting place of many musicians, drawn there both by the "Ivorian economic miracle" of the 1960s and by the biennial MASA (*Marché des arts africains*), hosted in Abidjan since 1992. In this country of sixty ethnic groups, where traditional music is very lively (from the mask celebrations of the Guere, Dan, Bete, Yacouba, and others to Senufo funeral ceremonies), many performers have accommodated regional styles to modern technology. The forerunner, Ernesto Djedje and his ziglibithy (derived from a Bete rhythm based on percussion, combining sopi, digba, and zaglobi rhythms), opened the way for Djimi Gnaore with the polihet, Kassiry with the gnama-gnama, Meiway with the zoblazo (inspired by rhythms of the N'Zema ethnic group), Aicha Kone with the Senufo poro rhythm, and many others.

The Nigerian Area

On the Gold Coast, colonization enabled the early meeting of European instruments and a rich musical tradition, namely a percussive one. A beautiful orchestral patrimony, inaugurated in Ghana by E.T. Mensah, resulted from it, along with a more intimate urban art, mainly in small drinking places. Across several decades, under various names, highlife developed: a hydra style always sprouting new heads (from juju to fuji, with much in between), particularly in vast Nigeria, linked with the musical traditions of the regional Yoruba, Ibo, and Hausa ensembles. Its charismatic figures include Fela Kuti (and his Afrobeat version of highlife), Ebenezer Obey, and Ayinde Barrister.

The heart of the triangular slave trade, the vodun lands have a strong specialization in the area of traditional music, but until recently have had great difficulty in bringing forth a modern idiom. In Benin, the first attempts can be attributed to Stan Tohon, who adapted the tchinkounme, a funeral rhythm, playing it on water calabashes, smaller gourds, and bells; or to Danielou Sagbohan, who was inspired by Kakagbo, Gohoun, and Agagoun rhythms. Angélique Kidjo achieved in her own right a mix of funk-rock and gogbahoun, a dance rhythm in her region of Ouida.

The Bantu Area

Music of Bantu inspiration extends over a vast area that includes Cameroon, Gabon, Congo, and the Democratic Republic of the Congo (formerly Zaire). Among its characteristics are the natural use of the voice, the prevalence of pentatonic structures, and the importance of choruses, often mixed. Its star instruments include the mvet (a zither based on a hollow stick resonator), slotted drums, xylophones, sanzas, drums, pluriarcs, horns, and flutes. Many foreign types of music made their way up the Congo River, most notably a type of Cuban music that would arrive in Kinshasa (formerly Léopoldville) and Brazzaville at their fullest phase of post-independence affirmation, bringing to flower a Congolese rumba—a syncretism of Latino and local rhythms—and rooting it in an orchestral tradition symbolized by Kabasele, Dr. Nico, Franco, Tabu-Ley Rochereau, and Papa Wemba. After turning into soukous, it delighted the dance floors of Africa for several decades, and its influence has left no modern African musician untouched. In Cameroon, the style that made the most interesting evolution was makossa, which Manu Dibango brought to international acclaim.

Africa of the Great Lakes

This region includes Uganda, Burundi, Rwanda, and a part of the Democratic Republic of the Congo. Its musical traditions are distributed according to both their linguistic background (Bantu or not: languages with tones have an effect on melodic structure and therefore on instrumental practice) and their work culture (herdsmen have one set of relationships to the world, farmers another). In Uganda, most of the music is pentatonic. Emblematic instruments of the area are the arched harp and the lyre (similar to the instruments of Pharaonic Egypt), which attest to the influence of Nilotic and Ethiopian cultures, and which are often linked to traditional nomadic bards. Linked formerly to royal courts, drum groups are now democratized and for the past two decades have traveled around the world.

Eastern Africa

On the Tanzanian and Kenyan coast, Arabic influence is manifest. The popular Kenyan sound used to be *omutibo*, based on Swahili song modes and played originally on guitar accompanied by a bottle tapped with a stick. On contact with the Congolese rumba, or perhaps South African kwela, *omutibo* gave birth to the benga style, formalized by Gabriel Omolo and subsequently Ochieng Kabaselleh. On the coast, from Somalia to Mozambique, and particularly in ports such as Zanzibar, taarab has evolved, with local variations, at the intersection of an Egyptian-stamped Arab music and Bantu influences.

The African Horn

Ethiopia is one of only a few countries on the continent to have remained independent throughout its history (except for a superficial Italian presence). Another peculiarity is that it has been a predominantly Christian nation for longer than many European nations have, with Jewish (the *Beta Israel*), Muslim, and animist minorities also part of the mix for centuries. Christian liturgical singing in the Ge'ez language has not left the domain of liturgy, but on the other hand, thanks to the *azmaris* (traveling musicians), bearers of the Abyssinian collective memory, and to the *tadjbet* (drinking places), Addis Ababa has been the heart of an urban traditional music based on the kraar (a lyre with six strings), the rebab (a one-stringed fiddle), the bägäna harp (heir to the famous "harp of David" in the Bible), and the sistrum (rattle) from ancient Egypt. First came the military brass bands, then rhythm and blues and rock (played over the airwaves by Radio Free Europe and Voice of America). In addition were the arrivals of accordion, guitar, and synthesizer, which gave birth in the 1960s to a very special Ethio-jazz, before a military junta—Stalinist with a touch of Amharic influence—overthrew the emperor in 1974. After a long intervening pause, this Ethio-jazz, symbolized by Mahmoud Ahmed, found its way onto international stages.

In neighboring Sudan, modern music has looked to Egypt (from the adoption of the oud and the violin in the 1930s to the contemporary jeel music). But the contributions of jazz (a word that indicates any Western addition) have also given birth to a specific style, a fusion of national rhythms (Nubian, Eddelibe, and Haddendawa), rhythm and blues, reggae, and funk, of which Abdel Aziz El Mubarak is the most prominent exponent.

Southern Africa

Vocals dominate the music of the Nguni peoples (including the Zulu, the Xhosa, and the Swazi), which revolves around polyphonic dance songs. Instruments, particularly the musical bow, are reserved for solo music. Apartheid, with its classifying obsession, favored the conservation of musical corpora in the Bantustans, while at the same time leading, via the mines, the *shebeens* (illegal bars in the ghettos), and the churches, to the emergence of hybrid styles such as marabi, kwela, mbaqanga, mapantsula, and kwaito—styles that would adapt many of the colonizer's instruments (pennywhistle, organ, accordion, guitars, brass) and would mimic many styles of American music (from the big bands to disco). In Zimbabwe, the Shona play the mbira, the lamellaphone linked to rituals of possession during the celebration of the ancestors. The adaptation of this mbira to the guitar was at the foundation of chimurenga music, which accompanied the fight for national liberation before becoming the modern sound of the country.

The Indian Ocean

At the crossroads of Africa, Arabia, Europe, China, and Indonesia, the islands of the Indian Ocean display a rainbow of styles, sound qualities, rhythms, and modes, and seduce us with the uniqueness of their instruments—particularly Madagascar, with its valiha (a zither built around a bamboo tube, identical to certain instruments in Southeast Asia), its 6/8 rhythm, its polyphonies, etc. Slavery has left its traces, as evidenced by the maloya of Réunion Island. Arabic influence can also be heard, especially in the Comoros, which has its own version of taarab.

Portuguese Africa

By imposing its language, the Portuguese colonists contributed to the unification of musical practices that were very dissimilar. Traditionally, Guinea-Bissau belongs more to the Manding area, while Mozambique offers pentatonic scales (such as those of the Tsonga) or an impressive orchestral tradition of timbila xylophones (from the Chopi of the coast). The fight for independence, however, has also given rise to a variety of urban music that can be heard throughout the Luso-African world, whether in Luanda, Maputo, or Praia, not to mention the diasporas in Holland, Senegal, France, and Lisbon.

Particular Areas

Some types of music, such as those of the Bushmen or the Pygmies, or the Ethiopian Coptic school, form a special category. The Pygmies, whose population straddles the borders of Rwanda, Uganda, the Central African Republic, the Congos, Gabon, and Cameroon, continue to fascinate us with their sophisticated polyphony, which evokes the *Ars Nova* of fourteenth-century Europe, and whose techniques (hiccups, yodels, ostinatos) have inspired many contemporary and avant-garde musicians (such as Anton Webern, Duke Ellington, Gyorgy Ligeti, and Luciano Berio). These polyphonies have been cheerfully plagiarized for world music recordings that have been extremely profitable. In Africa, these types of music have especially inspired jazz composers.

Musical Genres and Styles

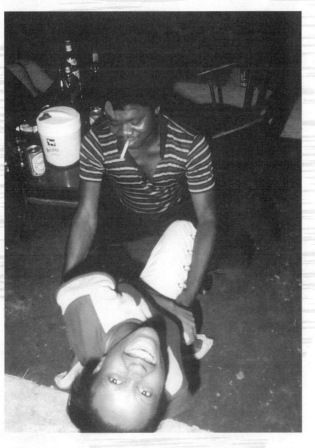

The ambience of a maquis in Douala (Cameroon), 1983.

The country where the genre was developed is indicated in parentheses. The representative artists of the genre are indicated with asterisks following each definition.

Afrobeat (Nigeria): A word used by Fela Kuti and his drummer Tony Allen to describe Kuti's music, a hybrid of jazz and highlife. *Fela and Femi Kuti, Tony Allen.

agooda (Sierra Leone): Music popularized by Abdul T-Jay.

ambas-bey (Cameroon): Street music that appeared in the 1920s and 1930s in the Bay of Ambas, close to Douala, played on the guitar and backed with bottles tapped with sticks or forks. Ambas-bey has mutated into assiko under Ghanian and Cuban influence. *Nel Eyoum.

apala (Nigeria): Yoruba music with vocals and percussion. *Aruna Ishola.

assiko or **ashiko** (Cameroon): Music based on Bantu rhythms and women's choirs, enriched by Cuban influences brought by Ashanti sailors from Liberia, and played on electric guitar backed by percussion, including a beer bottle hit with a knife. *Jean Bikoko.

batuka (Cape Verde): A celebration with songs and dances from São Tiago Island, featuring the txabeta dance and the finaçon song (q.v.).

bawlo (Djibouti): A style of Somalian or Afar ballad at the heart of the qaraami genre.

beko (Madagascar): A singing style with three or four voices, of religious inspiration, belonging to the Antandroy tradition. *Trio Salala.

benga (Kenya): A style that appeared in the 1960s, marrying local rhythms, especially those of the Omutibo, with Cuban or Congolese rumba and South African kwela, and forcefully performed with guitars and brass. *Gabriel Omolo, Maroon Commandos, Ochieng Kabaselleh, Daniel O. Misiani.

bikutsi (Cameroon): A style based on traditional rhythms of the Beti people, played originally with balafon, then adapted to the guitar. *Les Veterans, Anne-Marie Nzie, Les Têtes Brûlées.

brakka: A dance of young exiled Kenyans in the 1960s. *So Kalmery.

bubblegum (South Africa): A mix of disco, variety, and techno that appeared in the 1980s.

chimurenga (Zimbabwe): Music that accompanied the fight for national liberation in the former Rhodesia, based on Shona and Ndebele rhythms and spirituality, adapting the playing of the mbira (lamellaphone) and the hosho maracas. *Jonas Sithole, Thomas Mapfumo, Stella Chiweshe.

coladeira (Cape Verde): Successor to the funaná (q.v.); formerly dance music from São Vicente Island, becoming the favorite dance (in which couples are so close that they appear "glued" together) of the Cape Verdeans. *Os Tubarões, Finaçon.

didadi (Mali): Dance based on a trio of Bambara drums, from a region adjacent to Wassoulou in southern Mali. *Nahawa Doumbia.

eskista or eskeusta (Ethiopia): A dance during which one raises the chest and shakes the shoulders; also, the feeling that accompanies a trance achieved by this dance. *Mahmoud Ahmed, Aster Aweke.

Ethio-jazz (Ethiopia): Generic term given to urban Ethiopian music that appeared in the 1960s under the influence of rhythm and blues. *Mahmoud Ahmed.

finaçon (Cape Verde): From São Tiago Island (the most African island of the archipelago), improvised songs by women that have inspired many contemporary composers.

fuji (Nigeria): A variation of highlife that appeared in the 1960s, associated with Hausa Islamic religion. Vocals are backed by a lineup of dundun and iyalu percussion, led by a bell-shaped drum. *Ayinde Barrister.

funacola (Cape Verde): A hybrid of funaná and coladeira (q.v.). *Finaçon.

funaná (Cape Verde): The "blues" of escaped slaves (the badius), played on a diatonic accordion, accompanied by ferrinho. *Kodé di Dona, Katuta.

gnama-gnama (Ivory Coast): A dance popularized in the 1980s by Kassiry.

gnawa (Morocco): Therapeutic music led by the gimbri lute, using the trance of the lilas, ceremonies conducted by descendents of black slaves.

gogbahoun (Benin): Rhythm of the Ouida region. *Angélique Kidjo.

goumbe (Guinea-Bissau): A modernized version of the goumbe rhythm of the lambats (local griots). *Nkassa Cobra.

highlife or hi-life (Ghana, Nigeria): Dance music of Ghana and Nigeria that took off in the 1930s and 1940s from the intersection of Ibo and Akan traditions, palm-wine, military brass bands, jazz, and calypso, to give birth to a hybrid style that now dominates the region. *E. T. Mensah, Oriental Brothers, Sonny Okosuns, Osita Osadebe.

indlamu (South Africa): Traditional Zulu dance of martial origin. *Savuka, Juluka.

isicathamiya (South Africa): A name given to a cappella Zulu polyphony since the 1930s. *Ladysmith Black Mambazo, Colenzo Abafana Benkhokelo.

jiti (Zimbabwe): Music of the new urban generation, based on a sped-up rural rhythm. *Bundhu Boys, Virginia Mukwesha.

jive (South Africa): Electric pop.

juju music (Nigeria): A variation of highlife based on percussion of the Yoruba animist rites, similar to those of vodun. *Tunde Nightingale, I. K. Dairo, King Sunny Ade.

kalindula (Zambia): Modern music inspired by a traditional one-string bass.

kwassa-kwassa (Democratic Republic of the Congo): Variation on soukous popularized by Kanda Bongo Man.

kwela (South Africa): Traditional street music played in the 1940s and 1950s on pennywhistles. *Makgona Tshole Band.

makassi calculé (Democratic Republic of the Congo): A variation of soukous developed by Pepe Kalle and Empire Bakuba.

makossa (Cameroon): Syncretic rhythm and dance from the Douala area. *Ekambi Brillant, Guy Lobé, Moni Mbile, Sam Fan Thomas, Manu Dibango, Lapiro de Mbanga.

malogue (Réunion): A mix of maloya and reggae. *Né Essayé.

maloya (Réunion): A music of escaped slaves played with the rouleur, kayamb, bobre, and so forth, in *kabarés* (local fairs). A distinction is made between maloya roulé, a ritual music, and maloya pilé, accessible to all. *Firmin Viry, Lo Rwa Kaf, Granmoun Lélé, Danyel Waro.

mapantsula (South Africa): A variation of bubblegum music called the thug's dance on a 4/4 rhythm driven by loud drum and synthesizers. *Chicco, Yvonne Chaka Chaka.

marrabenta (Mozambique): popular urban fair and, by extension, music of Maputo, the capital, influenced strongly by the majika rhythm.

marabi (South Africa): Township jazz before mbaqanga. *Dorothy Masuka

mbalax (Senegal): Senegalese pop that appeared in the mid 1970s, based on vocals, drums held under the arms, and other percussion. *Xalam, Orchestre Baobab, Youssou N'Dour, Super Diamono.

mbaqanga or **umbaqanga** (South Africa): A combination of Zulu rhythms, rhythm and blues, and rock. The reigning music in ghettos under apartheid. *Mahlathini and the Mahotella Queens.

mbombela (South Africa): "Ghetto jazz." *African Jazz Pioneers.

mbube (South Africa): The tradition of Zulu choral singing with gospel inflections. *Ladysmith Black Mambazo, Black Umfosoli.

merdoum (Sudan): A modernized pentatonic rhythm from Kordofan. *Abdel Gadir Salim.

mogdo (Mozambique): A piece played by an orchestra of timbila (Chopi xylophones).

morna (Cape Verde): Cape Verdean blues, cousin to fado and samba, whose origin goes back to Angolan lundum, played with violas, guitars, cavaquinhos, and violins. *Cesaria Evora, Bana, Herminia, Titina.

mougue (Seychelles): A mix of Seychelles moutia and reggae.

mvet (Gabon, Cameroon): A spoken and sung epic form of the Fang, Beti, and Bulu peoples, simultaneously historical, prophetic, and cosmogonic, and conducted by a poet-singer-dancer (the *mbômô-mvet*), accompanied by the mvet, a five-string zither whose soundbox is made from gourds.

omutibo (Kenya): Music based on esukuti rhythms from Luyia culture (western Kenya) in which the litungu lyre and the siiriri fiddle are replaced by guitar accompanied by a bottle tapped with a stick. *Abana Ba Nasery.

osibi (Ghana): Traditional street dance accompanied by singing and percussion.

pachangue (Democratic Republic of Congo): A style devised by Franco that combines pachanga, merengue, and rhythms from Zairean territories.

palm-wine music (Sierra Leone): Music born in the bars that sold palm wine in English-speaking Africa in the 1920s and 1930s, combining local dialects and instruments from foreign sailors (guitar, harmonica, banjo). *S. E. Rogie and Daniel Amponsah.

pata pata (South Africa): A township dance from the 1950s.

pennywhistle jive (South Africa): A township dance of the 1950s led by a penny-whistle, replaced a decade later by the saxophone.

polihet (Ivory Coast): A dance rhythm. *Djimi Gnaore.

polyphonies These can be either vocal (in particular by Pygmies, by the Ethiopian Dorze, or on the high plateaus of Madagascar) or instrumental (from brass or ivory horns played by Bamoun blowers from Cameroon to horns made from hollowed roots by the Banda Linda of Central Africa).

qasida A form of vocal Arabic music found in East Africa.

roumbou (Mali): A trance ritual.

rumba (Congos): Music combining Caribbean and local Congolese influences, named after the Cuban rumba, which arrived via the ports of Matadi and Pointe-Noire in the 1940s. *Wendo Kolosoy.

salegy (Madagascar): A generic name for a modern Malagasy music founded on 6/8 or 12/8 time, whose origin can be traced back to the Sakavala tradition of the Indonesians who came to the west coast of the island from the sixteenth century on, and which still exists under various regional varieties (such as tusca, bassessa, and tsapika), and was later combined with outside influences (such as sega, benga, and rumba). *Eusèbe Jaojoby.

saova (Madagascar): Improvisations and games.

sebené (Zaire): Long improvisation or exercises in virtuosity by the lead guitarist in soukous.

sega (Réunion, Mauritius, Seychelles): Biguine of the Indian Ocean, with a combination of Malagasy salegy and the white settlers' quadrille. *Roger Augustin, Ti-Frère, Cassiya, Windblows, Patrick Victor.

seggae (Réunion): Cross sega and reggae with raggamuffin (dancehall) accents. *Racinetatane, Kaya.

semba (Angola): A Mbundu rhythm originally played with percussion (dikanzas), a musical bow (undu) and a guitar (kokoxa), forming the basis not only of modern Angolese music but also of the famous Brazilian samba (via slavery). *Bonga and Waldemar Bastos.

soukous or **soukouss** (Democratic Republic of the Congo): Essentially a Cuban rumba spiked with regional rhythms (such as mutuashi, makuandungu, and zebola), high-pitched voices, and cyclic guitars; now the generic name for modern Congolese music. Soukous has generated an impressive number of dances: the cavacha, the yucca, the makassi calculé, the kwassa-kwassa, etc. *Tabu-Ley Rochereau, Empire Bakuba, Papa Wemba, Diblo Dibala.

soundjoum A soukous devised by Tabu-Ley Rochereau in the 1970s.

taarab or **twarab** (East Africa, Comoros): A mix of music from the Arabian peninsula, Indian melodies, and Bantu rhythms. *Culture Musical Club, Bi Kidude (Zanzibar), Mohamed Hassane Mschangama (Comoros).

tassou (Senegal): A sort of traditional proto-rap, performed only by women, but adapted by rap groups.

tchamassi (Cameroon): A modernized traditional rhythm. *André-Marie Tala.

tcha-tcho (Zaire): A languorous variation of soukous devised by crooner Koffi Olomide.

tchinkounme (Benin): A funeral rhythm belonging to the Manhi people in the center of the country, based on water gourds (tohoun) and bells, at the source of a modern music that Stan Tohon baptized the Tchink System. *Fifi Rafiatou, Youssouf Cimpaore.

trombas (Madagascar): Spirit possession ceremonies.

tuku music (Zimbabwe): A fusion of rhythms from Zimbabwe. *Oliver Mutukudzi.

txabeta (Cape Verde): Part of the batuka celebration, featuring a dance by a woman to polyrhythms that other women drum on tightly folded cloths held between their legs. *Nacia Gomis.

wassoulou (Mali): A musical trend based on hunting rhythms, adopted by non-griots from the southeast part of Mali. *Oumou Sangare.

yela (Senegal): Tukolor music and dance based on the rhythms of women grinding millet. *Baaba Maal.

ziglibithy (Ivory Coast): A Bete rhythm modernized by Ernesto Djedje; a syncretism of sopi, zaglobi, and digba, it also became a dance. *Reine Pélagie.

zoblazo (Ivory Coast): A modernization of the *nzema* rhythm (southern part of the Ivory Coast), dances, and traditional instruments, led by Meiway.

zouglou (Ivory Coast): A musical movement that appeared during student protests in the 1990s. *Les Parents du Campus, les Salopards.

Glossary of instruments

Justin Vali and his valiha, 1994.

This selection encompasses the most commonly used instruments in contemporary music, or the ones through which musicians have given life to a genre or style. The African continent is a veritable El Dorado of stringed instruments, wind instruments, and percussion instruments with skins (membranophones) and without skins (idiophones), all bearing witness to the limitless human imagination for making sound and rhythm from one's environment. If possible, the name of a performer or group who has used the instrument in recordings is noted with an asterisk.

adungu (Central Africa): An arched harp.

agbahoun (Benin): A sacred drum. *Denagan Janvier Honfo.

alghaita (Niger, Chad): Derived from the Arab zurna, a conical double-reed wind instrument usually having four tone holes and played using continuous breathing techniques.

amashako (Burundi): In Burundian drumming, the drum that keeps a steady beat while the inkiranya drum plays more complex rhythms. *Tambours du Burundi.

ambio (Madagascar): Rounded percussion sticks.

amponga (Madagascar): A drum carved from a log and covered with two skins: "female" and "male."

ardin (Mauritania): A harp with a calabash resonator and eleven or fourteen strings, reserved for women. *Dimi Mint Abba.

asogwe (Benin): A sacred drum.

atenteben (Ghana): Bamboo flutes. *Pan African Orchestra.

atranatrana (Madagascar): A xylophone with mobile bars that sits directly on the knees, played exclusively by women.

bagana or bagabba (Ethiopia): A large trapezoidal lyre with eight or ten strings, formerly an instrument of the aristocracy and clergy. *Alemu Aga.

balafon[1]: A xylophone with seventeen to twenty-three wooden bars and gourd resonators, including three to four diatonic ascending and descending scales. The openings of the gourds are often closed with spider web. It has

---

[1] *Translator's note:* French word, from Manding *bala fo* (to play the bala).

numerous names: bala (Maninka), balanyi (Susu), balan-ru (Fulani).
*El-Hadj Djeli Sory Kandia, Mahama Konate, and Neba Solo.

bambol (Guinea-Bissau): A calling drum. *Kaba Mane.

bara (Burkina Faso): A hardwood drum, similar to the djembe, covered with goatskin. *Farafina.

bata (Nigeria): An ensemble of three double-headed drums.

bendir (Maghreb): A frame drum present in parts of the Sahara.

bigini (West Africa): A small fiddle.

bobre (Réunion): A musical bow struck with a bamboo stick (ticouti) and held at the same time as a rattle (kaskavel). Also called zezylava (Madagascar), bonm (Seychelles and Rodrigues Islands), and chitende (Mozambique). *Ti Fock.

bolon (Guinea): An arched harp with three strings, considered to be "the bass of the lords" in Manding song.

bougarabou (Senegal): One of several sizes of drums that can be attached together.

cavaquinho (Cape Verde): A small rhythm guitar with four strings. *Bau.

cherewa (Zanzibar): Maracas made out of coconuts.

conga or **tumba**: Afro-Cuban drums often used in highlife. *King Sunny Ade.

darbouka (Maghreb): A cup- or funnel-shaped drum with a ceramic body.

dikanza (Angola): A percussion instrument made of stripped bamboo and tapped with a wooden stick. *Bonga.

djembe: A large chalice-shaped drum cut from a log and covered with a tight goatskin. *Les Percussions de Guinée, Adama Drame, Mamady Keita.

doff: A small, square Nubian drum.

dondo (Ghana): A talking drum. Called gbedun in Nigeria.

doso ngoni (Mali): "Hunter's harp" with six strings.

doudouma: A large Manding drum.

doudoumni: A small Manding drum.

dourou: A large Manding drum made from a hollowed trunk and beaten with big wooden sticks.

enanga (Great Lakes region): A royal harp with eight strings that accompanies the epic chants of the Ganda people.

fer blanc (Indian Ocean): A dented milk can.

ferrinho (Cape Verde): Another name for the reco-reco: a scraper, usually made out of iron. *Kodé di Dona.

fiddle: Generic name for stringed instruments played by friction.

gabusi (Comoros): A five-stringed lute (two doubled strings, one single). *Ensemble Gabusi des Iles, Boina Riziki.

gadza (Comoros): A type of maracas.

gaita (Cape Verde): A diatonic accordion played in funaná. *Kodé di Dona.

godie (Niger): A one-stringed fiddle.

gorong: A long Wolof drum. See *sabar*. *Doudou N'Diaye Rose.

gotta (Benin): A drum made of a gourd covered with a skin, used in tchinkounmey, a rhythm for funerals. *Stan Tohon.

harp: An instrument distinguished from a lyre by its triangular shape and the unequal length of its strings. Called dilla (Chad), ouombi (Gabon), ngombi (Central Africa), loma (Liberia), kinde (Islamicized regions), and ougdye (Cameroon). Spread throughout Africa with a wide diversity of shapes (angled, arched), it is used commonly for praises, healing ceremonies, and bardic songs.

hoddu or **molo** (Senegal): A Tukolor lute with four, five, or nine strings. *Baaba Maal.

horn: Generic name for instruments often devised from tusks, horns, or hollowed roots (such as the polyphonic ensembles of the Banda Linda of Central Africa). Horns are sometimes equipped at the end with a gourd.

hosho (Zimbabwe): A rattle-gourd played together with the mbira.

ibishikiso (Burundi): In Burundian drumming, the drum that echoes the motifs played on the inkiranya. *Tambours du Burundi.

ilimba (Tanzania): A lamellaphone with forty metal blades, one of the largest on the continent. *Hukwe Ubi Zawose.

imzad: A one-stringed Tuareg fiddle, played by women.

inanga (Rwanda, Burundi): A cradle-shaped zither with seven or nine strings, associated with the tradition of narrators and poets. Its classic repertoire relates the genealogy of the nobles. *Médard Ntamaganya.

indonongo (Burundi): A rough fiddle.

ingoma (Burundi): Generic name for the drum. *Cécile Kayirebwa.

inkiranya (Burundi): In Burundian drumming, the calling drum in the center of the performance. Its rhythms are matched by the ibishikiso drum, on the right, and supported by the steady beat of the amashako drums on the left.

inungu (South Africa): A friction drum.

jejy lava or **pikilanga** (Madagascar): A musical bow with a rod, string, and gourd.

jejy voatavo (Madagascar): A zither on a stick with up to nine strings that accompanies epic songs.

jurkel (Mali): A guitar with only one string. *Ali Farka Toure.

kabosy (Madagascar): A small guitar with three to six strings, associated with cowherds, originally made from a turtle shell and covered with a zebra skin.

Strummed, its sound is reminiscent of the mandolin's or the banjo's. *Jean Emilien, Fenoamby.

kamelen ngoni (Mali): a harp with six or twelve strings, "instrument of the men in the golden years." *Oumou Sangare, Nahawa Doumbia.

kayamb or **caiambe** (Réunion): A wooden frame filled with grains that is shaken in a flat motion to give the 6/8 rhythm of maloya. *Waro, Granmoun Lélé, Firmin Viry.

kidumbak (Zanzibar): Singular of vidumbak, a set of cup drums similar to the Arab darbouka, used in taarab.

kilembe (Zaire): A lamellaphone of the Luba people of the western Kasai region.

kissanje (Angola): A lamellaphone similar to the sanza.

kokoxa (Angola): A guitar

konin: Manding guitar.

kora (West Africa): A harp-lute made out of a half-calabash covered with a skin, equipped with a long, braced handle, usually with twenty-one strings with a clear and pearly sound. *Lamine Konte, Jali Nyama Suso, Mory Kante, Toumani Diabate, Djeli Moussa Diawara.

kpahule (Benin): A vodun sacred drum. *Denagan Janvier Honfo.

kpezin (Benin): A vodun sacred drum.

kraar (Ethiopia): A harp with six strings made out of braided cow tendons, favorite instrument of the *azmaris* (traveling musicians).

lamak (Madagascar): A pair of zebu jaws that are clapped together.

lambe (Senegal): A large Wolof drum with a bass sound. See *sabar.* *Doudou N'Diaye Rose.

lamellaphone: Generic term for a resonator (wooden box or gourd) fitted with blades of metal, wood, or bamboo that are plucked with the thumbs. Also called a thumb piano, this type of instrument is known under dozens of names throughout Africa.

lesiba (southern Africa): A jaw harp with a tight string instead of a bar.

likembe (central Africa): A lamellaphone. *Antoine Moundanda.

litungu (Kenya): A seven-stringed lyre.

lokole (Zaire): A large drum from the Kasai region.

lukeme: A name for the lamellaphone in East Africa. *Geoffrey Oryema.

lute: Generic name for an instrument with plucked strings, having a neck and a resonating body, in which the strings are parallel to the soundboard. A lute can have one string (the molo in Senegal, the kountigui in Niger) or more (the konde in Burkina Faso, the xalam in Senegal, the komo in Nigeria). It is one of the favorite instruments of the griot.

macinko or **masinqo** (Ethiopia): A one-string hurdy-gurdy whose body is diamond shaped, with the string rolled around a wooden peg at the end of the handle.

mangada (Guinea-Bissau): A set of three drums. *Kaba Mane.

maravanne (Mauritius Island): An instrument similar to the Réunion kayamb, but in light wood onto which tin sheets are nailed. *Ti-Frère.

marimba (Angola): A xylophone belonging to the Mbundu culture.

marovany or **valiha vata** (Madagascar): A twelve-string zither on a rectangular body, having a deep sound.

mbung-mbung (Senegal): A Wolof drum that provides the rhythmic basis of mbalax, a style that has become associated with other percussion instruments (djembe, nder, gorong, tama, talmbat, ndende, bougarabous). See *sabar.*

mbira (Zimbabwe): A lamellaphone. *Stella Chiweshe.

messinqo (Ethiopia): A one-string fiddle played with a bow, a key instrument of the *azmaris.* *Betsat Seyoum, Abebe Fekade.

molo (Mali): A Tamasheq guitar with one string. *Ali Farka Toure.

mouth bow: An instrument in which part of the string passes between the lips so that the mouth serves as a resonator as the string is strummed with a stick. Called ngbiti by the Aka Pygmies, gana by the Nama.

msondro (Comoros): A terra cotta pitcher covered with a goatskin, used originally for taarab.

mvet or **mwett** (Gabon): A zither with one to five strings; also, name of the Fang epic repertoire it serves.

nanga (Uganda): A seven-string harp, cousin to the ancient Egyptian harp. *Geoffrey Oryema.

ndende (Senegal): A low-pitched Wolof drum.

nder (Senegal): A high-pitched Wolof drum.

ndzumara (Comoros): A small flute.

nay (Zanzibar): A cane flute used in taarab.

ngoma (Angola): A large drum with two skins.

ngombi (Central Africa): A harp of the Fang people with seven, eight, or ten strings, often shaped like a woman's body.

ngoni (Mali): A lute with four strings with a body made out of mango wood, dear to the griots. *Mah Dembra, Rokia Traore.

njarka (Mali): A one-string fiddle with a long neck and a gourd resonator. *Ali Farka Toure.

obukano (Kenya): A large lyre with eight strings, called "the double bass of Oriental Africa."

ondole (Zaire): Drums. *Papa Wemba.

oud or **ud** (Sudan): A pear-shaped lute played with a bow, used also in taarab. *Abdel Gadir Salim.

patsou (Comoros): A brass plate struck with two small sticks.

pennywhistle (South Africa): A small tin whistle with six holes.

pluriarc (equatorial Africa): An instrument similar to an arched harp but having a different neck for each of its three to seven strings.

puitas (São Tomé and Príncipe): A friction drum, played by rubbing a stick attached to the head; used in matcumbi.

qanoun or **kanoun** (Zanzibar): An Arab zither with seventy-two to seventy-eight strings, sitting horizontally on the knees and plucked with two plectra, one plectrum attached to the forefinger of each hand.

ravanne (Mauritius): A drum whose goatskin head must be heated before each use. Used in conjunction with the maravanne for the tipik sega. *Lelou Menwar.

reco-reco (Cape Verde): A wooden handle or iron armature with notches that the musician rubs with a wooden scraper or a nicked knife (in the funaná). *Kodé di Dona.

riti or **ziti** (Senegal): A one-string fiddle of kapok wood covered with lizard skin, used for exorcism ceremonies. Dear to Fulani shepherds, it is the only bowed instrument in the country.

rouleur or **houleur** (Réunion): A bass drum that is ridden like a horse. Used in maloya. *Zizkakan.

sabar (Senegal): A Senegalese tom-tom, the most commonly used, especially by the Manding, Wolof, and Serer. A set of Wolof sabars includes five instruments: the nder of the soloist (longest, and highest pitched), the mbung-mbung (to accompany the nder), the lambe (bass), the gorong talmbar (tenor), and the gorong mbabass devised by Doudou N'Diaye Rose.

samba (Nigeria): A small, square drum.

sanduku (Zanzibar): A percussion bass with one string, made from a tea chest. Similar models are found in southern Africa.

sanza (central Africa): A lamellaphone with a wooden soundboard and metal blades.

serdu (Guinea): A thirty-centimeter-long side-blown flute whose three or four holes are placed by the diviner according to a rite. Also called a tambin, khulé, or bur, it is one of the *nyamakala*'s instruments.

shakara (Nigeria): A drum. *King Sunny Ade.

shekere (Nigeria): A rattle. *Barrister.

shiwaya (southern Africa): A type of ocarina.

singbing: A Manding guitar with three to seven strings.

sodina (Madagascar): The national flute of Madagascar. *Rakoto Frah.

sokko (West Africa): A one-stringed Fulani instrument made from a gourd covered with a waral (large lizard) skin.

squashbox (South Africa): The concertina, adopted at the beginning of the twentieth century, which became the key instrument of *shebeens* (illegal bars in the ghettos). *Johnny Clegg.

talking drum (Ghana, Nigeria): A small drum with two heads, shaped like an hourglass and held under the arm, whose pitch can be adjusted to match the human voice. It is a lead instrument in Yoruba music, but it is known in other countries under a variety of names. *King Sunny Ade.

tama (West Africa): A talking drum. Tama is also the name of a male erotic dance. *Youssou N'Dour.

tidinit (Mauritania): A Tuareg lute in ebony wood with four or five strings, originally used only by men and especially the *iggawin* (Mauritanian griot). *Dimi Mint Abba, Ooleya Mint Amartichitt.

timbila (Mozambique): Plural of *mbila;* an orchestra of xylophones (up to thirty pieces) belonging to the Chopi of the coast. The instruments are classified as soprano (chilanzane), alto (sanje), tenor (dole), bass (dibhinda), and double bass (chinzumana); these xylophones are tuned according to an equiheptatonic scale in which the tonic is the first note of the soprano. *Eduardo Durão.

tohoun (Benin): A calabash turned over in a container filled with water and drummed with sticks. *Stan Tohon.

triangle (Mauritius): The third percussion instrument used in sega, along with the ravanne and maravanne.

tunni (Guinea): A straight flute with two reed tubes tied together and attached to a hollow gourd. *Nyamakala.

umuduri (Burundi, Rwanda): A musical bow. *Orchestre National Traditionnel.

umwironge (Burundi): A flute. *Cécile Kayirebwa.

ungu (Angola): A musical bow exported to Brazil under the name *berimbau*.

valiha (Madagascar): A round bamboo zither with eighteen to fifty-four strings, formerly the favorite instrument of Merina princes. It is always used in *tromba* possession rituals. The name comes from the Sanskrit word *vadya* meaning "musical instrument." *Justin Vali.

viola (Cape Verde): A name for the Spanish guitar.

xalam (Senegal): A Wolof lute which has from three to five strings. Called continko by the Malinke. In Guinea there is a twelve-string xalam. *Baaba Maal.

xylophone: Generic name for instruments consisting of struck wooden bars, often equipped with various types of resonators. E.g.: balafon, marimba, ambira, akadinda, and so forth.

zez (Seychelles): A one-string sitar.

zeze (Tanzania): A fiddle made with a handle and a gourd with four or six strings, played with a bow strung with raffia fiber. *Wagogo.

zither: Generic name for plucked or struck stringed instruments in which the strings are parallel to the resonating body.

Selected Discography

Empire Bakuba with Pepe Kalle (singing)
and the dwarf Emauro in concert, 1986.

This discography lists recordings valuable for a good understanding of musical styles, areas, and types. The cross-selections of both modern records and more traditional ones are intended to enable useful comparisons. As far as the main artists go, the choice of one recording is reductive, of course, but it was justified either by the importance of the album or by its place in the author's career or in the history of African music. Every recording mentioned should still be available, even if some have to be searched for in catalogs, on shelves, or in specialized stores.

Translator's note: In addition to more general search engines, the following Web sites may be useful for identifying, locating, and ordering recordings:

- www.afromix.org (an extensive but not complete discography, maintained by French aficionados)
- www.cdexpress.com (the mail and electronic ordering service of the Dutch firm Rockhouse, with an extensive searchable catalog)
- www.label-bleu.com (the Indigo–Label Bleu catalog, in English and French versions)
- www.mcm.asso.fr (Maison des Cultures du Monde)
- www.natari.com (Nick's African Tape and Record Import, England)
- www.ne.jp/asahi/fbeat/africa/contents.html (a Japanese site with some focused discographies)
- www.unesco.org/culture/cdmusic/ (UN Educational/Scientific/Cultural Organization CD catalog)
- www.utlib.ee/cgi-bin/cd.cgi?Ocora [*sic*] (a catalog of Ocora CDs at the University of Tartu library in Estonia—not an exhaustive list of Ocora recordings, but it includes the catalog numbers of many recordings not otherwise identified)

West Africa

BURKINA FASO
Farafina, *Faso Denou*, Real World–Virgin.
Saaba, *Koudougou*, Daqui–Harmonia Mundi.
Pays lobi, xylophone de funérailles, Ocora.

GAMBIA

Jali Nyama Suso, *L'Art de la kora*, Ocora–Radio France.

Seckou Sako et Ramata Kouyate, *Seckou et Ramata*, Island.

GUINEA

Kouyate Sory Kandia, *L'Epopée du Mandingue*, 2 vols., Bolibana.

El-Hadj Djeli Sory Kouyate, *Anthologie du balafon mandingue*, 3 vols., Budamusique.

Famoudou Konate with l'Ensemble Hamana Dan Ba, *Percussions et chants malinké*, Budamusique.

M'Bady and Diaryatou Kouyate, *Guinée: Kora et chant du N'Gabou*, 2 vols., Budamusique.

Kante Manfila, *Kankan Blues*, World Circuit–Night and Day.

Les Percussions de Guinée, 2 vols., Budamusique.

Les Nyamakala du Fouta-Djallon, Budamusique.

Bembeya Jazz, *Regard sur le passé*, Bolibana.

Bembeya Jazz, *10 ans de succès*, Syliphone-Syllart-Mélodie.

Mory Kante, *10 Cola Nuts*, Barclay.

Mory Kante, *Akwaba Beach*, Barclay.

MALI

Ali Farka Toure, *The Source*, World Circuit.

Ali Farka Toure and Ry Cooder, *Talking Timbuktu*, World Circuit.

Boubacar Traore, *Sa Golo*, Indigo.

Salif Keita, *69-80*, Sonodisc.

Salif Keita, *Soro*, Celluloid.

Oumou Sangare, *Moussoulou*, Mélodie.

Super Rail Band de Bamako, *Super Rail Band de Bamako*, Indigo.

Toumani Diabate, *Songhai*, Vol. 2, Hannibal.

Nahawa Doumbia, *Yankaw*, Africolor/Cobalt.

Moriba Koita, *Sorotoumou*, Africolor/Cobalt.

Mah Demba, *Nyarela*, Sony Music.

Sorry Bamba, *Sigui*, Cobalt.

Rokia Traore, *Mounaissa*, Indigo.

Les Dogon: Musique des masques et des funérailles, Inedit–Maison des Cultures du Monde.

Musique bambara du Baniko, VDE.

Toumani Diabate and Taj Mahal, *Kulanjan*, Hannibal-Rykodisc.

Musiques du Mali, 4 vols., Syllart–Media 7.

MAURITANIA

Dimi Mint Abba, *Musique et chants de Mauritanie,* Ethnic.

Aicha Mint Chighaly, *Azawan, l'art des griots,* Inedit–Maison des Cultures du Monde.

Ooleya Mint Amartichitt, *Praise Songs,* Long Distance.

NIGER

Baje Jibo, *Epopées zarma et songhai,* Ocora–Harmonia Mundi.

Anthologie de la musique du Niger, Ocora.

Harouna Goge, *Musique dendi,* Ocora.

SENEGAL

Toure Kunda, *Touré Kunda 1983–1984,* Celluloid.

Youssou N'Dour, *Set,* Virgin.

Doudou N'Diaye Rose, *Djaboté,* Real World.

Choral Julien Jouga, *Jama,* Indigo–Label Bleu.

Ismael Lo, *Diawar,* Syllart.

Positive Black Soul, *Salaam,* Mango.

Xalam, *Gorée,* Celluloid.

Baaba Maal, *Baayo,* Mango.

Wasis Diop, *Hyènes,* Mercury.

Cheikh Lo, *Né La Thiass,* World Circuit.

Africando, *Sabador,* Mélodie.

El-Hadj N'Diaye, *Thiaroye,* Sigi.

Lamine Konte, *Chant du nègre… chant du monde,* Arion.

Monks of Keur Moussa Abbey, *Messe et chants au monastère de Keur Moussa,* Arion.

Gulf of Guinea

BENIN

Angélique Kidjo, *Logozo,* Mango.

Wally Badarou, *Echoes,* Island.

CAMEROON

Manu Dibango, *Soul Makossa,* Accord.

Manu Dibango, *Négropolitaines,* 2 vols., Mélodie.

Anne-Marie Nzie, *Beza Ba Dzo,* Harmonia Mundi.

Francis Bebey, *Dibyé,* Pee Wee Music.

Sam Fan Thomas, *Makassi,* Africa Typic Collection.

Les Têtes Brûlées, *Ma musique à moi,* Bleu Caraïbes–Mélodie.

Les Vétérans, *Au Village,* Safari Ambiance.

Lapiro de Mbanga, *Ndinga Man Contre-Attaque: Na Wou Go Pay?,* Indigo.

Sally Nyolo, *Tribu,* Lusafrica.

GABON

Pierre Akendengue, *Lambarena: Bach to Africa,* Celluloid.

Hilarion Nguema, *Sida,* Safari Ambiance.

François N'Gwa, *N'Kang,* Mélodie.

Musique de Pygmées bibayak: Chantres de l'epopée, Ocora–Harmonia Mundi.

GHANA

La Musique de la Gold Coast des années soixante, Night and Day.

George Williams Aingo, *The Roots of Highlife,* Stern's.

E. T. Mensah, *All for You,* Harmonie.

The Pan African Orchestra, *Opus 1,* Virgin–Real World.

Osibisa, *Mystic Energy,* Terrapin Music.

IVORY COAST

Ernesto Djedje, *Tizeré,* Sacodis.

Alpha Blondy, *Cocody Rock,* EMI.

Alpha Blondy and The Wailers, *Jerusalem,* EMI.

Aicha Kone, *Adouma,* Bolibana.

Ismael Isaac, *Taxi Jump,* PolyGram.

Reine Pélagie, *Reine de feu,* Deg Music.

Zouglou, Buda.

Zagazougou, *Zagazougou Coup: Accordions from Abidjan,* Piranha.

Maître Gazonga, *Les Jaloux saboteurs,* Tangent.

NIGERIA

Juju Roots, 1930-1950, Rounder.

I. K. Dairo, M.B.E., *Juju Master,* Original Music–Night and Day.

Fela Anikulapo-Kuti, *Anthologie,* Barclay.

King Sunny Ade, *Juju Music,* Mango–Island.

Barrister (Ayinde Barrister), *New Fuji Garbage,* Globestyle.

Tempos/Ramblers/Uhuru: Giants of Danceband Highlife, Original Music.

Ebenezer Obey, *Je Ka Jo—Let Us Dance,* Virgin.

Babatunde Olatunji, *Drums of Passion,* Sony.

Segun Adewale, *Ojo Je*, Rounder.
Sonny Okosuns, *Liberation*, Shanachie.

SIERRA LEONE
Kru-Krio, Calypso Connection, Original Music.
S. E. Rogie, *Special Delivery*, Cooking Vinyl.
Sierra Leone—Musiques traditionnelles, Ocora.

TOGO
Bella Bellow, *Album souvenir*, Safari Ambiance.

Portuguese-Speaking Countries

ANGOLA
Bonga, *Angola 72—Angola 74*, Lusafrica.
Les Musiques urbaines d'Angola, 5 vols., Budamusique.
Waldemar Bastos, *Pretaluz*, Virgin.
Mario Rui Silva, *Luanda 50/60 Angola*, Night and Day.

CAPE VERDE
Bau, *Inspiração*, Lusafrica-BMG.
Cesaria Evora, *Miss Perfumado*, Lusafrica-Mélodie.
Bana, *Gira del sol*, Iris Musique.
Kodé di Dona, *Cap-Vert*, Ocora–Harmonia Mundi.
Herminia, *Coraçon Leve*, Celluloid-Mélodie.
Travadinha, *Le violon du Cap-Vert*, Budamusique.
Cap Vert: Anthologie 1959–1992, Budamusique.
Finaçon, *Funana*, Mélodie.

GUINEA-BISSAU
Ramiro Naka, *Salvador*, Cobalt.
Kaba Mane, *Best of Kaba Mané*, Mélodie.

MOZAMBIQUE
Eduardo Durão, *Timbila*, Globestyle.
Orchestre Marrabenta, *Independence*, Piranha.
Mozambique 2, Globestyle.
Saba saba!, Globestyle.
1975 - 1995 Independencia!, Lusafrica-Mélodie.

SÃO TOMÉ E PRÍNCIPE
Gilberto Gil Umbelina, *Vôa Papagaio, Vôa!*, Mélodie.

Central Africa

CENTRAL AFRICAN REPUBLIC
Musique gbaya, chants à penser, 2 vols., Ocora.
Musique pour sanza en pays gbaya, VDE.
Polyphonies banda, Auvidis–UNESCO.
Anthologie de la musique des Pygmées aka, Ocora.
Ongo Trogode, *Trompes banda linda,* Budamusique.

CHAD
Clement Masdongar, *SiYa,* Sankara.
Clement Masdongar, *Anastasia,* EMI.

CONGO (REPUBLIC OF THE CONGO, CONGO-BRAZZAVILLE)
Les Bantous de la Capitale, *Marie-Jeanne,* Sonafric.
Zao, *Ancien combattant,* Mélodie.
Antoine Moundanda, *Likembé géant,* Indigo–Label Bleu.
Pamelo Mounka, *L'argent appelle l'argent,* Sonics.

CONGO (DEMOCRATIC REPUBLIC OF THE CONGO, FORMERLY
    ZAIRE)
Jean-Bosco Mwenda, *Mwenda wa Bayeke,* Rounder.
Merveilles du passé: Grand Kallé et l'African Jazz, 2 vols., Sonodisc.
Ngoma: souvenir ya l'indépendence, Popular African Music.
Merveilles du passé: Franco et le TPOK Jazz, several volumes by year, Sonodisc.
Dr. Nico and the Africa Fiesta, *African Fiesta sous la direction de Docteur Nico,* 2
    vols., Sonafric.
Petites musiques du Zaïre, Budamusique.
Ray Lema, *Green Light,* Budamusique.
Lokua Kanza, *Lokua Kanza,* RCA.
Sam Mangwana, *No me digas no,* Mélodie.
Abeti Masikini, "Je suis fâchée," Bade Stars Music.
M'Pongo Love, *Hommage,* 3 vols., Sonodisc.
Wendo, *Marie-Louise,* Indigo–Label Bleu.

Papa Wemba, *Emotion,* Real World–EMI.

Zaiko Langa-Langa, *Subissez les conséquences,* Sonodisc.

Pepe Kalle, *Gigantafrique,* Globestyle.

Koffi Olomide, *Golden Star,* Sonodisc.

Kanda Bongo Man, *Kwassa Kwassa,* Hannibal.

Tshala Muana, *Biduaya,* Celluloid–Mélodie.

African Connection, Vol. 1: Zaïre Choc! (Empire Bakuba, Franco, 4 Etoiles, Papa Wemba, and others), Celluloid.

Great Lakes Africa

BURUNDI

Batimbo, *Burundi Drums,* PlayaSound.

Les Tambours du Burundi, *Live at Real World,* Real World.

Khadja Nin, *Sambolera,* BMG.

MALAWI

Donald Kachamba's Kwela Band, *Donald Kachamba's Band: Simanje-Manje and Kwela,* PAM Records.

Music Tradition of Malawi, UNESCO–Auvidis.

RWANDA

Médard Ntamaganya, *Chants de cour a l'inanga et chants populaires,* Inédit–Maison des Cultures du Monde.

Cécile Kayirebwa, *Rwanda,* Globestyle.

UGANDA

Geoffrey Oryema, *Exile,* Real World.

Ouganda: Aux sources du Nil, Ocora–Radio France.

The Kampala Sound, Original Music.

Ensembles villageois du Busoga, VDE-Gallo.

ZAMBIA

From the Copperbelt: Miners' Songs, Original Music.

Zambiance!, Globestyle.

Alick Nkhata, *Shalapo,* Retroafric

Shani! The Sounds of Zambia, WOMAD.

East Africa

ETHIOPIA
Mahmoud Ahmed, *Ere Mela Mela*, Crammed Records.
Ethiopian Groove, *The Golden Seventies*, Dona Wana.
Ethiopiques, 11 vols., Budamusique.
Polyphonies of the Dorzé, Le Chant du Monde.
Alemu Aga, *The Harp of King David*, Long Distance.
Betsat Seyoum et Abbebe Fekade, *Azmaris urbains d'Éthiopie*, Long Distance.

KENYA
Musiques du Nyanza, Ocora–Harmonia Mundi.
D.O. Misiani and Shirati Jazz, *Piny Ose Mer: The World Upside Down*, Globestyle.
Daniel Kamau, *Kenyafrica*, PlayaSound.
Kenya Dance Mania, Earthworks.
Abana Ba Nasery, *Classic Acoustic Recordings from Western Kenya*, Globestyle.
Guitar Paradise of East Africa, Earthworks.

SOMALIA
Maryam Mursal, *The Journey*, Real World.
Jamila, *Songs from a Somali City*, Original Music.

SUDAN
Abdel Aziz El Mubarak, *Straight from the Heart*, World Circuit.
Abdel Gadir Salim, *Le blues de Khartoum*, Harmonia Mundi.
Music of the Blue Nile Province, 2 vols., UNESCO.

TANZANIA/ZANZIBAR
Hukwe Ubi Zawose, *Tanzania Yetu*, Triple Earth Terra.
The Tanzania Sound, Original Music.
Remmy Ongala, *Songs for the Poor Man*, Real World.
Taarab, 4 vols., Globestyle.

Southern Africa

SOUTH AFRICA
Zulu Choral 1930-1960, Rounder–Média 7.
Miriam Makeba, *Sangoma*, WEA

Mahlathini and the Mahotella Queens, *Thokozile,* Celluloid.
Sounds of Soweto, Compilation, EMI–Pathé-Marconi.
The Indestructible Beat of Soweto, Earthworks-Shanachie.
Ladysmith Black Mambazo, *Zibuyinhlazane* (featuring "Homeless"), Celluloid.
Juluka, *Musa Ukungilandela,* Totem.
Savuka, *Cruel, Crazy, Beautiful World,* EMI.
The Kings and Queens of Township Jive, Earthworks-Stern's.
Lucky Dube, *Slave,* Celluloid.
Hugh Masekela, *Hope,* Triloka.
Chris McGregor and the Brotherhood of Breath, *Country Cooking,* Virgin.
The Elite Swingsters and Dolly Rathebe, *A Call for Peace,* Indigo.
African Jazz Pioneers, *The Best of the African Jazz Pioneers,* Celluloid.
Vusi Mahlasela, *When You Come Back,* Harmonia Mundi.

NAMIBIA
Namibie: Bushmen et Himba, Buda.
Chants des Bushmen ju'hoansi, Ocora.

ZIMBABWE
Thomas Mapfumo and the Blacks Unlimited, *Chamunorwa,* Mango-Island.
Dumisane Maraire, *Masters of the African Mbira,* Nonesuch.
Stella Chiweshe, *Ambuya? and Ndizvozvo,* Piranha.
Oliver Mtukudzi, *Tuku Music,* Putumayo.
Chiwoniso, *Ancient Voices,* Lusafrica–Média 7.
Zimbabwe Frontline, Earthworks.
Dorothy Masuka (sometimes treated as South African), *Pata-pata,* Mango-Island.

Indian Ocean

COMOROS
Baco, *Kara Lala/L'Eveil,* Night and Day.
Mikidache, *Kauli/Words,* Long Distance.
Abou Chihabi, *African Vibrations,* PlayaSound.
Boina Riziki and Soubi, *Chamsi na Mwesi,* Dizim Records.

MADAGASCAR
Rakoto Frah, *Flute Master of Madagascar,* Globestyle.
Madagascar Open Notes: Fruits des voyages, Musikela.

Madagasikara, 2 vols., Globestyle–Média 7.
Musiques de Madagascar, Budamusique.
Regis Gizavo, *Mikea*, Indigo–Label Bleu.
Bilo, *Malgache Connexion: Bilo*, Silex-Auvidis.
Feo-Gasy, *Feo-Gasy, polyphonies malgaches*, Mélodie.
Justin Vali, *The Genius of Valiha*, Unic Music–Night and Day.
Erick Manana, *Bonjour Madame La Guitare: A Tribute to Razilina*, Buda-Musidisc.
Madagascar—Possession et poésie, Ocora.
Madagascar—Pays antandroy, Ocora.
D'Gary, *Mbo Loza*, Indigo–Label Bleu.
Eusèbe Jaojoby, *Velono*, Indigo–Label Bleu.
Jean Emilien, *Miandraza*, Africolor/Cobalt.
Le Marovany de Madagascar, Silex.

MAURITIUS
Hommage a Ti-Frère, Ocora–Radio France.
Fanfan, *Sega ravanne*, Ocora.

RÉUNION
Granmoun Lélé, *Soleye*, Indigo–Label Bleu.
Firmin Viry, *Ti Mardé*, Harmonia Mundi.
Ziskakan, *Ziskakan*, Island.
Danyel Waro, *Batarsité*, Piros-Sonodisc.
Alain Peters, *Paraboler*, Takamba-Discorama.
René Lacaille, *Patanpo*, Daqui.

SEYCHELLES
Seychelles 2: Musiques oubliées des îles, Ocora.
Patrick Victor and Bwa Gayak, Totem Records.

Compilations

Masa (live recordings of the biennial *Marché des arts du spectacle africaines*), 2
    vols. (1997 and 1999), Indigo–Label Bleu.
Rendez-vous, compil de musique africaine, 12 vols., Syllart–Média 7.
Les Danses du monde, CNRS–Musée de l'Homme.
Les Voix du monde, CNRS–Musée de l'Homme.

Selected Bibliography

*Les Merveilles de Guinée
in action, 1995.*

Many of these titles have been reissued since their first publication.

Music

Akesson, Birgit, *Kallvatnets Mask: Om Dans i Afrika,* Atlantis, 1983. (*Le Masque des eaux vives. Danses et chorégraphies traditionnelles d'Afrique noir,* L'Harmattan, 1994.)

Arnaud, Gérald, and Henri Lecomte (coordinated by), "Musiques Africaines," *Ecoutez voir* magazine, 1990.

Arom, Simha, *Polyphonies et Polyrythmies instrumentales d'Afrique Centrale,* Sélaf, 1984.

Athcart, Jenny, *Hé! You, portrait de Youssou N'Dour,* Fine Line, 1989.

Balandier, Georges, *Sociologie des Brazzavilles noires,* Armand Colin, 1955.

Bamba, Sorry, *De la tradition a la world music,* L'Harmattan, 1996.

Barlow, Sean, and Banning Eyre, *AFROPOP! An Illustrated Guide to Contemporary African Music,* Book Sales, 1995.

Bastide, Roger, *Les Amériques noires,* L'Harmattan, 1996 (first edition: 1973).

Bebey, Francis, *Musique africaine,* Horizons de France, 1969. (*African Music: A People's Art,* Lawrence Hill Books, 1975.)

Belinga, Eno, *Littératures et Musiques populaires en Afrique noire,* Cujas, 1965.

Bemba, Sylvain, *Cinquante ans de musique au Congo-Zaïre,* Presence africaine, 1984.

Bender, Wolfgang, *Sweet Mother: Modern African Music,* The University of Chicago Press, 1984.

Bensignor, François, *Sons d'Afrique,* Marabout, 1982.

Berliner, Paul, *The Soul of Mbira,* The University of Chicago Press, 1992.

Blacking, John, *How Musical Is Man?,* The University of Washington Press, 1973.

Brandily, Monique, *Introduction aux musiques africaines,* Actes Sud, 1997.

Calame-Griaule, Geneviève, "Introduction a la musique africaine," *La Revue musicale,* 238, 1957.

Camara, Sory, *Gens de parole. Essai sur la condition et le rôle des griots dans la sociètè malinké,* Mouton, 1975.

"Chansons d'Afrique et des Antilles," *Revue Itinéraires,* L'Harmattan, 1988.

Clerfeuille, Sylvie, and Seck, Nago, *Les Musiciens du beat africain,* Bordas, 1993.

Conrath, Philippe, *Johnny Clegg, la passion zoulou,* Seghers, 1988.

Coplan, David B., *In Township Tonight,* Karthala, 1992.

"Culture hip-hop," *Africultures,* 21, October 1999.

Dampierre, Eric de, *Harpes zandé,* Kincksieck, 1991.

Davet, Stéphanie, and Tenaille, Frank, *Le Printemps de Bourges, chroniques des musiques d'aujourd'hui,* Gallimard, 1996.

Dibango, Manu, *Trois kilos de café,* Lieu commun, 1989. (*Three Kilos of Coffee,* University of Chicago Press, 1994.)

Drame, Adama, and Seen-Borloz, Arlette, *Jeliya, être griot et musicien aujourd'hui,* L'Harmattan, 1991.

Fampou, Francois. *Ku Sa: Introduction à la percussion africaine,* L'Harmattan, 1986.

Fatumbi Verger, Pierre, *Orisha, Les dieux yorouba en Afrique et au Nouveau Monde,* Métailié, 1982.

Friedson, Stephen M., *Dancing Prophets: Musical Experience in Tumbuka Healing,* The University of Chicago Press, 1984.

Gandoulou,. K. D., *Entre Paris et Bacongo,* Centre Georges-Pompidou, 1984

Grund, Francoise, and Cherif Khaznadar, *Atlas de l'imaginaire,* Maison des cultures du monde–Favre, 1996.

Hart, Mickey, *Drumming at the Edge of Magic,* Harper San Francisco, 1990.

Hurbon, Laënnec, *Les Mystères du vaudou,* Gallimard, 1993.

Idowu, Mabinu Kayodé, *Fela: Why Blackman Carry Shit,* Opinion Media, 1986.

Konate, Yacouba, *Alpha Blondy,* Karthala, 1987.

La Parole du fleuve. Harpes d'Afrique centrale, Cité de la musique, 1999.

La Selve, Jean-Pierre, *Musiques traditionnelles de la Réunion,* Azalées, 1995.

Lee, Hélène, *Rockers d'Afrique,* Albin Michel, 1988.

Lonoh, Michel, *Essai de commentaire sur la musique congolaise moderne,* SEI-ANC, Kinshasa, 1969.

Luveau, René, *Chants de femmes au Mali,* Luneau Ascot, 1981.

Mabika, Pie-Aubin, *La Chanson congolaise,* PAM, 1999.

Makeba, Miriam, and James Hall, *Makeba: My Story,* New American Library, 1987.

McGregor, Maxime, *Chris McGregor and the Brotherhood of Breath,* Bamberger Books, 1995.

Monteiro, Vladimir, *Les Musiques au Cap-Vert,* Chandeigne, 1998.

Moore, Carlos, *Fela, cette putain de vie,* Karthala, 1992. (*Fela, Fela: This Bitch of a Life,* Alison & Busby, 1982.)

Mortaigne, Véronique, *Cesaria Evora, la voix du Cap-Vert,* Actes Sud, 1997.

"La Musique africaine," UNESCO colloquium, Yaoundé, *La Revue musicale,* 288–289, 1970.

Ndachi Tagné, David, *Anne-Marie Nzié,* Sopecam, Yaoundé, 1990.

Nguyen Makoto, Bertrand, *Abeti, la voix d'or du Zaïre,* L'Harmattan, 1999.

Omotoso, Kolé, *Woza Africa! Quand la musique défie la guerre,* Le Jaguar, 1997.

Roberts, John Storm, *Black Music of Two Worlds,* Original Music, 1972.

Rouget, Gilbert, *La Musique et la Transe,* Gallimard, 1980.

Salée, Pierre, *Études sur la musique au Gabon,* ORSTOM, 1978.

Sans visa. Guide des musiques de l'espace francophone et du monde, Collective work, Zone Franche/IRMA 1995.

Saulnier, Pierre, *Bangui chante,* L'Harmattan, 1993.

Schaeffer, Pierre, *Traité des objects musicaux,* Le Seuil, 1966.

Schaeffner, André, *Le Jazz,* Jean Michel Place, 1988.

Schaeffner, André, *Le Sistre et le Hochet,* Hermann, 1990.

Sroulou, Gabriel, *La Chanson populaire en Côte d'Ivoire,* Présence africaine, 1986.

Tchebwa, Manda, *Terre de la chanson,* Duculot, 1996.

Tenaille, Frank, *Les Cinquante-six Afriques,* La Découverte, 1979.

Tenaille, Frank, *Touré Kunda,* Segher, 1987.

Titinga, Frédéric, *Le Langage des tam-tam et des masques en Afrique,* L'Harmattan, 1991.

Waterman, Christopher Alan, *Juju,* The University of Chicago Press, 1990.

World Music: The Rough Guide, Rough Guides–Penguin, 1994.

Zemp Hugo, *Musique Dan. La Musique dans la pensée et la vie sociale africaines,* Mouton, 1971.

Dance

La Danse africaine, c'est la vie, Maisonneuve et Larose, 1983.

Huet, Michel, and Keita Fodeba, *Les Hommes de la danse,* La Guilde du livre, 1954.

Savary, Claude, and Michel Huet, *Danses d'Afrique,* Le Chêne, 1994.

Tchimou, Famedji-Koto, *L'Art de danser en Côte-d'Ivoire,* L'Harmattan, 1996.

Tchimou, Famedji-Koto, *Le Langage de la danse chez les Dogons,* L'Harmattan, 1995.

Tiérou, Alphonse, *Dooplé, loi eternelle de la danse africaine,* Maisonneuve et Larose, 1989.

Zebila, Lucky, *La Danse africaine ou l'intelligence du corps*, L'Harmattan–Le
    Baobab, 1982.

Newspapers and Magazines

L'Affiche.
Les Cahiers de musique traditionnelle, published by Ateliers d'ethnomusicologie,
    directed by Laurent Aubert.
Diapason.
La Lettre des musiques et des arts africains, now *Africultures.*
Le Monde de la musique.
Paroles et musique, now *Chorus.*
Répertoire.
Trad'magazine.
Vibrations.
Visa permanent, newspaper of the Zone Franche Association, Paris.
Word.

Films

Djembefola, a Laurent Chevalier film, based on an idea by Pierre Marcault.
Djembé Oyé, a Laurent Chevalier film.
Doudou N'Diaye Rose, a Jean-Pierre Janssen film.
Doudou N'Diaye Rose, Djaboté, a Béatrice Soulé film.
Man No Run (about the bikutsi group Les Têtes Brûlées), a Claire Denis film.
Manu Dibango, a Béatrice Soulé film.
Papa Wemba, a Jimmy Glasberg film.

Radio stations

Africa Numéro Un.
Radio France Internationale.
Radio Nova.

acknowledgments

Every type of popular music is best appreciated in its environment. For me, to speak of African musics is to follow a chain of linked memories of nights spent in clubs, *les circuits,* with musicians, singers, seasoned amateurs, many of whom, unfortunately, I can no longer name. Photographer Bill Akwa Betote, whose pictures illustrate this book, has been, for more than two decades, a part of this group of crazy fanatics of live music who accompany me. He is certainly a large piece of this puzzle. As are, in the name of Afro-optimism, a handful of fellow journalists who are enamored of . . . gumbo sauce. I also tip my hat to Suzanne Aguiar, Sylvie Coma, Luigi Elongui, Gilles Fruchaux, Philippe Gouttes, Remy Kolpa Kopoul, Jacques Matinet, Christian Mousset, Corinne Serres, and Manda Tchebwa, who know why. Myriam Astruc, Dominique Bach, Isabelle Béranger, Maryse Bessaguet, Nicole Courtois-Higelin, Alice Lepers, Yazid Mamou, Catherine Michel, Eliane Petit, Liliane Roudière, and Muriel Van den Bosche helped edit this book, commissioned by Bernard Magnier for Actes Sud. Many pages also owe their comprehensibility to Françoise Dastrevigne, Pascale Neyron, Anne Quentin, and the sharp eyes of Aïté Bresson and Claire Simonin. Of course, in the final count, these musical dispatches are dedicated to Jean and Marie-Jeanne Bourret, who enabled a child to grow up in the midst of griots—*bilakoro* who were sure that, with their koras and balafons, in the heat mirages, they made chameleons dance.

iNDEX

FRANK TENAiLLE

A journalist specializing in world music, Frank Tenaille is considered one of the leading experts on African music. He has contributed to numerous magazines and radio shows (*Le Nouvel Observateur, Le Monde de la Musique, Radio France Internationale,* and *La Cité de la Musique*). A founding member of *Zone Franche* (an association of world-music professionals in Europe) and the *Académie Charles Cros* (recognized for the quality of its prize list), he is also artistic advisor on musical performances for the Festival de Radio France Montpellier. He has written and contributed to more than a dozen books, including *Les Cinquante-six Afriques* (1979), *Patrice Lumumba* (1985), *Le Roman de Coluche* (1986), *Guide de la chanson française* (1986), *Touré Kunda* (1987), *Polac, droit de se taire* (1987), *Bedos, histoire d'un rire* (1990), and *Le Printemps de Bourges* (1996).

AKWA BETOTE

Born in Douala, Cameroon, Akwa Betote moved to France in 1972. Chronicling the black presence in European and African music, his photographs have been widely published (*Le Monde, Le Nouvel Observateur, Libération, Jeune Afrique,* and *Newsweek*). He has also collaborated on a number of books. His photographic oeuvre extends over thirty years, during which time his lens has captured all the stars of African music.